A History of Advertising

A History of Advertising

Stéphane Pincas and Marc Loiseau

Foreword by Maurice Lévy

TASCHEN

HONG KONG KÖLN LONDON LOS ANGELES MADRID PARIS TOKYO

To stay informed about upcoming TASCHEN titles, please request our magazine at www.taschen.com/magazine or write to TASCHEN America, 6671 Sunset Boulevard, Suite 1508, USA-Los Angeles, CA 90028, contact-us@taschen.com, Fax: +1-323-463.4442. We will be happy to send you a free copy of our magazine which is filled with information about all of our books.

© 2008 TASCHEN GmbH
Hohenzollernring 53, D-50672 Köln
www.taschen.com

Project management: Anne Gerlinger, Julius Wiedemann, Cologne
Production: Horst Neuzner, Cologne
Cover design: Sense/Net, Andy Disl und Birgit Reber, Cologne

Printed in China
ISBN 978-3-8365-0212-2

The original version of this book was created in 2006 in a non-commercial edition entitled "Born in 1842. A History of Advertising". It was done exclusively for the members of the Publicis Groupe to pay homage to the 100th anniversary of Marcel Bleustein-Blanchet, the founder of Publicis.

© 2006, Mundocom (Publicis Groupe), Paris, for the original edition

Original concept: Stéphane Pincas and Marc Loiseau
Consultant editor: Yasha David
Contributors: Howard Davis, Richard Myers, Dan O'Donoghue
Special contributors: David Droga, Pat Fallon, Miguel Angel Furones, John Hegarty, Bob Isherwood and Linda Kaplan
Editorial coordination: Valérie Beun, Claire Burgess, Robert Fridovich and Stephanie Owen
English translation: Liz Attawell, Kim Sanderson and Kelly Pennhaligon
Documentation and sources: Beth Callahan, Sally De Rose, Johanna Hunt, Paige Miller, Sarah Okrent and Ilana N. Pergam
Production: Jean-Claude Le Dunc, Brigitte Crapoulet, Alain Djebali, Patrick Franckhauser, Olivier Marchand, Marie-Pierre Millet, Christian Naudet and Jean-Claude Pelleray

The authors thank the institutions and companies who have made archives available and given permission for their use. They equally express their gratitude to some of the creators of this story who generously gave their time to discuss the finer details. The authors would like to express their sincere thanks to their colleagues, without whom this project would not have come to a successful conclusion.
Réjane Bargiel, Gérard Baumann, Jean-François Bauret, Nicole Bazerque, Jean-Louis Broust, Luc Byleveld, Philippe Calleux, Patrice Cazes, Michèle Chalvet, Deborah Chinnock, Jean Collette, Bruno Desbarats, Katie Dishman, Lynn Eaton, Corinne Evesque, Paul Faccheti, John A. Fleckner, Simon Gallo, Paule Gendre, Carla Grad, Simone Guibert, Chantal Jan, Michèle Jasnin, Oluf La Lau, Eric Marchin, Claude Marcus, Meredith Metcalf, Roland and Yvette Michau, Philip Mooney, Nancy Palley, Gérard Pédraglio, Serge Perez, Albert Pfiffner, Philippe Quidor, Jacqueline Reid, Ed Rider, Salomon Salto, Vangphet Sananikone, Bruno Suter, Nicola Weston and Daniel Wormeringer

Contents

7

Foreword

by Maurice Lévy

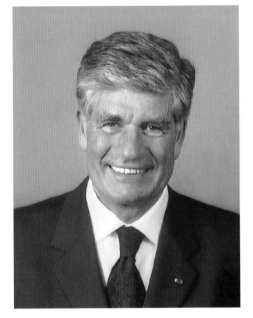

Maurice Lévy,
Chairman and CEO, Publicis Groupe.

This book is something different, and it is a difference that is very important to me. When I read it, I can feel deep down how much I love working in advertising. I can feel how the rhythm of my life is dictated by advertising. How much my life is coloured by the satisfactions and frustrations of the job. And what a job!

Half way between a craft and a business, rooted in both art and social science, one moment giving objective advice and the next at the very heart of the action, advertising can fill one's life and fill it well. It is common knowledge that the profession feeds off inventiveness, imagination and daring. What is less well-known is that discipline and rigour are hidden behind the image of the 'ideas person'. Behind the superb campaigns featured in this book, I can picture the feverish excitement, the last-minute meetings, the impassioned debate. I can picture this all the more clearly because that is the life I live every day, and every day I spend living this life gives me an emotional buzz.

At the other end of the emotional scale, the advertising profession requires a real sense of responsibility. Advertising agencies are accountable to their clients for the work they do and a successful campaign can be a formidable asset. A successful campaign can give the brand a competitive advantage in its market or boost the launch of a product or service and make the difference between success and failure. In financial communications, besides the figures, the difference between a successful stock market flotation and one that is mediocre often stems from the quality of the communications. But a sense of responsibility extends much further to cover the brand's consumers. Consumers being third parties, are absent from the formal contract between the client and the advertising agency but are central to that relationship. On occasion, I have been known to say no: no, we will not do this or that campaign because it is not compatible with our ethical stance. Being an adman also means knowing when to say no, even to one's most important clients, when one believes that this is in their ultimate interest.

I love this profession for many and varied reasons and for the experiences it brings by the dozen. I love it because advertising is an exercise in modesty. I know this will come as a shock to some people, but advertising on behalf of a brand means having the discretion to speak on its behalf yet not to steal its place in the limelight. It also means having the patience to listen to what consumers are saying and having the intelligence not to set oneself up as always being the sole arbiter of popular taste. At Publicis, we have refined these self-effacing ethics: we work behind the scenes in order to leave the stage to the brand, the communications and the client.

But there is another deeply-rooted reason I am in advertising. I like persuading people! I like the exchange of ideas with my teams and my clients. I like conveying a conviction and I like seeing that conviction translated into reality. Nothing can compare to the adrenaline rush that accompanies the presentation of a campaign plan, and it is even a pleasure to feel the fear and tension that grips one on the opening night of a new campaign.

This book embraces over a century of history. It begins in the middle of the nineteenth century in the United States, when the seeds of the story were sown. Of course, advertising first appeared somewhat earlier –in a way it first appeared with the invention of the printing press in the mid-fifteenth century and the emergence of newspapers a century later. It would be easy to demonstrate, by going back so far into the past, that the first posters and advertisements were European! However, the major difference between these first advertisements and the modern industry, the shape of which began to emerge in the nineteenth century, lies in the context of consumption. Modern advertising was clearly born alongside the brands and the mass consumption made possible by the industrial revolution.

On reflection, it is striking to note how quickly the fundamental principles of the profession became established. Consumer studies, the use of radical modes of communication and the consideration of major sociological issues were all integrated into the advertising practice from the early days. One might say that advertising has always had an extraordinary, malleable quality, and in recent years this adaptability has allowed it to meet the challenges presented by the internationalisation of its clients and their brands, and by the challenge of the new communications technologies.

The timeframe of this book is measured in generations. Our own working life fits, for the most part, squarely into the last chapter. Only

The door of the office at 17, rue du Faubourg Montmartre, in Paris, where in 1926 Marcel Bleustein took the first steps in creating Publicis as it is known today.

a few of us are now able to claim that we played any role during the period covered by the penultimate chapter. Personally I can claim that privilege —but only just! I freely admit that I possess both the grey hairs and too many years of experience!

The retrospective view taken in this book renews my great respect and admiration for my predecessors. They succeeded in inventing a profession, succeeded in refining its working methods, and also succeeded in building up brands which made a mark on the public consciousness. I am acutely aware of being part of a long, unbroken line of advertising professionals. Among these people, Marcel Bleustein-Blanchet occupies, for me, an exalted position; it is alongside him that I made my debut. I have said it many times before and I will say it again: I learnt my passion for advertising from 'The Rage to Persuade'[1], Marcel Bleustein-Blanchet's rage to persuade! He was my teacher, my mentor and the person who directly, daily, instilled this passion in me. However, the reader can leaf through this book and find all the other talented pioneers, from Europe, North America and around the world. Neither I nor the reader will have had the chance to meet them all in person. And yet, like me, the reader will be struck by the humanity of such giants of advertising as Francis W. Ayer, William C. D'Arcy, Theodore MacManus, Leo Burnett and Maurice Saatchi.

As an heir to this long tradition I feel under an obligation which has two aspects which at first appear contradictory: to uphold but also to change tradition. In fact, these two aspects complement one another. Continuity is one of the cornerstones of this profession, and an agency must be a place where creative ideas can serve our clients' brands in the long term. This is our 'raison d'être'; it created the profession and it continues to underpin the profession's existence.

Change is, dare I say it, the only other thing of any import. Let me take Publicis, for example. In the seventies, the agency was still essentially a French agency, with 80% of its business conducted on French soil and the remainder in Europe. Today, Publicis Groupe business activity fairly closely reflects the economic weight of the continents, with North America in the lead. Measured in economic terms, the change that has occurred is considerable. In cultural terms, it is even more considerable. As I lead the company through this evolution, I believe I am staying true

[1] Chelsea House, New York, 1970.

to the legacy of our founder. Change has been a 'sine qua non' simply to keep our traditions alive, and now, adapting to the economy of the new millennium is the new challenge to preserve the spirit of the company he founded.

For a man who prefers action a book about the past, rather surprisingly, makes a great springboard to propel myself into the future. The story of advertising is always written with an eye to the future. Through careful observation of the phenomena which populate this story, it is possible to discern some of the main forces which seem to be shaping the future of the profession. The future seems to depend on the profession's ability to meet four challenges.

Advertising was born and grew up alongside the 'consumer society'. It normally feeds off consumer confidence. However, as the world today has not turned out to be so secure and stable, the first challenge for advertising is to contribute, as far as possible, to restoring consumer confidence. This will restore the necessary preconditions for an economy which fosters growth and dynamic consumption. It entails bringing optimism and hope to people who, these days, are exposed to so many uncertainties, constraints, anxieties and fears.

As for the second challenge, the past provides ample evidence that advertising has won hearts where it has been diverting, sometimes amusing, and often moving. Advertising runs on optimism and a light touch. Saturation of the consumers' world with advertising is one of the major issues facing tomorrow's advertisers. How can we continue to guarantee our clients effective communication programmes without being accused of intruding into the consumer's personal space?

Advertising experienced a golden age during the booming thirties, a period of double-digit growth which the economies of Europe then forgot all about for over twenty years. The baby boomers were the economic and cultural drivers of the following prosperous period and advertising has become accustomed to singing the praises of youth. Now demographers have alerted us to a new phenomenon: Western economies are getting inexorably older. The third challenge for advertising is to learn how to address these 'ex-youngsters' in a credible, appealing way.

Finally, the fourth challenge is that of the future of brands. This is a question that is clearly of concern to both clients and agencies.

The front of the Publicis building, at the top of the Champs-Élysées, where the headquarters of the Group is located.

Increased competition sometimes forces companies to adopt short-term strategies –lowering prices can seem like the quickest and most reliable means of defending market share. This is inevitably detrimental to the brand and, more seriously, detrimental to the profit margin. The logical consequence is that consumers are likely to turn away from major brands –if the added value of the brand is no longer significant, why pay the price differential? This phenomenon can most easily be seen at work in hard-discount stores. The new broader communications industry must now demonstrate that brands can retain their power of attraction.

I am confident; I know how inventive advertising people can be and this book illustrates this beautifully. Advertising is always faced with challenges. That is the way it became the formidable growth engine it is, driving the economy in general, and the growth of companies in particular. Advertising has also amply demonstrated an instinct for sociocultural insight to track down trends and shifts in mindset, and to adjust to or even anticipate them. The profession has always succeeded in holding fruitful dialogue with contemporary artists and personally, I am greatly committed to making this exchange flourish. In return, advertising has produced campaigns that are sometimes real works of art. It has usually found the right balance between creativity and craftsmanship, between industry and art, between reality and the world of the imagination. Advertising has always drawn on talent and technology in constantly updating its creativity.

My modest contribution to this story is to accompany some big brands, awaken some feelings, and find the right resonance with some consumers. Most of all, I would like to praise the talent, humanity and vision of the great men and women who made the last century and a half so full of ideas.

The communication industry has come of age and will go on to seduce you.

Viva la Difference!

"It's not advertising *anything*, damn it!"

Introduction

"It's not advertising <u>anything</u>, damn it!" says the father to his son wondering which brand supports the rainbow. This cartoon from the New Yorker provides a useful reminder that the whole world does not revolve around advertising. But it also shows that a child who has grown up surrounded by advertising may well believe that it was ever thus. It is easy to forget the way advertising has developed alongside production and distribution, easy to overlook the part brands have played in the creation both of a consumer society, and in improving our living conditions. Conversely, it is also true that paying too much heed to advertising can lead us to criticise it as pure and all-powerful –to believe it is capable of making rainbows.

This book tells the story of advertising. Our story begins in 1842, starting point of both the advertising industry and Publicis Groupe. It is true that a history of advertising could begin as early as the 1630s, when Frenchman Théophraste Renaudot placed the first advertising notices in La Gazette de France. Or perhaps in the United Kingdom in 1786, when William Tayler began to offer his services as "Agent to the Country's Printers, Booksellers, etc." in the Maidstone Journal. But it was in 1842 that the history of modern advertising began. That was when a certain Volney B. Palmer first uttered the words "advertising agent". That year, he created the first advertising agency in Philadelphia. And his agency just happens to be one of the founders of Publicis Groupe.

Our story brings us to 2006. This is a key date, the hundredth anniversary of the birth of Publicis' founder, Marcel Bleustein-Blanchet.

This long-term view of advertising allows us to identify its salient features more easily. What will we be able to observe? Firstly, we will see that advertising works best when it is fed on a diet of emotion mixed with rationality. In some places and at some times in its history, the advertising profession has binged on one or other of these. But the real challenge is to find the right balance between the two, to express a rational argument whilst appealing to the emotions.

Secondly, we will witness the variety of rhythms in advertising. Advertising sometimes entirely concentrates on short-lived 'eureka' moments. Some brands found their own message, and a means of encoding it, immediately having appeared on the scene. Yet other brands have worked more slowly, perhaps even laboriously, waiting

Cartoon by Charles E. Martin,
The New Yorker, 24 September 1966.

months or years until they found their own, distinctive angle. Marlboro is one brand which looked for a long while before finally finding its famous cowboy. Remarkably, given the industry's ephemeral, disposable image, some advertising images outlive fashions –and even generations. We will witness the (exceptionally) committed relationship between the agency N.W. Ayer & Son and Bell System, which spanned the period from 1908 to 1994.

Flexibility is another of the industry's key characteristics. Advertising emerged as a commercial phenomenon during the industrial revolution, selling first goods then services. Two world wars gave it a chance to help mobilise forces, but advertising was equally at home supporting the Russian revolution or promoting the American New Deal. It found words and images to accompany student protest and major appeals as well as promoting financial performance and corporate policy. Advertising is also astonishingly adaptable in adopting new techniques for new technologies. Although it grew up in print, it has since learned to live harmoniously with radio, cinema and television, developing specialist audiovisual skills. And the new electronic media now emerging are encouraging the industry to adopt even more new and original ideas.

As readers, we will marvel at the way advertising moulds itself to different cultures. This fourth characteristic was first observed when advertising had not spread far beyond the opposite sides of the Atlantic. It became more starkly apparent when commercial communication methods reached the command economies of Central and Eastern Europe. Such cultural confrontation was repeated many, many times as advertising was adopted in Asia, Africa and Latin America.

As to its fifth observable feature, it is undeniable that, through the adaptations it has made to accommodate different cultures and technologies, advertising has established an enviable ability to revitalise itself, in terms of both the issues it addresses and its approach. Much as we admire the skill of the industry's pioneers, who leapt out of the starting blocks with such success, we must not forget the tenacity of those who have taken up the baton and run with it over the past hundred and fifty years. They have all been creative, and this is not something to be dismissed lightly. Over the years, advertising has

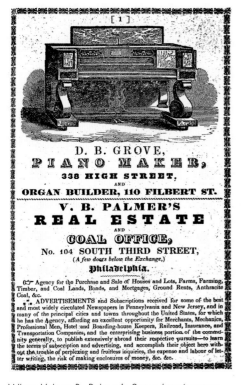

When Volney B. Palmer's first advertisement was published in M'Elroy's Philadelphia Directory in 1842, advertising was not yet the company's main focus.

invented a hundred and one ways of making the consumer connect with a brand —through humour or affection, prose or poetry, information or appeal, by whispering or shouting and even with fireworks.

The sixth phenomenon we will observe is how advertising constantly borrows from contemporary art —and lends in return— in terms of ideas and talents. The Container Corporation of America from the United States ran the most impressive campaign to illustrate this, calling on the greatest artists of the time. The list of contributors looks like a catalogue from a modern art museum! In Europe in general —and France and Italy in particular— most major film directors have worked on commercials.

There is a seventh and final observation we can make: advertising has always interacted with the media. This is partly because the advertising profession was born when newspapers delegated the sale of advertising space to brokers. Advertising's heritage explains why, for a long time and in many countries, agencies' remuneration was based on a percentage commission of the cost of the space or time their advertisements occupied, rather than a fixed fee. If we look deeper, we will see that media and advertising have always been an odd couple, with a relationship of complicity and competition. It is understandable that journalists worry about the potential for confusing fact and fiction, but it is also clear that writers and advertisers are united in the way they tap into social and cultural change.

This book outlines the main stages in the process by which the Publicis Groupe was formed. The founding agency, Volney B. Palmer, soon became part of N.W. Ayer & Son. Ayer's was an exceptional agency: with its hundred-and-thirty year lifespan, it is the grande dame of the United States advertising scene. The second branch of the US advertising family tree began with D'Arcy, an agency born in Saint Louis, Missouri, in 1906. Over its long lifetime, the agency associated with MacManus, from Detroit, then formed alliances with Masius from London and the New York-based Benton & Bowles network. It would ultimately found the DMB&B family. The third branch of the North American family descended from Leo Burnett. This agency had its roots in Chicago at the end of the Great Depression, and eventually grew into a global network, notable for its purchase of the London Press Exchange.

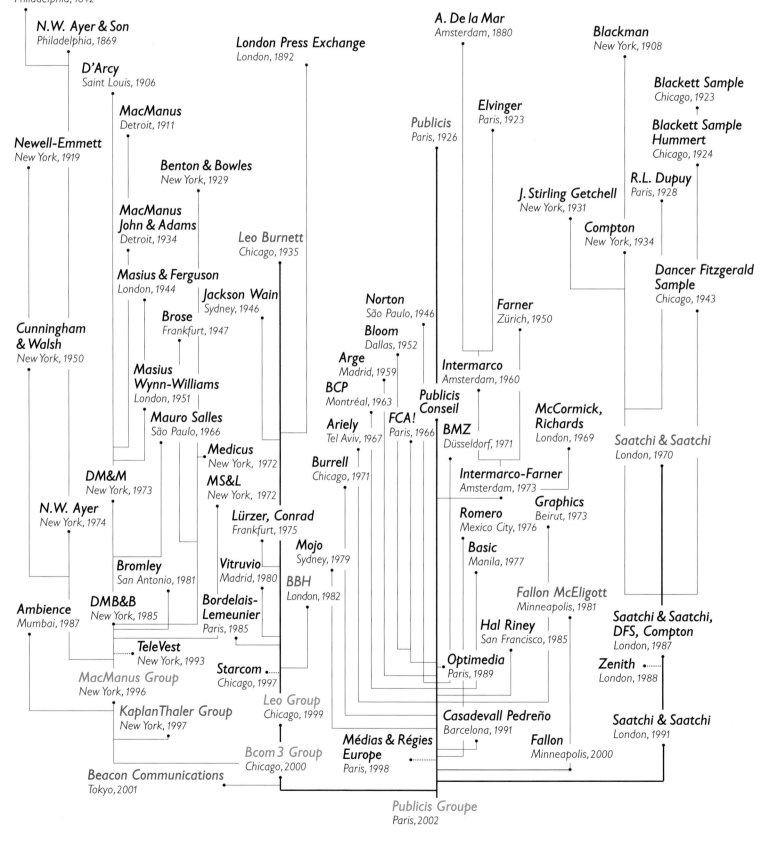

Volney B. Palmer
Philadelphia, 1842

N.W. Ayer & Son
Philadelphia, 1869

D'Arcy
Saint Louis, 1906

MacManus
Detroit, 1911

Newell-Emmett
New York, 1919

Benton & Bowles
New York, 1929

MacManus
John & Adams
Detroit, 1934

Masius & Ferguson
London, 1944

Jackson Wain
Sydney, 1946

Brose
Frankfurt, 1947

Cunningham
& Walsh
New York, 1950

Masius
Wynn-Williams
London, 1951

Mauro Salles
São Paulo, 1966

Medicus
New York, 1972

DM&M
New York, 1973

MS&L
New York, 1972

N.W. Ayer
New York, 1974

Lürzer, Conrad
Frankfurt, 1975

Mojo
Sydney, 1979

Bromley
San Antonio, 1981

Vitruvio
Madrid, 1980

BBH
London, 1982

Ambience
Mumbai, 1987

DMB&B
New York, 1985

Bordelais-
Lemeunier
Paris, 1985

TeleVest
New York, 1993

MacManus Group
New York, 1996

Starcom
Chicago, 1997

KaplanThaler Group
New York, 1997

Leo Group
Chicago, 1999

Bcom3 Group
Chicago, 2000

Beacon Communications
Tokyo, 2001

London Press Exchange
London, 1892

Leo Burnett
Chicago, 1935

A. De la Mar
Amsterdam, 1880

Publicis
Paris, 1926

Elvinger
Paris, 1923

Norton
São Paulo, 1946

Bloom
Dallas, 1952

Arge
Madrid, 1959

BCP
Montréal, 1963

Ariely
Tel Aviv, 1967

FCA!
Paris, 1966

Burrell
Chicago, 1971

Publicis
Conseil

Intermarco
Amsterdam, 1960

Farner
Zürich, 1950

BMZ
Düsseldorf, 1971

McCormick,
Richards
London, 1969

Intermarco-Farner
Amsterdam, 1973

Romero
Mexico City, 1976

Graphics
Beirut, 1973

Basic
Manila, 1977

Fallon McEligott
Minneapolis, 1981

Hal Riney
San Francisco, 1985

Optimedia
Paris, 1989

Casadevall Pedreño
Barcelona, 1991

Médias & Régies
Europe
Paris, 1998

Fallon
Minneapolis, 2000

Blackman
New York, 1908

Blackett Sample
Chicago, 1923

Blackett Sample
Hummert
Chicago, 1924

R.L. Dupuy
Paris, 1928

J. Stirling Getchell
New York, 1931

Compton
New York, 1934

Dancer Fitzgerald
Sample
Chicago, 1943

Saatchi & Saatchi
London, 1970

Saatchi & Saatchi,
DFS, Compton
London, 1987

Zenith
London, 1988

Saatchi & Saatchi
London, 1991

Publicis Groupe
Paris, 2002

The Publicis Groupe can also count Saatchi & Saatchi among its number. This major British agency became a strong global network after it had taken over two american agencies, Compton and Dancer Fitzgerald Sample.

Meanwhile, the Group can trace its roots back to the birth of the Dutch agency De la Mar, one of the oldest in mainland Europe, and above all to Marcel Bleustein, who created an agency called Publicis in Paris in 1926. This agency began to expand into the international arena in the early '70s, when it purchased two European networks. The first was Intermarco, the second Farner –which encompassed the De la Mar in the Netherlands and Elvinger, already a presence on the French market. Publicis' expansion continued apace, uniting in 1989 with the US-based international network Foote, Cone & Belding. When this union foundered, Publicis set out in 1996 to build its own network.

Besides these major historic brands, the Publicis Groupe also encompasses newer arrivals. There is Fallon, from Minneapolis, the Kaplan Thaler Group, whose home is New York, and London-based BBH (in which the Group owns a large minority share), not to mention Beacon Communications from Tokyo, in which Dentsu, the prominent actor of the Japanese communication scene which contracted an alliance with Publicis Groupe in 2002, has also an interest.

With such a vast territory to explore, this book has had to limit its scope. The first limitation applied was on the agencies portrayed. Many companies are mentioned, but many more are not. Indeed, although their work is rich and varied, specialist advertisers –who focus either on particular subject areas such as corporate or financial communications, health or sport or on special skills like design, publishing, electronic communications, public relations, events, direct marketing or sales promotion– have not received their just deserts. We might say the same of media operations, like ZenithOptimedia, Starcom MediaVest or Médias & Régies Europe. These feature only briefly here, despite playing an increasingly crucial role in the communications industry.

Nor does the book do justice to the multitude of communications techniques in existence. The traditional advertising media (posters, the press and audio-visual advertisements) feature heavily here, to the detriment of new media. What is more, printed material, such as

Development stages of a global communication group: founding dates of the main agencies and their successive mergers until their absorption into the group. In red, the main networks as of 2006, in blue the holding companies. The links between advertising agencies are shown by solid lines, those between media agencies are dotted.

posters and newspaper advertisements, predominates simply because that is what packs a punch in a publication such as this.

We also chose advertisements that stood out for their strategic or representational brilliance in linking art with advertising. Which is not to say our choice of advertisements was easy. We were interested in art based both on words and images. For the more distant periods covered –where we had the luxury of hindsight– the choice was easier. We could rely on the opinions of others, such as advertising historians and members of professional bodies, who had assessed the output of the period. For the later periods, the opinions of the Group's creative directors proved invaluable. In many cases, the work we chose has won awards, but we have streamlined our commentary and have therefore chosen not to list them.

It is worth mentioning briefly that the names of agencies are cited as they were at the time when the work shown was produced. And we have not listed all the names of our colleagues within the Group who made such excellent contributions. However, we have tried wherever possible to supply the names of featured artists, illustrators, photographers, musicians, directors and actors from outside the Groupe.

From a geographic viewpoint, we were keen to allow each continent to showcase its wares. Nevertheless, we cannot deny the truth: ever since its inception, advertising has been an overwhelmingly western phenomenon which started in North America and spread to Europe. Thus a large proportion of the book's advertisements originate from the US, UK and France, but no more than is fitting for three countries that have played such a large part in the history of advertising in general. In recent times, of course, this Western bias has begun to lessen as the global scene has become remoulded and other continents' works have emerged.

This book is a journey through the history of advertising, and it has a fixed destination. It aims to give all sorts of products their due, from the everyday and ubiquitous to the lavish and luxurious, as well as the latest technologies. By reviewing such a vast landscape of consumption, we can discern how mindsets and lifestyles evolved in the course of time.

Raymond Savignac's "Garap" poster for Paris Advertising Week, 1953.

It is a journey which aims to revisit the evolution of the way advertising is expressed. This means looking at the artistic facet of advertising, but it also means reviewing the technology employed. We will look at typography, developments in colour printing and the route advertising took from its beginnings in illustration through photography and into the digital revolution.

This book is ordered chronologically. It is divided into five chapters, all built round the same principle. From the first page of each chapter, we will encounter a selection of agencies that came to prominence in the Publicis Groupe during the relevant period. Each chapter opens with an overview of the politics, society and arts of the era in question. Then the main body of the chapter comprises a series of double-page spreads, each dealing with a major campaign or issue. All consumption sectors are addressed. The final two chapters also deal with key social causes which have come to the fore in recent years –Saatchi & Saatchi is one agency which has been particularly successful at this sort of work.

At the end of the book, we will encounter contributions from the creative directors of the six major advertising networks that form the Groupe. Each supplies their own unique vision of the challenges advertising will have to face in future.

"It's not advertising anything" –or perhaps "everything is advertising"? To mark the Paris Semaine de la publicité (Advertising Week) in 1953, Savignac produced this poster to advertise something called "Garap". It was a tremendous success, and everyone was talking about it. But the famous product didn't actually exist. What Savignac was really illustrating was the power of advertising. But he had his tongue firmly in his cheek: he explained that "Garap" was short for "gare à la pub.", or 'be wary of advertising'. So Savignac was probably just like you and I –someone who knows and likes rainbows for what they are.

Chapter I

1842-1920

Volney B. Palmer

N.W. Ayer & Son

De la Mar

London Press Exchange

D'Arcy

Blackman

Mac Manus

The Pioneers

Times Square, New York. The name reflects the New York Times' presence from 1904 onwards. The first electric sign shone out on the corner of Broadway.

On the page opposite are listed the names of the advertising agencies which created the works illustrating this chapter. All of them were founded during the period covered by the chapter. A similar list will appear at the beginning of the four following chapters, adding the agencies founded during the period and those founded previously and still in existence at that time.

The first advertising people were primarily people who pioneered the idea that the industrial revolution could bring about mass consumption through mass communication. In the United States, two people had a key impact on laying the foundations for the profession: George P. Rowell, who published the first media directory in 1869, and Francis W. Ayer who, a short time later, offered his clients a transparent, commission-based, payment system. This took courage considering that some of the first steps taken in advertising were far from promising: fanciful advertisements flaunting charlatans' potions, and middlemen duping both the newspapers, for whom they were supposed to be selling advertising space, and the advertisers, who paid a high price for promises of placements which were not always kept.

Fortunately, advertising succeeded in breaking with this dubious tradition. In the space of a single generation, the foundations for the profession had been laid both in the United States and the major European economies. Consumer motivation came into play. Jobs in advertising became professional roles. Buying advertising space was now conducted according to quantitative, objective criteria. A whole range of media was tested in a short space of time: mobile advertising, sandwich boards, and brochures. The first of what we now call posters appeared on public transport in London in 1847, and catalogues appeared in France at the turn of the century.

It followed that the major advertisers of the time thought fit to convert to this new respectable, efficient way to do business. Brands became an essential weapon in the armoury of manufacturers setting out to conquer their national markets. These manufacturers were no longer content to rely on local distributors to promote their products.

During these years, the world was changing at mind-boggling speed. The upheaval of the Civil War in America and the revolutionary movements in Europe left their mark on the popular psyche. However, the industrial revolution was in full swing and standards of living advanced immeasurably between the mid-nineteenth century and the eve of the First World War. The first country to give women the right to vote was New Zealand in 1893. Freud was exploring the unconscious mind; cubism and expressionism were laying down new aesthetic challenges to traditional art. The world had changed beyond recognition.

Women in Ads

Corsets had a firm grip on women's bodies and men's minds. Questions asked about the status of women during this era would remain unanswered until after the First World War. Women were still mainly portrayed as objects of desire.

1

2

Green for hope and fertility, purple for dignity and white for purity: these were the colours of the Women's Social and Political Union, founded by Christabel Pankhurst in Manchester in 1903, with the aim of campaigning for women's suffrage. Votes for Women was the suffragettes' monthly publication, launched in 1907. The Union's three colours are shown in this 1909 poster created by the militant artist Hilda Dallas (1). Recognition of the political rights of women was slow in coming, but their role in society was nevertheless changing and this was reflected in advertising. In a break from societal convention women were shown reading the press, implied by this 1895 advertisement by E. Pickert for the New York Times, in the Art Nouveau style (2). In another advertisement, which appeared in the United States in 1896, the French actress Sarah Bernhardt promotes Lowney's bonbons (3). While the brand benefited from her testimonial, the actress would also have expected to benefit. In fact, this advertisement was a subtle means by which she could promote the American tour she was planning.

3

The portrayal of women was a major source of inspiration for posters of the day. Jules Chéret and Alphonse Mucha in France, and Edward Penfield in the United States were just some of the artists to cover the walls with such work. The French painter Henri de Toulouse-Lautrec produced this poster in 1896 for his friend, the photographer Paul Sescau (4). There was also passionate enthusiasm in this Belle Époque for the latest technical discoveries, celebrated in several international exhibitions. In this poster for Ivens & Co of Amsterdam, which dates from around 1900, the Dutch painter and poster artist Johan G. van Caspel uses the image of a woman in an allegorical way, to represent science and technology (5). This increasing use of artists to create posters was due to both their graphic skills and their mastery of lithography, a process invented by Aloys Senefelder in 1796, which allowed large format posters to be printed in large numbers.

4

5

Kub and Dada

The paths of advertising and art often cross. Artists have influenced advertising, which —being so widespread— has had an impact on their work. Here, art shook off tradition and went out onto the street. New artistic directions emerged, drawing on everyday life and on advertising.

1

Julius Maggi & Cie was founded in Switzerland in 1872 and from 1907 marketed a meat concentrate, the stock cube, or Kub in German. After an initial fruitless attempt, the Swiss company was finally established in France in 1897. The company had always attached great importance to advertising; from the 1880s, it had its own advertising department. The launch of the stock Kub was synonymous with communication on an even grander scale. The plan was to fight off imitators, as two German firms, Liebig and Springer, had copied the product, and also to counter violent attacks from French nationalists. Maggi therefore registered the name Kub and created the slogan 'Exiger le K' (Ask for the K). Posters flooded towns and cities; in 1911, Maggi turned to the Italian painter and poster artist Leonetto Cappiello. Capiello was a pioneer of lithography applied to posters and also succeeded in bringing together text and image in a creative way (2). This advertising campaign also employed boards and enamelled signs (Maggi was the first food producer to use the latter), which were displayed in kiosks, on walls and in shop windows (1).

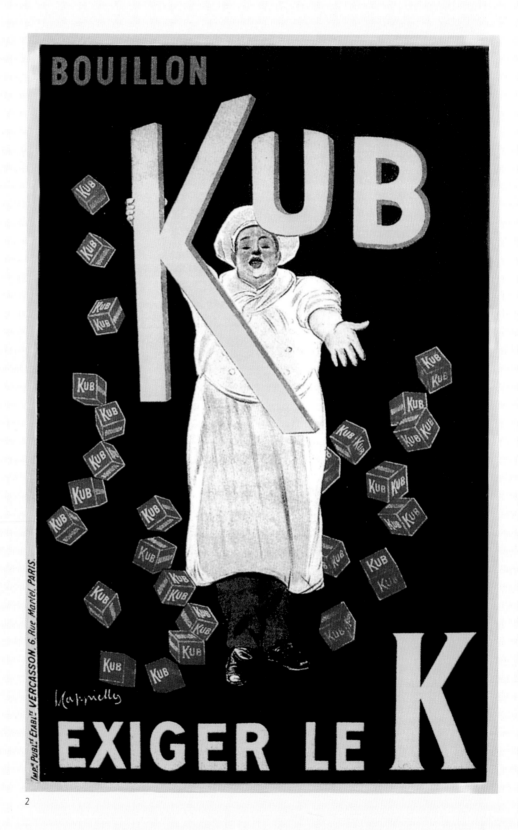

2

3

At the dawn of the twentieth century, Paris was the crossroads at which all the new talented artists met. Working at the time of the major influence of the Kub advertisement, Pablo Picasso painted "Paysage aux affiches" (Landscape with posters) (3) in 1912, placing the famous cube (5) alongside a Pernod Fils bottle and the logo of the hat maker Léon (4). In 1914, Piet Mondrian inserted the —clearly legible— word Kub into his work "Composition dans l'ovale avec plans de couleurs 2" (Composition in oval with colour planes 2). The critics rushed to denounce "these painters who offer themselves, body and soul, to advertising." Against this backdrop, the Cubist movement emerged. Could it be that the modest little Kub had lent its name to a whole movement? There are certainly close ties between the Kub and Cubism. In 1911, Guillaume Apollinaire wrote an article entitled "Le Kub", in which he noted that Matisse "made fun (…) of cubism" even though "he thought up the name himself." In 1916, at Zurich's Cabaret Voltaire, a group of artists including Tristan Tzara and Hans Arp launched a new movement, the manifesto for which was inspired by a local advertisement for a hair strengthening tonic called 'Dada' (6). Thus the Dada movement was born!

4

5

6

Your country needs you

With the coming of the First World War, propaganda turned to posters in a show of strength. Skill and artistry supported war efforts from 1914 to the Russian Revolution in October 1917.

The choice and expression of themes used by the parties to the first global conflict in their posters were singularly similar. Although their ideologies were opposed, the formulae they used to promote joining the cause were identical. The themes and the gestures (finger and gaze fixed on the viewing public) were identical; the words were almost identical. At the beginning of the war, the UK tried to recruit soldiers on a voluntary basis. Thus it was the UK that fired an opening salvo in 1914 with this poster by Alfred Leete, depicting Lord Kitchener of Khartoum, then Minister of War (3). In 1915, the same theme was taken up in Germany, illustrated by a soldier with a rank of private addressing the viewer in a familiar tone: "You too should enlist in the army of the Reich" (2). Besides recruiting, the warring nations needed to raise money. Once again, they turned to posters as the medium for this message. In 1917, Achille Lucien Mauzan created this poster for Credito Italiano, to go towards the war effort: "Everyone should do his duty!" (1).

I WANT **YOU**
FOR U.S. ARMY
NEAREST RECRUITING STATION

4

5

In 1917, the United States *staged a massive*
recruitment drive and commissioned
James Montgomery Flagg to produce a poster;
the result was inspired by the British poster,
but featured Uncle Sam (4). *In June, the members*
of the Associated Advertising Clubs of the World
met in St. Louis and signed-up to the war effort.
They revisited Flagg's poster –this time Uncle
Sam invites the citizen to buy a liberty bond (6).
In 1920, when battles were raging between the
Bolsheviks and the White Russians, the Soviet
illustrator Dmitri S. Moor picked up the same
theme, asking: "You, have you volunteered?" (5).

6

Advertising becomes a profession

The job of advertising agent was emerging. They had been newspaper sales representatives, working for commission; now agencies offered a comprehensive service. The rudiments of the profession appeared in Europe, but the United States gave advertising the shape we recognise today.

2

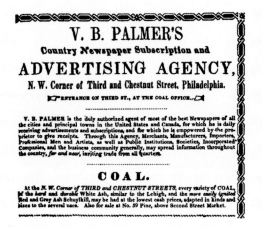

V. B. PALMER'S
Country Newspaper Subscription and
ADVERTISING AGENCY,
N. W. Corner of Third and Chestnut Street, Philadelphia.

☞ ENTRANCE ON THIRD ST., AT THE COAL OFFICE. ◁

V. B. PALMER is the duly authorized agent of most of the best Newspapers of all the cities and principal towns in the United States and Canada, for which he is daily receiving advertisements and subscriptions, and for which he is empowered by the proprietor to give receipts. Through this Agency, Merchants, Manufacturers, Importers, Professional Men and Artists, as well as Public Institutions, Societies, Incorporated Companies, and the business community generally, may spread information throughout the country, *far and near*, inviting trade from all quarters.

COAL.

At the N. W. Corner of THIRD and CHESTNUT STREETS, every variety of COAL, of the hard and durable White Ash, similar to the Lehigh, and the more easily ignited Red and Gray Ash Schuylkill, may be had at the lowest cash prices, adapted in kinds and sizes to the several uses. Also for sale at No. 59 Pine, above Second Street Market.

1

*Volney B. Palmer, considered to have been the world's first agency, was founded in Philadelphia in 1842. It issued its own advertisement in 1849 (1) in McElroy's Philadelphia Directory and the term 'advertising agency' was used for the first time. It later became Coe, Wetherill & Co. and was bought by **N.W. Ayer & Son**, an agency established in 1869, also in Philadelphia by Francis Wayland Ayer, a young, religious newspaper representative. Ayer sought to achieve professional status for his line of work. He no longer thought of himself as a newspaper representative, but as a supplier to industry. In 1876, he defined the transparent relationship he would henceforth enjoy with industry in what has been called "the open contract." Ayer's own advertisements regularly appeared in the professional press, as can be seen from this 1893 advertisement (3). The firms that had a permanent presence in the papers were those that had understood the message "Keeping everlastingly at it brings success." From 1886 onwards, this became the agency's motto. In 1906, **D'Arcy** had just been established in St. Louis and was sharing Coca-Cola's advertising with another agency, Massengale, based in Atlanta. D'Arcy chose the letter "D" with an arrow through it as its monogram (2). D'Arcy used this monogram in the advertisements it produced for Coca-Cola in which an arrow also appeared alongside the slogan "Whenever you see an arrow, think of Coca-Cola."*

COASTING ➤

is the term given by bicycle riders to their practice of taking the feet from the pedals and allowing the machine to run with the momentum acquired from previous effort.

This is the season when many business men are tempted to try "coasting" with their Newspaper Advertising.

The newspapers themselves however do not "coast." They are regularly issued, and regularly read, and the advertisers who have learned that

Keeping
EVERLASTINGLY AT IT
Brings Success

are regularly represented therein. They would no more "coast" with their advertising than with their employees, or any other every-day business necessity.

Coasting is a down-grade exercise. Success is an up-hill station. We have been there ourselves. We have gone there with many successful Newspaper Advertisers. We will be glad to start with you.

Correspondence solicited.

N. W. AYER & SON,
Newspaper Advertising Agents,
Philadelphia.

3

4

In 1880, the agency **De la Mar** was created in the Netherlands. It would join Publicis much later in 1972. Its brochure stated that the agency "is to the advertising customer what the compass is to the seafarer" (5). Besides handling mass-market goods, this agency, which produced financial advertising, sold advertising space and had links with the news agency Reuters. Oscar H. Blackman created his own agency in New York in 1908. A year later, it also bore the name of his associate Frederick Ross. This 1919 advertisement explains why an agency needs a "manager of advertising" (6). **Blackman** changed its name again in 1935, to become Compton. An International Advertising Exhibition took place in London in 1920. This poster by Frederick Charles Herrick features some of the great advertising icons of the time, including the Michelin Man, the Bisto kids, Mr. Punch, the Kodak girl and the Johnnie Walker striding man (4).

5

6

The birth of a brand

Follow the arrow and you will go far! In 1906, when Coca-Cola
entrusted some of its advertising to the D'Arcy agency,
no one, perhaps, realised that they were creating what would
become one of the best-known brands in the world.

2

1

In 1886 John S. Pemberton, *a pharmacist from
Atlanta, perfected a tonic with a name inspired
by one of its ingredients, coca, which would soon
be expressed in "Spencerian script." Two years
later, Asa G. Candler acquired the business and
added carbonated water to the syrup. In 1892,
the Coca-Cola Company was created, and in
1895, the new drink found widespread favour.
Bottling and distribution were contracted out but
Coca-Cola retained the secret recipe for its soda
as well as ownership of the brand and its image.
Originally a specialist medicinal product, Coke
became a "delicious, refreshing, thirst-quenching"
drink. D'Arcy ran a campaign based on the arrow
theme in an initial attempt to give a graphic
personality to the brand's advertising materials.
For more than ten years, this theme ran through
all the advertisements. The three examples
shown here are drawn from a rich seam of
material and illustrate the drink's availability (1),
its effect on dehydration (2), and Coca-Cola as
a source of pleasure (3).*

3

The originality of this advertisement, which appeared in 1914, lies in the skilful use of the first and last pages of the monthly magazine in which it appeared (4). The illustration in the advertisement, on the left, echoes the cover illustration, on the right. Thus the brand generates a greater presence in the magazine. The following year, the glass manufacturer C.S. Root put the finishing touches to the famous Coca-Cola bottle, drawing his inspiration from the coca bean, and designed a logo in relief. The brand graphics and bottle shape would change little in the years to come (5).

5

Mere commodities no more!

Mass-market goods, especially groceries, had previously been sold loose; now they were sold in packets. Brands were committed to ensuring the quality of their products and packaging also provided them with a new way of expressing their identity.

2

1

In 1898, three U.S. bakery groups came together to establish the National Biscuit Company, later known by its acronym Nabisco. The company cooperated with **N.W. Ayer & Son** on the launch of the first packaged soda crackers. Shops had previously sold crackers loose and there was no guaranteeing their quality or freshness.
A cardboard packet, lined with greaseproof paper, would now protect the product against humidity. This technical innovation was represented in the company's advertisement by the boy's oilskin raincoat (6). A brand name was required –in this case, Uneeda Biscuit was chosen, a clear phonetic statement. A quality seal was also added to each packet. It bore the words "inner seal" (later simplified to "in er seal" as in this advertisement), to indicate that the flavour was locked inside; the idea of freshness was used to promote the crackers: "The Bakers' Best From The Oven To You In The Package With This Seal" (1). The company also built an innovative and sophisticated brand architecture (2).
All its brands bore the National Biscuit Seal and Uneeda endorsed a wide range of products (there were forty-four in 1908) (3).

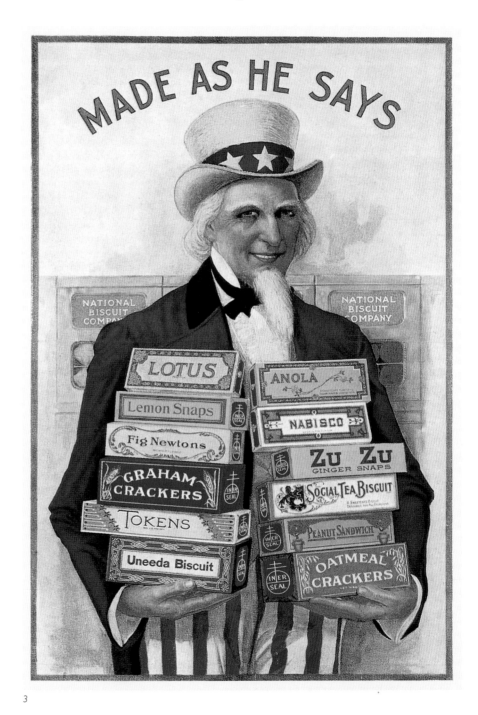

3

The Rueckheim brothers sold snacks made of popcorn, peanuts and molasses, which were very popular on the streets of Chicago. Around 1893, they found a way of packaging their snacks that helped them keep longer and stopped them sticking together. They named these sweets Cracker Jack, which according to the slang of the time meant 'exceptional'. The job of advertising these sweets went to N.W. Ayer & Son. Shortly afterwards, the image of a sailor boy appeared, accompanied by a dog, and in 1919 this picture was added to the packaging (4). Robert, the grandson of one of the Rueckheim brothers, and his dog Bingo, inspired the sailor and his dog. The slogan "The more you eat, the more you want" dates from the same era and is still in use. Morton's Salt is also N.W. Ayer & Son advertising; once again packaging and a character came into play. The selling point of Morton's Salt was that it was so well packaged it stayed dry and flowed well, free from the effects of humidity, hence "When it rains, it pours" (5). This slogan, too, has been retained ever since its inception in 1911. The little girl under the umbrella, an image used to express the same idea as the slogan, was also created in 1911. Her image remains, but the style in which she is represented has been regularly updated.

5

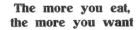

4

6

A million for the boy

It was said to be the first time a brand had invested a million dollars in an advertising campaign.
In today's money, given the rise in the retail price index, this represents roughly twenty million dollars.
The name of the million-dollar boy in a yellow oilskin raincoat was Gordon.

1

Nabisco and its agency N.W. Ayer & Son spent
big money on promoting Uneeda. Their
campaigns were many and varied: advertisements
in magazines and newspapers, small signs on
tramcars, small posters, and a whole series of
postcards (1) and large posters (2). In fact, it used
all the media available at the time, including
immense murals. All these campaigns were highly
consistent: their single message was borne by the
boy in a yellow oilskin raincoat. As with the other
mascots created by N.W. Ayer & Son, this little
boy was inspired by a real person: in this case,
Gordon Stille, the nephew of a staff member
at the agency. The brand name, Uneeda Biscuit,
was popularised in chirpy verse, which made it
easy to remember: "Lest you forget, We say it yet:
Uneeda Biscuit." The result was commensurate with
the funds invested; Uneeda achieved enormous
success at a time when the first chain stores, like
Woolworth, were emerging.

2

eda Biscuit
IN ER
SEAL
THE
NATIONAL
FOOD
NATIONAL BISCUIT COMPANY

"Ol' Joe"

When a cigarette becomes the top brand in the
United States within five years, with a 40% market share,
it cannot be put down to luck. Indeed, a camel named
"Ol' Joe" played the starring role in this brand's success.

2

1

The year was 1913 and American taste was
turning irrevocably towards cigarettes. Brands
were all regionally-based and R.J. Reynolds was
seeking to repeat the nationwide success of their
Prince Albert pipe tobacco. To launch the first
national cigarette brand in the States, they stuck
with **N.W. Ayer & Son**, whom they had worked
with successfully in the past. As the fashion was
for all things Oriental, they prepared a refined
blend of Turkish and American tobaccos.
They needed a name so they registered Camel,
a simple word with exotic connotations, reminiscent
of the animal names they gave to the original
chewing tobacco –Humming Bird, Old Rat, Duck
Leg, Red Rabbit. To create the illustration for the
packet, they drew inspiration from a photograph
of "Ol' Joe", the dromedary from the Barnum &
Bailey circus then in town (1). In 1914, the brand
was launched in the press, and the launch was
based on a series of four advertisements that
played on the brand name and placed "Ol' Joe"
centre stage (3). One last original feature: where
other brands offered free gifts in their packets,
Camel states that the tobacco used is too
expensive to allow such luxuries (2).

3

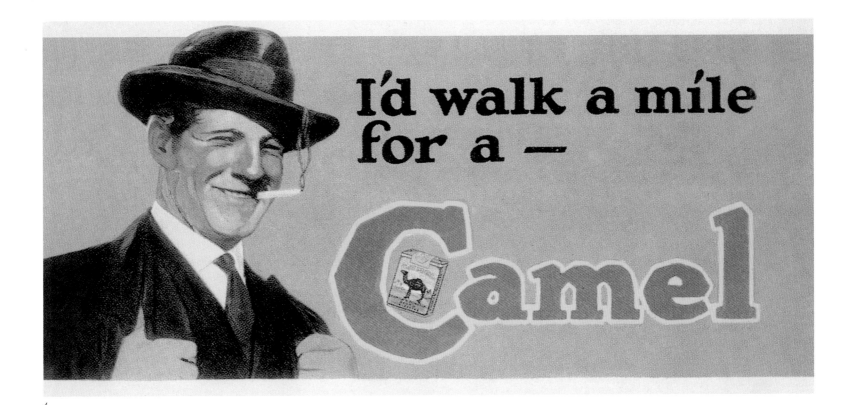

4

After their successful launch, *Camel and N.W. Ayer & Son explored another avenue. In 1921, a series of advertisements was developed containing a selection of characters. A farmer straight from the rural heart of America declared "I ought to know. I grow tobacco, you can't beat a Camel." A businessman ("Mellowness is rich, fragrant mildness Camels") and an office worker ("Folks who appreciate really fine tobacco become wedded to Camels") were also portrayed. Research undertaken at the time showed that all the advertisements were well-received, but one was especially popular. It featured a mature man, who seems virile and self-assured, with an air of both the country gent and the city businessman; he smiles and says "I'd walk a mile for a Camel" (4). This message was translated into the various languages of the melting pot of American society (shown here in Chinese, Norwegian and Spanish) (5), in a precursor of today's ethnic communications. This slogan became the brand's signature until 1929, and was revived in the forties when the agency Dancer Fitzgerald Sample was engaged for the brand's advertising work.*

5

The power of words

*Some words are strong enough to stand alone as the starting point for a campaign.
Words which, years later, remain fresh in the viewer's mind, still expressing
the soul of a brand and still remaining inextricably linked to that brand.*

1

*Established in 1902, Cadillac was soon advertising
–witness this 1903 example from the stable of
N.W. Ayer & Son (1). In 1909, General Motors
bought Cadillac; Cadillac was the jewel in the
crown of the future American giant but, in 1914,
encountered technical problems with the engine
for a new model. Seizing its chance to exploit this
moment of weakness in a normally formidable
competitor, Packard launched an offensive.*
***MacManus**, an agency established in Detroit in
1911, which was to join D'Arcy in 1971, was asked
to respond; the agency, which believed strongly
in the power of words, created "The Penalty of
Leadership." This advertisement appeared only
once, on 2 January 1915 in the Saturday Evening
Post (3). The text is skilfully written. In essence,
it implies that the virulence of the attacks made is
proportionate to the excellence of the Cadillac:
in other words, critics are testament to the strength
of the brand. The image of excellence recurs in
future years, as demonstrated by George Harper's
1925 advertisement for a vehicle with a ninety
degree V engine (2). No vehicle is shown, but
the text incorporates the expression "The Penalty
of Leadership."*

2

The PENALTY OF LEADERSHIP

IN every field of human endeavor, he that is first must perpetually live in the white light of publicity. ¶Whether the leadership be vested in a man or in a manufactured product, emulation and envy are ever at work. ¶In art, in literature, in music, in industry, the reward and the punishment are always the same. ¶The reward is widespread recognition; the punishment, fierce denial and detraction. ¶When a man's work becomes a standard for the whole world, it also becomes a target for the shafts of the envious few. ¶If his work be merely mediocre, he will be left severely alone—if he achieve a masterpiece, it will set a million tongues a-wagging. ¶Jealousy does not protrude its forked tongue at the artist who produces a commonplace painting. ¶Whatsoever you write, or paint, or play, or sing, or build, no one will strive to surpass, or to slander you, unless your work be stamped with the seal of genius. ¶Long, long after a great work or a good work has been done, those who are disappointed or envious continue to cry out that it can not be done. ¶Spiteful little voices in the domain of art were raised against our own Whistler as a mountebank, long after the big world had acclaimed him its greatest artistic genius. ¶Multitudes flocked to Bayreuth to worship at the musical shrine of Wagner, while the little group of those whom he had dethroned and displaced argued angrily that he was no musician at all. ¶The little world continued to protest that Fulton could never build a steamboat, while the big world flocked to the river banks to see his boat steam by. ¶The leader is assailed because he is a leader, and the effort to equal him is merely added proof of that leadership. ¶Failing to equal or to excel, the follower seeks to depreciate and to destroy—but only confirms once more the superiority of that which he strives to supplant. ¶There is nothing new in this. ¶It is as old as the world and as old as the human passions—envy, fear, greed, ambition, and the desire to surpass. ¶And it all avails nothing. ¶If the leader truly leads, he remains—the leader. ¶Master-poet, master-painter, master-workman, each in his turn is assailed, and each holds his laurels through the ages. ¶That which is good or great makes itself known, no matter how loud the clamor of denial. ¶That which deserves to live—lives.

Cadillac Motor Car Co. Detroit, Mich.

3

A dubious cleanliness

Education about cleanliness in body and home was increasing in the late nineteenth century and buoyed up sales of all sorts of new detergents. However, the concept of cleanliness could go overboard, leading to racist, chauvinist forms of expression.

2

If we could teach the Indians to USE **SAPOLIO** it would quickly civilize them

1

This is the maid of fair renown
Who scrubs the floors of Spotless Town.
To find a speck when she is through
Would take a pair of specs or two,
And her employment isn't slow,
For she employs

SAPOLIO

3

This is the butcher of Spotless Town,
His tools are bright as his renown.
To leave them stained were indiscreet,
For folks would then abstain from meat,
And so he brightens his trade you know
By polishing with

SAPOLIO

4

The Sapolio brand of soap, launched in 1868 by Enoch Morgan Sons, played in hundreds of ways with the central tenet "Use Sapolio". For example, it suggested that the use of Sapolio by Native Americans would take them a long way down the road towards civilisation (1). It also associated the soap with a maid, happy to go down on all fours and scrub the floor because she uses Sapolio (2). In an era when the effect of slogans and rhyme in advertising was being discovered, James Kenneth Fraser, the future head of the **Blackman** agency, invented "Spotless Town." The inhabitants of this town each had their own signs on trams; here are the maid (3), the butcher (4) and the 'spotter' (5).

Good for the Spotter of Spotless Town! He spotted a spot on the Butcher's gown.
'T would not be meet, for justice' sake, to roast the Butcher at the steak,
And so behind the bars he'll go.
Bars of what?——— **SAPOLIO**

5

Roosevelt scoured Africa — The **GOLD DUST TWINS** Scour America

"Let the **GOLD DUST TWINS** do your work"

6

7

From 1891, N.W. Ayer & Son worked on advertising for N.K. Fairbank. This was the Chicago company that, in 1884, had produced the all-purpose washing powder Gold Dust, a product as yellow and fine as its name suggests. Goldie and Dusty, the twins who represented the brand (7) were inspired by a cartoon by E.W. Kempel that appeared in the English magazine Punch. "Let the Gold Dust twins work for you" was the theme which ran through the campaign; this was certainly cynical, but also a sign of the times. The same idea, just as unsympathetic, was applied in George Henry Edward Hawkins' 1910 creation (8). In the same year, and in the same vein, this advertisement was posted on walls a week after U.S. President Theodore Roosevelt returned from a hunting trip to Africa (6).

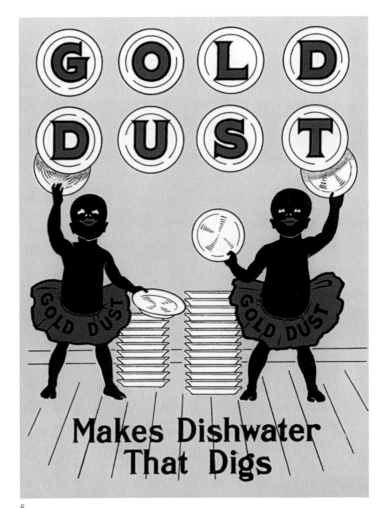

GOLD DUST

Makes Dishwater That Digs

8

White-collar man

*Cluett Peabody was one of the first advertisers to offer the consumer
an idealised, aspirational alter ego instead of simply showcasing the product.
This was a real departure from the dominant strategies of the day.*

1

2

3

The "white-collar man" *was Charles Beach, who
was Canadian. He had been a secretary, an
accountant, an agent and then assistant to Joseph
Christian Leyendecker, one of the most popular
illustrators in the United States at the beginning
of the twentieth century. But above all, for almost
fifty years, he was Leyendecker's model for the
man with the Arrow collar. Our story begins in
1885, when George B. Cluett bought a New York
company that specialised in detachable collars,
established in 1851, and then joined forces with
Frederick F. Peabody, who was selling his collars
under the brand name Arrow. The two associates
retained the name and added shirts to their
range. In 1905 they approached an illustrator,
Joseph C. Leyendecker and then engaged
N.W. Ayer & Son for their advertising.
He illustrated the Arrow advertisements until
1931; no illustrator would replace him as
photography replaced drawing and painting in
most of the advertising of the 1930s. Much later,
when Arrow once again wanted to capture the
style of these advertisements, they returned
to Leyendecker's drawings, which had become so
closely identified with the brand. By creating the
idealised image of the man about town at that
time, Leyendecker created a timeless picture
of elegance (1), (2), (3). This is fashion that never
goes out of style.*

In Europe at the end of the nineteenth century, posters were entrusted to painters and were therefore directly influenced by the art of the time. In the United States at the beginning of the twentieth century, cartoonists and illustrators started to produce the advertisements. Advertisers and agencies believed that an illustrators' realistic style was also more accessible and better reflected the tastes of people. Leyendecker is an excellent example of this trend. He is known for his Arrow work (4), (5) but he also worked for other brands, such as Chesterfield cigarettes. Leyendecker also regularly illustrated covers for the Saturday Evening Post: 321 to be precise! It was Leyendecker who created the most enduring image of American manhood, real or imagined. Other illustrators also constructed strong American archetypes, as Charles Dana Gibson did with the 'Gibson Girl.' Norman Rockwell, who was a highly-detailed, often sardonic, and always affectionate observer of family life, also designed many covers for the Saturday Evening Post. Earnest Elmo Calkins promoted the artistic side of advertising illustrations; his stated ambition was to educate the public through art as expressed in his book 'The Business of Advertising'. The other great American professional of the day, Claude C. Hopkins, opposed him on this, preferring 'reason why' to 'fancy' advertising as stated in "My Life in Advertising."

4

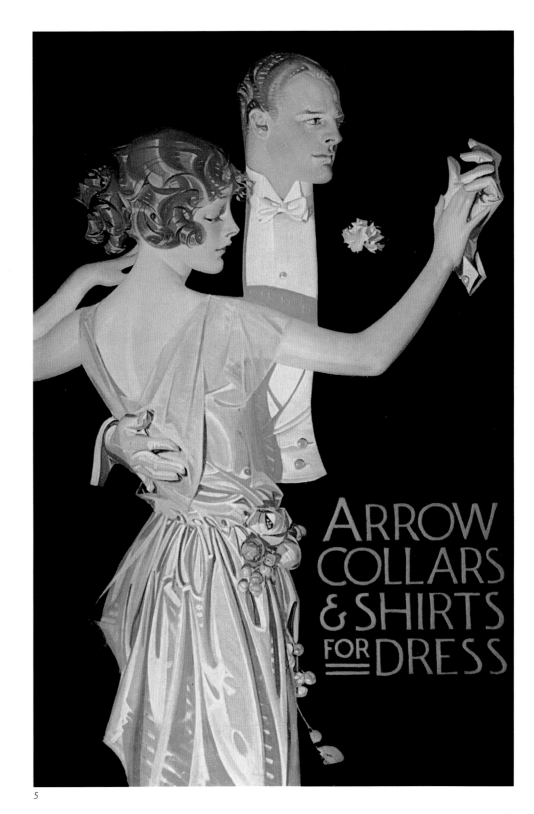

5

Son et lumière

Times were now easier: gas lighting had arrived in towns and cities about 1800, oil lamps about 1880, and then electricity. Leisure pursuits were also expanding: the phonograph was born in 1877 and Brahms made his first cylinder recording in Vienna in 1889.

1

Philips was established in Eindhoven in the Netherlands in 1891 by the engineer Gerard Philips, who was later joined by his brother Anton. The firm quickly grew in influence when it developed its first electric lightbulbs. **De la Mar** was one of the firm's preferred agencies. Initially, Philips' bulbs worked on the basis of a carbon filament placed in an imperfect vacuum; the filament would end up burning. Then, after much experimentation, improvements in industrial techniques made it possible to manufacture a new type of bulb with a tungsten filament surrounded by a rare gas, argon. These bulbs produced better light, lasted longer and were more economical. Philips produced the new bulbs under the brand name Arga from 1915 onwards. The shortage of coal and gas due to the war meant electric lighting was more than welcome (1). In 1918, Philips celebrated the end of the conflict with this poster by Albert Hahn, which symbolically depicts the victory of light over darkness (2).

2

3

STEINWAY

The Instrument of the Immortals

There has been but one supreme piano in the history of music. In the days of Liszt and Wagner, of Rubinstein and Berlioz, the pre-eminence of the Steinway was as unquestioned as it is today. It stood then, as it stands now, the chosen instrument of the masters— the inevitable preference wherever great music is understood and esteemed.

STEINWAY & SONS, Steinway Hall, 107-109 E. 14th Street, New York

Subway Express Stations at the Door

4

N.W. Ayer & Son convinced Steinway, the piano makers, not to content themselves with the presence of their instruments in concerts. They needed to address a wider audience. The first advertisements speak simply of pianos, as this 1908 example (3) demonstrates. Raymond Rubicam, a copywriter who joined the agency in 1919 with a brilliant advertising career ahead of him, noticed that many Steinway pianos had belonged to great musicians, and invented the line "The Instrument of the Immortals" (4). Originally intended for this one advertisement only, the line became the brand's signature for more than ten years. The photograph by Lejaren A. Hiller was a 'painted photograph'. Carefully staged, bathed in an unearthly light, a figure resembling the 'immortal' Franz Liszt plays the piano. In 1895, the Englishman Francis Barraud depicted his dog listening to a phonograph; he sold the painting to the British Gramophone Company, whose parent company changed its name to Victor Talking Machine Company, and in 1901 enlisted the services of N.W. Ayer & Son. The concept of a dog recognising "His Master's Voice" became a world-wide quality symbol (5).

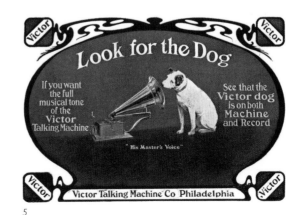

5

Chapter II

1921–1940

N.W. Ayer & Son

De la Mar

D'Arcy

Newell-Emmett

Elvinger

Blackett Sample Hummert

Publicis

Benton & Bowles

J. Stirling Getchell

MacManus John & Adams

Compton

Leo Burnett

A Testing Time

The Eiffel tower, Paris. Built by Gustave Eiffel for the 1889 Exposition Universelle and illuminated for the 1925 Exposition des Arts Décoratifs.

This was a terrible time in which one war followed another and the Great Depression shook all the Western economies to their very foundations. Then came the rise of totalitarianism. In the United States, as in Europe, the Twenties were productive, overall, but in October 1929 came the shock: the Dow Jones, which only a month earlier had reached an all-time high of 381 points, fell to 230. A pattern of recovery and fall continued until July 1932. By then, the index had lost almost 90% of its September 1929 value. The ravages of inflation had begun to affect the economies of the German-speaking world some years earlier and other European economies were to be affected slightly later, with damaging effects being felt until the Second World War.

Advertising survived, but at a price. Considerable adaptation saw advertising turn increasingly towards the hard-sell and away from emotion. The price of products was mentioned more often. Comparative advertising, competitions and promotions emerged. The aesthetic sophistication which flourished in the Twenties was called into question. The aim was to combat consumer apathy.

In spite of all these difficulties, this period was marked by the appearance of a major innovation in North America and across Europe- radio. In Spain, for example, fifteen radio stations were established in 1924. In France, in 1935, Marcel Bleustein launched Radio-Cité. Questions were raised in the Thirties which still have a modern ring to them today. What sort of content should be invented for this new medium? What new forms of advertising should be created? One answer to these questions was 'the soap opera', a series of dramas or comedies. 'Soap Operas' were specially created by agencies in order to promote the brands they managed, and the expression came into its own in television some time later.

This was the time of the second industrial revolution. The oil- and electricity-powered economy was born. Western civilisation came to be characterised by jazz, cinema, comic strips and cartoons –Walt Disney's characters started life in 1930. A different way of life was spreading that utilised credit and cars (numbers of which quadrupled during this period), and there was incredible progress towards a comfortable everyday standard of living.

The celebration of consumption

The industrial aesthetic decreed that utensils should combine form and function. Major exhibitions celebrated this new perspective on mass consumption.

2

1

This poster designed by Fritz Schleifer for the Bauhaus exhibition in 1923 reworks the emblem created a year earlier by the painter Oskar Schlemmer (1). The Bauhaus school, founded by Walter Gropius in Weimar, Germany in 1919, encompassed all disciplines from art to design via typography, and came to influence the aesthetics of everyday life. The theme of the exhibition, "Art and technology –a new unity" was a clear statement of the Bauhaus view that beauty and function should be combined. Modern art, for its part, gave advertising legitimacy as a real art form. A group of artists established the Union des Artistes Modernes (Modern Artists Union) in Paris in 1929. Among them were architects like Le Corbusier, poster artists like Paul Colin, Jean Carlu and A.M. Cassandre and interior designers such as René Herbst.
That same year the World Advertising Congress in Berlin embodied this new spirit demonstrated in this poster by Lucian Bernhard and Fritz Rosen (3).
In 1933, using a similar visual approach, the Englishman Austin Cooper created this poster for the "Art in the home" exhibition in London (2).

3

4

6

The first major event of its kind, "The Great Exhibition of all Nations" was held at London's Crystal Palace in 1851. Over time, these exhibitions became moments of celebration of the industrial ethos. The competitive show of household appliances held in Paris from 1923 onwards was to become the Salon des arts ménagers. In 1933, Francis Bernard, official poster artist to the Salon, created this 'Mechanical Marie' (4). In 1937, advertising, which had found it hard to win acceptance in France, officially became part of the establishment. It was permitted its own pavilion at the Paris World Exhibition of Art and Technology for Modern Living (5). The poster artist Jean Carlu and the architect René Herbst were commissioned to create this building. They drew inspiration from Oscar Nitzchké's plans for a House of Advertising which was due to be built on the Champs-Élysées in 1935. This exhibition was a precursor of the 1939 exhibition in New York, the advertising for which was entrusted to **N.W. Ayer & Son**. As the leading exponent of the new trend towards graphic art, Joseph Binder produced the exhibition's official poster (6).

Constructivism and surrealism

A new visual culture emerged from the ashes of the First World War. It combined the aesthetics of speed, a move away from ornamentation and a commitment to society.

2

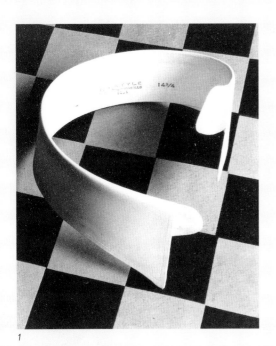

1

3

In 1914, Clarence White opened *a school of photography in New York. He encouraged his students to apply their talent and technique to commercial photography instead of confining themselves strictly to art. This approach eased the emergence of many new talents including Anton Bruehl, Margaret Bourke-White and Paul Outerbridge. In 1922, the latter created an advertisement for Ide collars, published in Vanity Fair (1). In France that same year, Sonia Delaunay revolutionised textile design with her geometric motifs in contrasting colours and rhythms. The strength of this approach is clear from the advertising mock-up she created for a cooker manufacturer (2). While art influenced advertising, advertising also influenced art. In 1924, the North American painter Stuart Davis, on the lookout for popular subjects that depicted modern life, became fascinated with Odol. This mouthwash had been launched in Dresden in 1892 by Karl August Lingner, for whom, later on in 1928, Hanns Brose would work. Inspired by its packaging, and by the style in which the name was written, Davis painted a whole series of pictures showing the famous Odol bottle (3).*

In the Soviet Union, **Vladimir Maïakovsky** created posters providing a commentary on contemporary politics. They were displayed in the windows of ROSTA, the Soviet telegraph agency, and took the place of newspapers. He also produced dozens of posters for state-owned shops and, in 1923, worked with Alexander Rodchenko on commercial advertisements. The two saw themselves as 'Advertising-Constructors.' To them, publicity work was akin to agit-prop in industry and commerce: "We cannot leave the weapon of commercial propaganda in the hands of (...) the foreign bourgeoisie." Their 1923 poster for Resinotrest rubber teats for babies caused an outcry: "The best teats that ever existed. You could suck them all your life" (4). Maïakovsky retorted that the advertisement would continue to contribute to be a civilising influence "for as long as people in the countryside still stuff dirty rags into babies' mouths." Kurt Schwitters, the German painter, sculptor, poster artist and poet, is well-known for his compositions incorporating 'found objects' discarded by consumer society. He became interested in advertising, and in 1924 produced this advertisement for Pelikan Indian ink, combining typography and photo-montage. It was published in his magazine Merz (5). The work of the Belgian surrealist painter René Magritte owes much of its subversive power to the unexpected juxtaposition of words and images. One of his most popular and enigmatic pictures is "Ceci n'est pas une pipe" (This is not a pipe) from 1928, which poses questions about reality and appearances (6). Advertising was to benefit from this move towards expressing ideas using shortcuts in expression and seeking to make an impact by juxtaposing words and images. Simply supplying a faithful reproduction of the product was no longer enough.

4

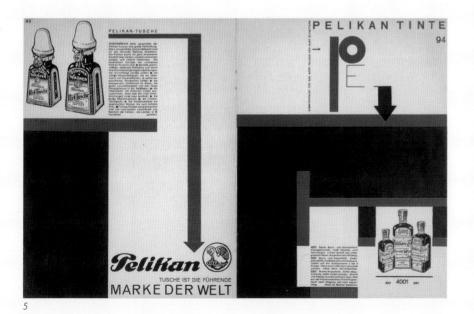

5

6

Advertising advertising

As they gained in strength and respectability, advertising agencies came to play a full part in economic life and began to promote themselves.

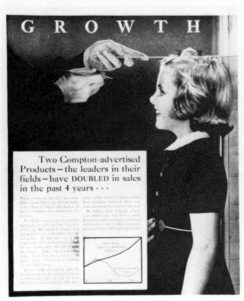

1

The effects of the Great Depression were still being felt and the public at large was now concerned with the health of the stock market. This is most probably why, in 1934, E.A. Pierce & Co., a financial company that was to merge with Merrill Lynch in 1940, created a 'live poster' showing the Dow Jones Index hourly (3).
N.W. Ayer & Son continued to place its own advertisements in the professional press, as it always had done. It is estimated that the firm placed hundreds of advertisements in titles such as Printer's Ink, Advertising & Selling and Fortune. A 1931 example is shown here (2).
By explaining what the advertiser's job entails and what clients can expect, these notices did not simply serve the agency's interests, they also promoted advertising as a whole. The **Compton** agency, which emerged from Blackman in 1935 and would, in 1943, take over **J. Stirling Getchell**, an agency established in 1931, also undertook its own promotional activity. In a series of advertisements Compton emphasised the growth its clients attained due to advertising, despite the economic downturn (1).

The **SUPREME COURT**

★ ★ ★   of business

SHE IS IMPARTIAL in her decisions . . . the American wife and mother . . . and exacting in her standards. She looks on qualities with clear, penetrating eyes. In her management of the home, she puts to practical daily tests soaps, linen, kitchenware. She finds out intimately the aesthetic values of rugs, reading-lamps . . . the virtues of clocks, refrigerators.

She and her 29,000,000 sisters comprise, so to speak, the supreme court of decision for all merchandise for their families and homes. Here before them, foods, clothes, household appointments face their conclusive test. Here, patents and processes receive their final trial, values their ultimate appraisal.

Addressing these wives and mothers on the printed page becomes increasingly an art. They are increasingly discriminate in their buying. In a sense, they are still the chief competitors business has—in more or less clinging to their accustomed ways of fire-tending, long hours of cooking, sweeping.

Yet they are also a most alert, responsive market. They buy an overwhelming majority of the merchandise sold. They are the reason for endless experiments in commercial kitchens; constant research in laboratories. They keep their homes bright, comfortable, healthful . . . their children well-dressed, well-nourished . . . themselves amazingly young . . . through selections they make with their cool, sure decisions.

These 29,000,000 justices of the supreme court of American business have in their hands the spending of $52,000,000,000 every year. Naturally they base their decisions on the facts they glean from advertisements, backed by day-by-day experience in the home. It follows with equal force that the manufacturer whose goods are sound, and ably promoted, has the best chance of getting a favorable verdict. . . . For in the weighing and assaying of relative claims and values these are the most just, the most discerning and unbiased judges in the world.

N · W · A Y E R   &   S O N, INC. ADVERTISING

Washington Square, Philadelphia   •   New York   •   Boston   •   Chicago   •   San Francisco   •   Detroit   •   London

2

3

4

Only a bunch of optimists would have opened
an ad agency on a day like that—and we still are

Leo Burnett Company, Inc., Advertising
CHICAGO · NEW YORK · HOLLYWOOD · TORONTO · MONTREAL

5

In 1933, in order to boost the economy, *Franklin D. Roosevelt's administration passed the National Recovery Act and General Hugh S. Johnson was entrusted with its implementation. Johnson commissioned a symbol to identify the corporations contributing to the programme: the blue eagle (4). It was the work of Charles Coiner, art director of N.W. Ayer & Son. The story was that he actually borrowed the General's pen to colour in the eagle. In Chicago on the 5th of August 1935, Leo Burnett opened his own agency and a bowl of apples was left in reception on offer to visitors. (Apples, at that time, were a very emotive symbol as many unemployed people would make themselves a bit of money by selling apples for 5 cents each). The tradition of the bowl of apples lives on in all the* **Leo Burnett** *agencies; the memory of it was very much alive in this 1960 advertisement (5). As a professor at Columbia University, Francis Elvinger had reflected long and hard on the relationship between producers and distributors. In 1923, he opened an agency,* **Elvinger**, *in Paris and three years later, in 1926, Marcel Bleustein also created his own agency* **Publicis**. *Well aware of the importance of radio and cinema, Bleustein developed media brokering companies (regies): "Get your Brand name heard on Publicis' airwaves; Get your Brand name seen on Publicis screens" 1936 (6).*

6

The real Father Christmas!

One of the most heart-warming stories in advertising reads like
a Christmas carol. And with good reason: it is the story of Father Christmas
as children around the world know him today.

1

The character of Father Christmas seems to have
been inspired by Saint Nicholas, whose feast
day we celebrate on the 6th of December. On that
day, he is traditionally shown handing out presents
to children as a reward. Father Christmas was
introduced to the United States in the seventeenth
century by immigrants from Northern Europe;
in 1821 he appeared as Santa Claus in a poem
written by a pastor. The poem described him as
a mischievous figure, and it rapidly became very
popular. In 1863, a draftsman called Thomas Nast
provided the first visual image of Santa, but his
appearance was not yet established, and it wasn't
until 1930 that he took on the form we now know.
The D'Arcy agency, which had already successfully
applied itself to making Coca-Cola a year-round
success, developed a specific winter campaign for
which it planned to rely on the one character
who embodied the whole season – Father Christmas.
It asked Haddon Sundblom, a painter and illustrator,
to create the character. Sundblom already knew
the brand well, and he gave Father Christmas
a jovial, bon viveur image, dressing him in
the Coca-Cola colours of red and white (1).
Since this was not long after the stock exchange
crash of 1929, the advertisements also bore
glad tidings of recovery (2).

2

3

This very first representation of Father Christmas, as created by Haddon Sundblom, was displayed on the front wall of a bottling plant in Memphis at Christmas time 1931 (3). The amiable figure tips his hat to the slogan D'Arcy had introduced two years earlier: "The pause that refreshes." For many years, this signature and Father Christmas himself were to remind everyone, everywhere and in all seasons, of the unstinting presence of their favourite drink. The character Sundblom created was used in every way imaginable: on window display panels, in display units, and many other forms. What is more, the artist painted him in a different situation every year: alone or with children, with or without a bottle of Coca-Cola (4). The slogans also changed: "The pause that keeps you going" in 1934, "The pause that refreshes me too" in 1936, "Somebody knew I was coming" in 1940, but Father Christmas always remained the same. Until 1964, the last year he worked on this, Haddon Sundblom renewed his portrayal of the character whom D'Arcy placed in tightly defined visual guidelines. All aspects were thought through in advance and carefully defined (colours, typeface/location of the bottle). The precision in the illustration, the quality of the situations and their endlessly refreshed recurrence, were clearly the determining factors in imprinting the character on the public's imagination. This phenomenon was to grow further when it arrived in Europe towards the end of the Second World War. Coca-Cola and Father Christmas were then present in forty-four countries, fulfilling the plans of Ernest Woodruff, President of Coca-Cola in 1923, for a Coke to be "within arm's reach of desire" of people worldwide.

"Merry Christmas to you."

4

The beauty of the product

The product is a source of unlimited inspiration in advertising. Especially when artists glorify its sensuality with talent and present its attributes through a sweet Hawaiian countryside.

2

1

In 1901, soon after the young state of Hawaii joined the American territory, James Dole founded the Hawaiian Pineapple Company. As many others, the company met with great difficulties at the beginning of the 1930s during the Great Depression. **N.W. Ayer & Son** helped the company prosper with a campaign that was very original at the time and in the country, and brought a new luxury image to the brand. This campaign mixed tropical exoticism and refined sensuality by relying on the works of contemporary artists who didn't subscribe to the popular realist tradition but instead experimented with the essence of the brand in a more symbolic manner. In particular, French poster painter A.M. Cassandre created two advertisements in 1938 for Dole pineapple juice (1), (3) and one for its 'pineapple gems' (2). Afterwards, Dole solicited Georgia O'Keeffe. Born in 1887, this great American artist was very quickly convinced that realism was a dead end, and from 1915, she began the search for a personal language with a series of charcoal drawings considered to be the most innovative in American art at the time. In 1940, Ayer asked her to paint a pineapple, but instead she presented this magnificent mock bird of paradise flower that she had brought back from a trip to Hawaii (4).

3

•Hawaiian Pineapple Company, Ltd., invited the world-famed American artist, Georgia O'Keefe, to visit Hawaii and paint her impressions of the color and brilliance of the Islands. She chose the magnificent Haliconia flower, called by some the "Mock Bird of Paradise."

PAINTED IN HAWAII, HOME OF DOLE PINEAPPLE JUICE, BY GEORGIA O'KEEFFE

Hospitable Hawaii cannot send you its abundance of flowers or its sunshine. But it sends you something reminiscent of both—golden, fragrant Dole Pineapple Juice. As you drink this pure, unsweetened juice of luscious, sun-ripened pineapples, you will know that only Nature could give Dole Pineapple Juice its marvelous flavor. For breakfast... when you are tired or thirsty between meals... whenever you, your children or guests crave refreshment, serve tall glasses of **DOLE PINEAPPLE JUICE FROM HAWAII**

4

The Green Giant

The Minnesota Valley Canning Company was among the first clients of a new agency to open its doors in Chicago in 1935 – Leo Burnett. Over very many years, the two firms worked together like peas in a pod.

1

Established in Le Sueur, Minnesota, in 1903 the Minnesota Valley Canning Company decided in 1919 that, in order to develop the tinned goods industry and differentiate itself from its competitors, it needed to concentrate on creating unique products. The company began by replacing white with golden cream-style corn, which is sweeter and more tender, although this variety had previously been reserved for feeding horses! It marketed this corn in 1924 under the Del Maiz brand. A year later, the company began to sell a new variety of peas, larger than those usually consumed, which it called Green Giant (1). The company decided to protect this name, which at the time was considered to be generic, by associating it with a character who appeared on the label three years later. Like a reworked image from a Grimm's fairytale, the character initially was small and mischievous and he wasn't even green! One of the first things **Leo Burnett** did was to make him into a real green giant. In 1936, he finally looked friendly and stood up as a character in his own right, the Jolly Green Giant, making the brand distinct from the generic product. Now the character could be used more widely to represent not just peas but also a new brand of sweet corn, Niblets (2). In a move to firmly establish the distinctiveness of the brand, consumers were advised to look for the Green Giant on the label (3).

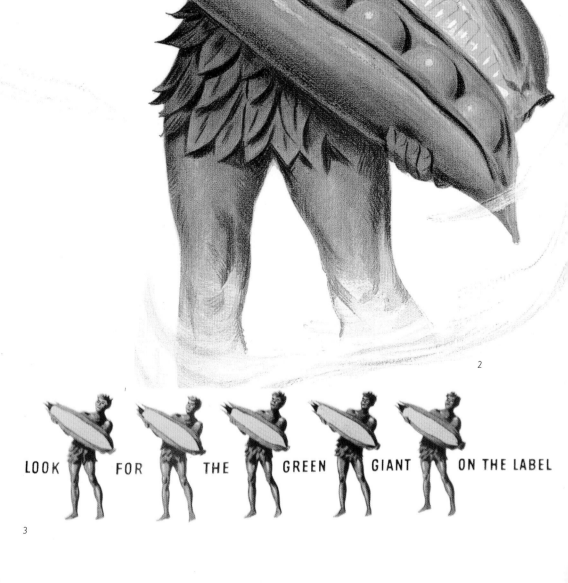

2

LOOK FOR THE GREEN GIANT ON THE LABEL

3

Leo Burnett also worked with the illustrator Norman Rockwell, already well-known for producing many covers for the popular weekly Saturday Evening Post. For the Minnesota Valley Canning Company, he produced four paintings illustrating traditional American family values and the warmth of childhood memories. As Leyendecker had for Arrow and Sundblom had for Coca-Cola, Rockwell plucked his models from everyday surroundings, in keeping with the realist school much prized in advertising. The first advertisement in 1938 was a full page spread featuring his youngest son (4). He produced three other advertisements in the same vein for the same product. Reproductions could be obtained by returning the coupon at the bottom of the advertisement. The promotional offer was aimed at adults; others were aimed at children –like this 1941 example, for the launch of the film Dumbo, the latest favourite from Walt Disney (5). Eleven years had passed since the first national advertisement by the Minnesota Valley Canning Company, and the Jolly Green Giant could take his place easily among Disney's characters.

Sweet nothings

Two continents, two sweet products on the same quest for originality: a touch of humour for Life Savers, a hint of poetry for Verkade.

1

2

As everyone knows, chocolate has an irritating tendency to melt in summer. Clarence Crane, a chocolate maker from Cleveland, Ohio, decided in the summer of 1912 that, at that time of year, he'd be better off making mints. In those days mint sweets were imported from Europe and were square in shape. Crane turned to a pill producer who made him some pretty little round sweets with a hole in the middle. As they looked like miniature lifebelts (life savers) Crane had an instant brand name and registered it. A certain Edward Noble from New York found the idea interesting, met with the chocolate maker and bought the brand for 2,900 dollars. It was he who made it the worldwide success we know today, and few brands have made such an impression on our consciousness. Right from their inception, Pep-O-Mint Life Savers created a strong, distinctive personality for themselves, and have maintained it in the face of time and tide. Three advertisements produced by the agency **N.W. Ayer & Son** in the early 1920s show with wit where the brand's inspiration came from (1), (2), (3). The famous "mint with a hole" reinvented itself in new flavours but never abandoned its playful, gently teasing charm.

3

4

BESCHUIT
VERKADE

Verkade, a Dutch manufacturer of sweets and biscuits, gave its advertising account to **De la Mar** in 1924, and the modern version of the agency still has it today. In 1933, the Dutch poster artist Kees Dekker produced this very modern-looking poster for Verkade's biscuits (4). Whilst in 1936, a fresh film for the cinema, part fairytale, part Arabian nights, told of the love between a deliciously exotic cocoa bean with a certain sensuality and a severely smitten sugar loaf (6). From this marriage of cocoa and sugar a superb bar of chocolate was born (5). Georges Méliès pioneered the use of cinema for advertising. However, it was in an animated form that advertising commercials took off in cinemas and on television, both in Europe and in the United States.

5

6

Thoroughly modern miss

When it came to marketing manufactured cigarettes, advertising addressed men and largely ignored women. However, women had been the first cigarette smokers.

1

Three major manufacturers had been competing with one another for several years: R.J. Reynolds with Camel, Liggett & Myers with Chesterfield and American Tobacco with Lucky Strike. Their advertisements targeted men because, in the male dominated society of the day, it was thought that women should not smoke in public! In 1927, R.J. Reynolds, with **N.W. Ayer & Son**, employed a creative way to avoid upsetting social convention. A poster represented a woman looking at the famous Camel image (1). Then, in 1928, advertisements presented elegant scenes in which men smoked, surrounded by women who didn't. But in 1930, Camel stepped up the pace by presenting a woman offering a man a cigarette (2). And the well-known Camel slogan: "I'd walk a mile for a Camel" gains a caveat, a punning use of the saying "A miss is as good as a mile."

2

In 1911, after fourteen solid years at the American Tobacco Company under James B. Duke, Liggett & Myers struck out on their own. In 1926 they ran their first campaign aimed at a female audience. This was for the Chesterfield cigarette brand and was produced with the **Newell-Emmett** agency. Established in New York in 1919, Newell-Emmett later became Cunningham & Walsh before finally joining N.W. Ayer & Son. The skill of their campaign lay in employing a standard theme in the brand's communications (3), usually used in a purely masculine context, but shifting it into a romantic, night-time setting (4). However, neither in this Chesterfield advertisement, nor in the one for Camel, are women to be seen smoking —and certainly not smoking alone. Women were always portrayed alongside men, with the brands attempting to appeal to both sexes. Women represented 5% of the American cigarette market in 1923, rising to 18% by 1933. It was only in the 1960s that a newcomer, Philip Morris, launched a cigarette brand specially designed for women: Virginia Slims.

"I can tell that taste in the dark"

CHESTERFIELD

3

4

Critical mass

The development of the automobile confronted industry with a critical, challenging, new question: how to mass produce with reliability, innovation and low cost?

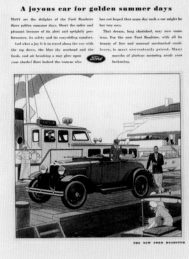

3

First Pictures of the New Ford Car

Get complete details **TODAY** at Ford salesrooms

FORD MOTOR COMPANY
Detroit, Michigan

1

Henry Ford established Ford Motors in Detroit in 1903 and launched the Model T in 1908. Six million sold across the globe. The Model T was replaced in 1928 by the Model A, which came with a three-speed gearbox and in a choice of colours! Its launch was entrusted to **N.W. Ayer & Son**, who would soon open agencies in London, Buenos Aires and São Paulo to serve their new client. The campaign began with an announcement signed by Henry Ford (2). When this text was presented to the founder's son, who was then head of the company, he asked that the word 'perfect' be replaced with 'correct' since "nothing is perfect." No illustrations of the car, no technical information, and no prices were featured in this first advertisement; it was followed by a second and a third, still with no pictures or prices. Only in the fourth and final advertisement was the car, and its price, revealed to the world (1). This teasing approach to car launches persists even today.

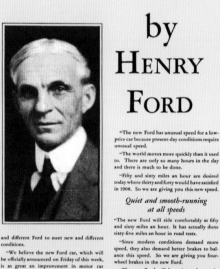

THE NEW FORD CAR

An announcement of unusual importance to every automobile owner

by HENRY FORD

NINETEEN years ago we made and sold the first Model T Ford car. In announcing it to the public we said:

"We will build a motor car for the great multitude. It will be large enough for the family, but small enough for the individual to run and care for. It will be constructed of the best materials, by the best men to be hired, after the simplest designs modern engineering can devise. But it will be so low in price that no man making a good salary will be unable to own one.'

"If I were starting in business today, or asked to restate my policy, I would not change one sentence or one word of that original announcement. In plain, simple language it gives the reason for the very existence of the Ford Motor Company and explains its growth.

"IN THE last nineteen years we have made 15,000,000 Ford cars and added to the world nearly 300,000,000 mobile horse-power. Yet I do not consider the machines which bear my name simply as machines. I take them as concrete evidence of the working out of a theory of business which I hope is something more than a theory of business—a theory that looks toward making this world a better place in which to live.

"The Model T Ford car was a pioneer. There was no conscious public need of motor cars when we first conceived it. There were few good roads and only the adventurous few could be induced to buy an automobile.

"The Ford car blazed the way for the motor industry and started the movement for good roads. It broke down the barriers of time and distance and helped to place education within the reach of all. It gave people more leisure. It helped people everywhere to do more and better work in less time and enjoy doing it. It did a great deal, I am sure, to promote the growth and progress of this country.

"We are still proud of the record of the Model T Ford car. If we were not, we would not have continued to manufacture it so long. But 1927 is not 1908. It is not 1915. It is not even 1926.

We have built a new car to meet modern conditions

"We realize that conditions in this country have so greatly changed in the last few years that further refinement in motor car construction is desirable. So we have built a new car. To put it simply—we have built a new

and different Ford to meet new and different conditions.

"We believe the new Ford car, which will be officially announced on Friday of this week, is as great an improvement in motor car building as the Model T Ford was in 1908.

Smart new low lines and beautiful colors

"The new Ford is more than a car for the requirements of today. It goes farther than that. It anticipates the needs of 1928, of 1929, of 1930.

"The new Ford car is radically different from Model T. Yet the basic Ford principles of economy of production and quality of product have been retained. There is nothing quite like the new Ford anywhere in quality and price.

"The new Ford has exceptional beauty of line and color because beauty of line and color has come to be considered, and I think rightly, a necessity in a motor car today. Equally important is the mechanical beauty of the engine. Let us not forget this mechanical beauty when we consider the beauty of the new Ford.

"The new Ford has unusual speed for a low-price car because present-day conditions require unusual speed.

"The world moves more quickly than it used to. There are only so many hours in the day and there is much to be done.

"Fifty and sixty miles an hour are desired today where thirty and forty would have satisfied in 1908. So we are giving you this new speed.

Quiet and smooth-running at all speeds

"The new Ford will ride comfortably at fifty and sixty miles an hour. It has actually done sixty-five miles an hour in road tests.

"Since modern conditions demand more speed, they also demand better brakes to balance this speed. So we are giving you four-wheel brakes in the new Ford.

"The new Ford will be quiet and smooth-running at all speeds and you will find it even easier to handle in traffic than the old Model T Ford.

"The new Ford has durability because durability is the very heart of motor car value. The Ford car has always been known as a car that will take you there and bring you back. The new Ford will not only do that, but it will do it in good style. You will be proud of the new Ford.

THIS new Ford car has not been planned and made in a day. Our engineers began work on it several years ago and it has been in my mind much longer than that. We make automobiles quickly when we get in production. But we take a long time planning them. Nothing can hurry us in that. We spent twelve years in perfecting our former Model T Ford car before we offered it to the public. It is not conceivable that we should have put this new Ford car on the market until we were sure that it was mechanically correct in every detail.

"Every part of it has been tested and retested. There is no guessing as to whether it will be a successful model. It has to be. There is no way it can escape being so, for it represents the sum total of all we have learned about motor car building in the making of 15,000,000 automobiles.

The new Ford will sell at a low price

"The price of the new Ford is low in accordance with the established Ford policy. I hold that it is better to sell a large number of cars at a reasonably small margin of profit than to sell a few cars at a large margin of profit.

"We never forget that people who buy Ford cars are the people who helped to make this business big. It has always been our policy to share our profits with our customers. In one year our profits were so much larger than we expected that we voluntarily returned $50 to each purchaser of a car. We could never have done that if this business had been conducted for the sole benefit of stockholders rather than to render service to the public.

"No other automobile can duplicate the new Ford car at the Ford price because no other manufacturer does business the way we do.

"We make our own steel—we make our own glass—we mine our own coal—we make virtually every part used in the Ford car. But we do not charge a profit on any of these items or from these operations. We would not be playing fair with the public if we did so. Our only business is the automobile business. Our only profit is on the automobile we sell.

"WE ARE able to sell this new Ford car at a low price because we have found new ways to give you greater value without a great increase in our own costs.

"We did not set out to make a new car to sell at such-and-such a figure. We decided on the kind of car we wanted to make and then found ways to produce it at a low price.

"The new Ford car, as I have said, will be officially announced on Friday of this week. In appearance, in performance, in comfort, in safety, in all that goes to make a good car, 't will bear out everything I have said here. We consider it our most important contribution thus far to the progress of the motor industry, to the prosperity of the country, and to the daily welfare of millions of people."

Henry Ford

FORD MOTOR COMPANY
Detroit, Michigan

© 1927, Ford Motor Company

2

Everything
you want or need in A Modern Automobile

EVERYTHING you want or need in a modern automobile is brought to you at a low price in the new Ford . . . beauty of line and color—steel body—speed of 55 to 65 miles an hour—mechanical, internal expanding-shoe type four-wheel brakes to balance this speed and to provide the safety demanded by present-day motoring conditions—flashing pick-up and ease of control that put a new joy in motoring—power for any hill because of a remarkably efficient engine which develops 40-brake-horse-power at only 2200 revolutions a minute —new transverse springs and four Houdaille hydraulic shock absorbers for easy-riding comfort—the economy of 20 to 30 miles on a gallon of gasoline, depending on your speed—three-quarter irreversible steering gear—reliability and low cost of up-keep.

Check over these features and you will find that not one essential thing that you require of a motor car is omitted from this list.

Yet the completeness of the new Ford goes farther even than this. It extends to every least little detail of finish and appointment and to the equipment which is standard on the car.

This includes speedometer, ammeter, gasoline gage on instrument panel, electric windshield wiper on closed cars, five steel-spoke wheels, four 30 x 4.50 balloon tires, dash light, mirror, combination stop and tail light, oil indicator rod, theft-proof coincidental ignition lock, high-pressure grease gun lubrication, and Triplex shatter-proof glass windshield.

All Ford cars have roomy interiors, wide, deeply-cushioned seats, rich upholstery, and are finished in a variety of beautiful two-tone color harmonies.

Five years ago—three years ago—one year ago—it would have been impossible to produce such a really fine car at such a low price. It is possible today only because of the development of new machines, new manufacturing methods and new production economics that are as remarkable as the car itself.

The Ford Motor Company did not set out to make a new car at a certain figure. It decided on the kind of car it wanted to make and then found ways to build it at the lowest possible price.

Every purchaser shares the benefits of the Ford policy of selling at a small margin of profit, of owning or controlling the source of raw materials and of constantly giving greater and greater value without greatly increased cost.

As Henry Ford himself has said: "We make our own steel—we make our own glass—we mine our own coal. But we do not charge a profit on any of these items or from these operations. Our only profit is on the automobile we sell."

When you know the joy of driving the new Ford—when you see its outstanding performance under all conditions—you will know that it is not just a new automobile—not just a new

Proudly at home in any company is the new Ford Tudor Sedan. Distinguished by its low trim lines and the quiet good taste of every detail of finish and appointment.

model—but the advanced expression of a wholly new idea in modern, economical transportation.

FORD MOTOR COMPANY
Detroit, Michigan

The sturdy strength and sweeping lines of the new Ford are shown in this view from the driver's seat. Windshields in all the new Ford cars are made of Triplex shatter-proof glass—an important safety feature.

4

A series of advertisements were to follow the launch, all built around the same idea: encouraging people to dream (3), (4). In this same era, Ford Motors took up another challenge: aeronautics. Aviation was in its infancy and air travel was not yet part of everyday life. Ford's new Tri-motor aircraft was to open the way to air travel, but first the advantages of this form of transport needed to be publicised. N.W. Ayer & Son conducted this awareness-raising campaign. Seventeen advertisements, all drawn by the illustrator who had worked on the Model A Ford and all written with the help of engineer William B. Stout, appeared between 1927 and 1929. "Lift up your eyes" came the cry that acted as a reminder. After railways and automobiles, aeroplanes were the coming form of transport (5).

LIFT UP YOUR EYES!

How long ago did Wilbur Wright circle the drill field at Fort Myer while a few score of astonished witnesses stared open-mouthed at the sight of this first man to fly with wings for more than an hour? . . .

How long ago did the intrepid Bleriot hop in his flimsy, scorched monoplane from France to land precariously on the cliffs of Dover? . . .

How long ago did Graham-White circle the Statue of Liberty, struggling dexterously with his hands to maintain equilibrium? . . . *It seems only yesterday!*

Yet in the few brief years since then man has learned a new technic in existence. He has explored the earth's atmosphere, his noble machine climbing on after human faculties had failed. . . . He has skimmed lightly over the impenetrable ice barriers of the polar regions. . . . He has taken in his flight not only the gray, fog-blanketed waters of the North Atlantic, but the empty blue seas of the South Atlantic—the Mediterranean—the Pacific—the Indian Ocean—the Gulf of Mexico. . . . He has soared confidently over the sands of Sahara and the Great Arabian Desert, where only the camel had dared venture before. . . . He has skimmed the terrible dark jungles of the Amazon, and scaled high above the silent places of Alaska. . . . He has flown in squadrons from the Cape of Good Hope to London. . . . In squadrons he has circled South America. . . . In squadrons he has circumnavigated the globe! And in the ordinary routine of transportation service he travels on fixed schedules over airways that streak the skies of Europe and North America. Mail. Passengers. Express. The world is rapidly assigning special duties to this safe vehicle that cuts time in two.

Is there any epoch in all history that has been so sudden in growth from birth to universal achievement? . . . so dramatic in its nature and accomplishments? . . . so rich in promises for the future?

Perhaps the most significant thing in the great accomplishment of young Colonel Lindbergh is that in him the world sees the first outstanding example of a generation that is born air-conscious! Just as the past generation was born to steam, accepting railway transportation as an accomplished fact—and just as the present generation has accepted the automobile as a customary vehicle—so does the rising generation lift up its eyes to the skies! It may be hard still for many of us to accept the fact, but it is certain that the aeroplane will give as great an impetus to advancing civilization as did the automobile.

In this firm belief the Ford Motor Company is devoting its activities and resources to solving the problems that still face commercial aviation. In factory equipment, in laboratory experiment, in actual flights, the Ford Motor Company is establishing a foundation for one of the greatest industries the world has yet known. Within the last two years pilots have flown over the established Ford air routes, carrying freight, on regular daily schedules, a distance of more than 700,000 miles.

5

A new look

North American advertising moved smoothly from realistic illustrations to photography.
But, for a brief period, Modern Art made a fleeting appearance thanks to a French cubist.

1

2

Adolphe Mouron, born in 1901 in Kharkov (which was then in Russia), arrived in France in 1914 and began to work in advertising in 1922 under the pseudonym Cassandre. Inspired by the new directions modern art was taking, and by Cubism in particular, his style moved away from the traditionalist, somewhat everyday, approach of contemporary realist illustrators. Mouron suggested the message by means of symbols rather than representing the product or even the consumer, and he played with typography, skilfully integrating it into the image. A retrospective of Mouron's posters was organised at the Museum of Modern Art in New York in 1936 and that gave him the opportunity to visit the United States. He stayed until 1939, working at the magazine Harper's Bazaar and in 1938, he was approached by **N.W. Ayer & Son**, who commissioned a poster advertising the Ford V8 (2). This poster, which made a striking impact on the streets, became one of Cassandre's best-known (1). It was a turning point between two periods. Behind lay the last gasps of the realistic and romantic notion of automobile advertising and ahead lay photography's slow rise to dominance across all sectors. A.M. Cassandre's individual approach was a notable exception to both.

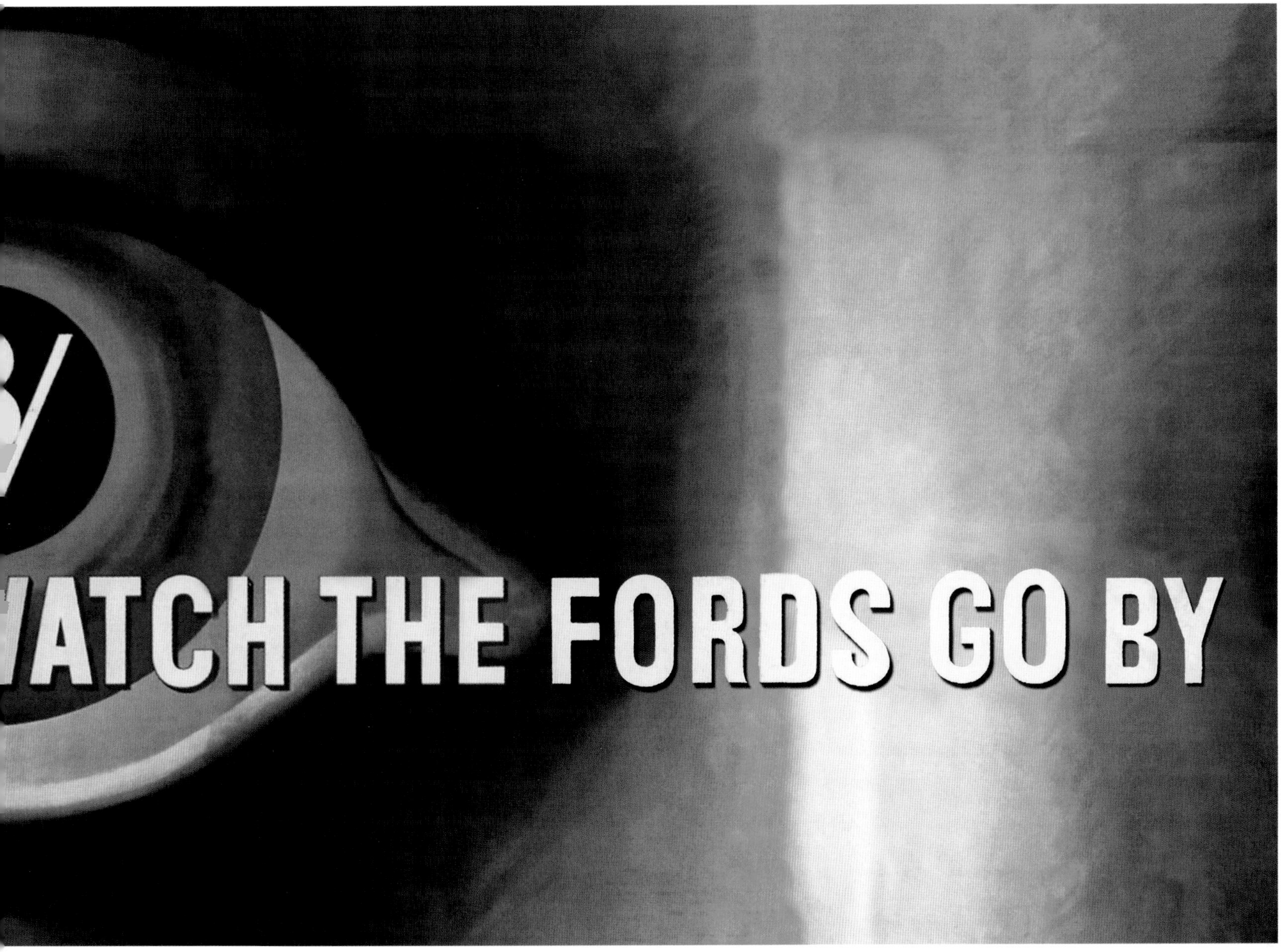
ATCH THE FORDS GO BY

Read all about it!

*What could Chrysler do when faced with Ford and their successful launch
of the Model A or with General Motors, who covered all sectors of the market?
They advised the prospective purchaser to 'read up' before buying!*

1

*Automobile advertising of this era employed
flattering illustrations of all the models, evoking
travel and escape. The MacManus agency
provides us with magnificent examples of this
tradition in the shape of these two advertisements
designed for Cadillac by the illustrator J.M. Cleland.
One dates from 1919 (1); the other, for the launch
of the new V8, from 1929 (2). The Plymouth
however, created by Chrysler on the eve of the
Great Depression, had not been selling well. The
J. Stirling Getchell agency, established in 1931,
and later taken over by Compton in 1943, was
already working for DeSoto, a division of Chrysler.
The agency came up with a bold campaign in the
spring of 1932 which involved encouraging the
potential customer to compare the Plymouth with
the General Motors' Chevrolet 6-cylinder and
with Ford's 8-cylinder (3). Without naming names,
the advertisement explains that the new suspension
of its 4-cylinder engine gives the Plymouth
a comparable comfort to its two competitors. The
advertisement introduces a new journalistic style
to advertising, with a black and white photograph
(here showing Walter Percy Chrysler himself)
and a headline. It immediately propelled the
Plymouth into a leading position.*

CADILLAC

*Creates a New
Luxury in Motoring*

ALL discussions end the moment the exquisite design and lavish luxury of the new Cadillac
are revealed—to be obliterated forever when the powers of its 90-degree, V-type, eight
cylinders begin to manifest themselves. As this car proclaims itself first among the fine automobiles of America and Europe in newly created beauty of design—so the immensely advanced
V-type engine records itself as the most perfect performance factor in the world today.

More than 50 exclusive body styles by Fisher and Fisher-Fleetwood

CADILLAC

A Notable Product of General Motors

2

"Look at All Three!

BUT DON'T BUY ANY LOW-PRICED CAR UNTIL YOU'VE DRIVEN THE NEW PLYMOUTH WITH FLOATING POWER"

"It is my opinion that any new car without Patented Floating Power is obsolete."

THOUSANDS of people have been waiting expectantly until today before buying a new car. I hope that you are one of them.

Now that the new low-priced cars are here (including the new Plymouth which will be shown on Saturday) I urge you to carefully *compare* values.

This is the time for you to "shop" and buy wisely. Don't make a deposit on any automobile until you've actually had a demonstration.

It is my opinion that the automobile industry as a whole has never offered such values to the public.

In the new Plymouth we have achieved more than I had ever dared to hope for. If you had told me two years ago that such a big, powerful, beautiful automobile could be sold at the astonishing prices we will announce on Saturday . . . I'd have said it was absolutely impossible.

I have spent my life building fine cars. But no achievement in my career has given me the deep-down satisfaction

A STATEMENT BY
WALTER P. CHRYSLER

that I derive from the value you get in this 1932 Plymouth. To me, its outstanding feature is Floating Power. We already know how the public feels about this. Last summer it was news, but today it is an established engineering achievement.

It is my opinion, and I think that of leading engineering authorities, that any new car without Floating Power is obsolete. Drive a Plymouth with Patented Floating Power, and note its utter lack of vibration . . . then drive a car with old-fashioned engine mountings and you will understand what I mean. *There's absolutely no comparison.*

We have made the Plymouth a much larger automobile. It is a BIG car. We have increased its power, lengthened the wheelbase and greatly improved its beauty.

In my opinion you will find the new Plymouth the easiest riding car you have ever driven. Yet with all these improvements we have been able to lower prices.

Again let me urge you, go and see the new Plymouth with Floating Power on Saturday. Be sure to look at all THREE low-priced cars and don't buy *any* until you do. That is the way to get the most for your money.

FIRST SHOWING NEXT SATURDAY, APRIL 2nd, AT DESOTO, DODGE AND CHRYSLER DEALERS

3

The development of photographs

As it had done with posters and then illustrations, advertising turned to artists when photography started to be popular. But what type of photograph was to be used?

2

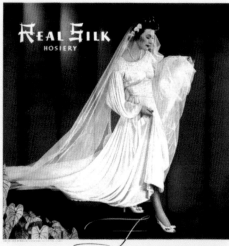

1

Proponents of photographic realism approached this new discipline as the illustrators had before them, and their photos were essentially descriptive and figurative. They reflected a true-to-life reality that the public could easily decode. These two portraits of women, very classically inspired, were shot in 1935 by the agency **Leo Burnett** for Real Silk Hosiery Mills, a lingerie manufacturer from Indiana (1), (2). The company remained particularly loyal to Mr Burnett. In fact, it had followed him when he left the agency Homer McKee in 1930 to join Erwin, Wasey & Co. Then, in 1935, with two other clients of that agency (Minnesota Valley Canning and Hoover), they urged Mr Burnett to start up his own business and even invested half the capital he required. The special relationship between Real Silk and Leo Burnett was to last until 1943 and, from their liaison, such gems as this advertisement for men's socks would emerge (3). Groucho Marx, the Hollywood funny man, played a Real Silk sales rep and under the punning headline he launched, with great seriousness, into a tale of misadventure.

The *Psychology* of *Psocks*

by GROUCHO MARX

ADVERTISER'S NOTE—We engaged Groucho Marx to write this advertisement, reimbursing him at his regular rate. The result is a hilarious burlesque of the Realsilk Representative calling on Mr. Marx on his Hollywood set and making the sale.

This is a true pstory, which I have translated from the Russian, first, however, putting on a neat Russian blouse to get the "feel" of that difficult language. It concerns the sox-life of the former Grand Duke Grouchidor ("Tiger Rose") Marxisoxsky.

ONE DAY a commoner came to my castle in Hollywoodograd. He caught the Grand Duke with a hole in his sock. Imagine catching the Grand Duke with a hole in his sock. Imagine catching anyone with a hole in his sock. I felt chagrin creeping all over me. I blushed through my tunic.

The commoner took one look at the rosy ducal toes and playfully said, "This little pig went to market; this little pig stayed home."

"Enough," I cried, "quit profaning the Grand Duke's toes and come to the point." Hastily I threw my *mantilla* over the offending members.

"Don't let the hole in the sock get your goatsky," he said. "You'd be surprised how many holes in socks, or stockings for that matter, go on under cover. In fact, I just came from the exclusive Malibu Beachsky section, where I found three leading men and an ingenue with holes in their hosiery. I helped them, and I can help you, too."

"You have moved me strangely," said the Grand Duke. "Who are you?"

"The Realsilk Man—come to bring you the glad tidings of wonderful socks—wholly without holes—and of such quality that Grand

Dukes, and even people with regular jobs, are proud to sheathe their feet within them."

He started firing questions at me rapid-fire.

"Is your sox-life a happy one?

"Can a Grand Duke do first-class duking in socks like those you now wear?

"Do you feel at ease when you take off your shoes in company?"

By this time we were both in tears. I dried his and vice versa.

"Shako," I said at last, doffing my own with a bow, "but why are you taking so much trouble just for a poor old broken-down Grand Dukeovitch?"

"You look good for at least a dozen pairs of these non-rippable, extra quality, super-guarded toed, double-decked soled, handsomely patterned, longer-wearing famous Realsilk socks. I feel sure that I have shown you the error of your previous sox-life. Shall I put you down for two or four dozen pairs?"

Of course, a Marxisoxsky never takes the first figure offered, so I got him down to one dozen pairs before I bought. And I can truthfully say, it was the turning point in the Grand Duke's life.

Now, on the set, when the boys and girls have recess from the hurly-burly of lights, cameras, sound mixers, directors and gagmen, and have gathered together for a moment's relaxation, instead of importuning me to do my card tricks, bird calls, or ocarina solos, they say:

"Grouchidor, show us your socks," —and I'm proud to say that I do!

To Women: If you have read this sock ad please know that the Realsilk Representative who calls at the home also brings a complete line of women's fine hosiery and lingerie, as well as wearables for all members of the family.

THE SOCKS WITH SEVEN EXCLUSIVE FEATURES

① **Six-Ply Toe**—which is the best wearing sock toe in the world (patent pending). ② **High-Spliced Heel**—to prevent those exasperating holes where the shoe rubs. ③ **Double-Layer Sole**—longer wear. ④ **More Compact Weave**—more actual fabric—more actual wear—and better looks for the money. ⑤ **Longest Silk Leg Found in Any Socks**—the bigger the foot size, the longer the leg. ⑥ **Double-Thick Garter Bands**—non-rippable—comfortable. ⑦ **Triple-Fast Hygienic Dyes**—fast to light, washing and perspiration. Color cannot harm the feet. Realsilk Hosiery Mills, Inc., Indianapolis, U.S.A. World's largest manufacturers of silk hosiery. Branches in 250 cities.

REAL SILK
SOLD ONLY IN OFFICE AND HOME

3

4

The leading edge of photographic artists were
freeing themselves from the confines of realism.
Edward J. Steichen was the main proponent of a
more modernist approach. At the beginning of
the century he was linked to the Photo-Secession
movement created by Alfred Stieglitz in 1902
which published the influential Camera Work
magazine. The name of the movement was
inspired by Secession, a group of artists Klimt
had established in Vienna in 1897. Some years
later Steichen distanced himself from this and
abandoned pictorialism for the effectiveness of
light and shade and tight framing. In so doing he
opened the way to a new and original means
of expression for photography in advertising.
He worked for Vogue and Vanity Fair, specialising
in portraits and fashion and then, from 1923, in
beauty product brands. **N.W. Ayer & Son** chose
him in 1935 to work for their client, Cannon Mills,
which, from its beginnings in North Carolina in
1928, had acquired a great reputation for the
quality of its blankets, cotton napkins and
household linen, and for innovative designs.
At the time, Steichen was seeking to promote his
photographic vision so he offered his work to both
the Woodbury line of cosmetics and to Cannon.
The same model, Dixie Ray, was used for both
campaigns (4). On the theme of "Towel Talks",
a whole series of compositions with the artist's
signature were issued to promote the brand (5).
This was the first major campaign featuring
nudity in the history of advertising.

5

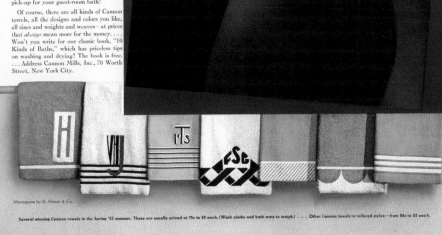

"... out of the ivory palaces, whereby they have made thee glad."

The soap Ivory, which emerged at the end of the nineteenth century, is an icon in the world of communications. The brand cleverly adapted to trends by regularly creating new products without ever altering its personality.

1

IVORY SOAP

99.⁴⁴⁄₁₀₀% PURE
—it floats

Guards loveliness—

William Procter and James Gamble, were two brothers-in-law from Cincinnati, Ohio. One manufactured candles and the other soap, and they decided to join forces in 1837. In 1878, James' son, James Norris, bought the formula for a new soap which would bear the name Procter & Gamble White Soap. The name was clear and simple, but lacked personality. The following year, William's son, Harley T. Procter, listening to a psalm (45:8), was struck by one word: 'ivory' and thus he baptised the soap! Like ivory, it was white, compact, long-lasting and evoked ideas of luxury and purity. Two rational arguments were considered to establish the product's superiority. The first, discovered by accident, was that if the soapy mixture was left on the heat too long it filled with air yet did not lose any of its desirable properties and, what was more, it floated! Secondly, on hearing his competitors' claims to purity, Procter had analysed his own soap which he found to be 99.44% pure –purer than any other, and the first advertisement appeared in 1882 in a religious weekly.

...silent, speaking hands...

*be sure they say
nice things about you
—always*

WHETHER they accent a sentence with a tiny, gay gesture, or lie quiet and slim and listening—your hands say things about you.

And busy hands, hands that look skilful and supple, can be lovely, can say the nicest things of all—if only their beauty has not been squandered! If only their white smoothness has not been parched by harsh soaps. If only they have been protected *while* they were doing their tasks.

If yours are homekeeping hands, they need protection a dozen times a day. And Ivory Soap, which guards so gently the bloom and beauty of complexions, will befriend your hands, too.

When you wash your shining dishes and your gleaming silver—when you rub your downy woolens and shimmering silks and dainty cottons—whenever you need to use soap-and-water for a household task —use Ivory and your hands will be safeguarded.

Women who know Ivory and think of it as a true and constant friend, long ago learned that its quick, lasting suds clean everything with housewifely thoroughness. But they value it chiefly, perhaps, because its purity protects the loveliest complexion or the prettiest hands.

With Ivory as their guardian all through the day, your hands can say nice things about you *always!*

PROCTER & GAMBLE

IVORY SOAP

KIND TO EVERYTHING IT TOUCHES
99 ⁴⁴⁄₁₀₀% pure - It floats

IVORY
FLAKES

2

If you want a baby's clear, smooth skin use a baby's beauty treatment

Cherish your complexion—indeed, your complete loveliness—as gently as if you were a baby. See how gratefully your skin will respond to a baby's beauty treatment. Entrust your charm to Ivory, the soap that keeps millions of babies so adorable. Ivory is advised for babies by doctors and nurses, because its touch is as gentle as a kiss to the most sensitive skin.

Don't take risks with a less pure soap. Even when your hands are busy with housework, with dishes and cleaning, let Ivory turn every soap task into a beauty bath.

To protect or regain that baby-smooth look, use gentle Ivory . . . 99 44/100% PURE.

© 1932, P. & G. Co.

Ivory Soap

3

"THERE'S SOMETHING I READ IN YOUR FACE"

I KNOW why daddy likes to look at your face, mother. It's just the face I'd have picked for you if I could have done the picking.

I've admired you many times when you thought I was just kicking the air or blowing lacy bubbles. I've been watching particularly to see how you care for your face. And it does my heart good to see that you're using my beauty soap. Goodness, mother, what would our complexions be—if it weren't for our Ivory Soap?

Don't ever let me hear of your buying perfumed or colored soaps for your sensitive skin. Remember what fancy "beauty" soap did to the baby next door. It made her skin feel so cross that she yelled and yelled. Let that be a warning never to use an impure soap!

No question about it, our doctor knows what he is talking about. He told both of us, "A sensitive complexion needs a pure, gentle soap, and I'm sure you've got that soap in your home—it's IVORY . . . 99 44/100% PURE!"

If you want a baby-clear, baby-smooth skin, use a baby's beauty treatment

IVORY SOAP

4

Procter & Gamble first turned to an advertising agency in 1923. The agency was Blackman, which was later to become Compton. Blackman produced this 1927 poster by Andrew Loomis (1) and this 1928 advertisement by Harry M. Meyers (2), both of which illustrate the theme of female beauty, using a style in keeping with the realistic spirit of the day. Later, in 1932, the brand would use a more novel subject, babies' skin (3).
A baby experiencing its mother's soft skin (4) and sharing soap with her (5) became the advertising focus. By then, photographs had replaced illustrations. Later, Compton was to publicise another Procter & Gamble brand: Camay soap.

"I'm sharing my soap with Mother now"

[DOCTOR'S ORDERS]

Yes, doctors must pure, gentle Ivory Soap for the sensitive skin of babies and for grown-up complexions. Recently a leading medical journal wrote every doctor in the United States, asking which soap they advised for babies' and grown-ups' skin. More doctors replied "Ivory" than any other brand of toilet soap.

Procter & Gamble make Ivory Soap. If you write them, saying you have read this advertisement, they will send you a useful surprise gift. Mail post card to Ivory Soap, Dept. FP, Box 687, Cincinnati, Ohio. Offer good until May 30, 1941.

Try baby's beauty treatment for your skin, too. Ivory Soap—99 44/100% pure.

5

First, a 'soap opera'

To get to number one in the detergent market, Oxydol orchestrated its communication with great effect. Oxydol is also recorded in the annals of advertising history as the brand which started the 'soap opera.'

1

2

Oxydol washing powder was launched in 1914 by William Waltke and, in 1927, Procter & Gamble bought the brand. The company was not satisfied with second place on the market, behind Lever Brothers' Rinso and at the time, Oxydol used traditional, stereotyped images, as shown in this poster by Marshall Reid (2). In 1930, the agency **Blackett Sample Hummert**, established in Chicago in 1923 —and later to join the ranks of Saatchi & Saatchi after an interim existence as Dancer Fitzgerald Sample— handled a radical relaunch with granules replacing flakes, thus modernising the product's formula. The packet was simplified to improve its impact and its communications were in the comic strip tradition which competitor, Rinso, had used to great effect. A promotional campaign was born (1). In December 1933 the agency created the first 'soap opera', "Ma Perkins" which was sponsored by Proctor & Gamble and in 1939, Oxydol became the first detergent brand designed for washing machines.

Content providers

In the early days of radio in the 1920s it was thought that, in order to protect the intimate atmosphere in the home, no broadcast advertisements should really be allowed to intrude. But radio advertising was to find forms of expression that would make it very popular.

1

Almost all the big names in radio belong to the post-First World War generation: the BBC was born in 1922 in the United Kingdom, NBC (1926) and CBS (1929) in the United States. The development of radio as a medium depended on households buying radio sets from manufacturers who were very active in selling their wares. Philips, who began production in 1927, reached sales of a million sets in 1932. Philips used an advertisement created by **Elvinger** (an agency established in Paris in 1923, which was later to join forces with **De la Mar** in 1960 to form Intermarco) which emphasised sound quality as its selling point. It claimed that you could hear laughter over Philips radios as if you were in the same room (1). De la Mar also worked for Philips in the Netherlands; their work is shown in these poster for Miniwatt lamps (2). The Philips brand symbol, with its waves and stars, was used for the first time on the packaging for these lamps and became the brand's official logo in 1938.

2

A HERO WITH FIVE MILLION FOLLOWERS...

Jack Armstrong, "All American Boy" of the N.B.C. Airwaves

who are learning some good lessons in healthful living

Late this afternoon, some four to five million boys and girls from 6 to 16 years of age will take 15 minutes from their work or play to tune in to the latest thrilling venture of Jack Armstrong, radio's "All American Boy"—a program sponsored by General Mills, Inc., for Wheaties.

And the same thing will happen tomorrow, and next day—five days a week, straight through the season. A mighty potent force, is it not, to so continuously draw one of the largest juvenile audiences in America?

But how does this phenomenon interest you? In this respect: that the Jack Armstrong broadcast, due to the nature of its important portion of its daily message, is an instrument for child education which we believe merits your notice.

In the box at right are the three Jack Armstrong "Training Rules" which have been an integral part of the sponsor's message on this broadcast for more than three years. Look them over.

We believe they will strike you as a notable example of truthful, beneficial advertising. The sort of message that, in addition to publicizing a product, performs a desirable social service.

In formulating this and similar advertising policies, we acknowledge a deep indebtedness to the invaluable counsel of your Association's Council on Foods. We, too, believe that sound educational propaganda is a valuable adjunct to truthful advertising.

Jack Armstrong's TRAINING RULES

1. Get plenty of sleep, fresh air and exercise.

2. Make a friend of soap and water, because dirt breeds germs and germs can make people sickly and weak.

3. For sound nourishment and keen flavor, eat this "Breakfast of Champions"—a big bowlful of Wheaties, with plenty of milk or cream and some kind of fruit.

General Mills, Inc.
MINNEAPOLIS, MINN.

"Breakfast of Champions" is a registered trade mark of General Mills, Inc.

WHEATIES *"Breakfast of Champions"*
WITH MILK OR CREAM AND FRUIT

3

In 1922, N.W. Ayer & Son created two 'radio talks' for its clients and the following year the agency produced the first musical programme, "The Eveready Hour", for National Carbon, a battery manufacturer. **Newell-Emmett** *ran a similar show on behalf of Texaco: the Texaco Star Theatre which broadcast concerts from the New York Metropolitan Opera, beginning in 1930. Frank Hummert joined* **Blackett and Sample** *in 1927 and produced with his wife, Anne Ashenhurst, a dozen of 'serial dramas' (which were christened 'soap operas' when Procter & Gamble chose them as its preferred mode of operation on the radio). Amongst them was the youth adventure serial created for Wheaties, a General Mills cereal brand, broadcast daily from 1933 to 1951. By the end of its run it was called "Jack Armstrong of the SBI". Jack, the hero, originally played by Jim Ameche, teaches his young public the principles of a healthy diet (3). Hummert also created in 1938, for Oxydol, "Ma Perkins", a soap opera which lasted thirty-seven years and became a televised series. This is a photograph of a recording session with the cast that would play it (5). Blackett and Sample also launched, in 1924, for Gold Medal Flour, a brand of the Washburn Crosby Company, which became part of General Mills, a new type of programme: a cooking show featuring "Kitchen-Tested" recipes of Betty Crocker (4).*

Starting
Next Monday, Sept. 21st

Keep this page for reference
Read details below

FREE *to* WOMEN!

Famous GOLD MEDAL "Kitchen-Tested"
Recipes by Radio—*three times each week*

In our own model kitchen—conducted by home economics teachers and cooking experts—we are constantly studying and working on the food problems that worry housewives.

For many years we have been sending to women throughout the country the results of our experiments; for example, household helps, balanced menus, and the famous Gold Medal "kitchen-tested" recipes for the handy Gold Medal Flour Recipe Box.

So great has been the response that we have continually sought ways and means to bring this service into more direct contact with all of you who have been so appreciative of our efforts.

We have found at last, we believe, the ideal way: *the radio!*

And so we are happy to announce that starting next Monday, September 21st, you can now tune in three times each week on the "Betty Crocker, Gold Medal Flour, Home Service Talks".

Every Monday—Wednesday—and Friday. At approximately 10:45 in the morning. Check the stations at the side and tune in Monday on your favorite. We know you will like it, Thousands of women are proving this to us by their letters of appreciation to our own Gold Medal Station, Minneapolis-St. Paul.

Send today for your free booklet—giving full program for 29 weeks. Just send name and address. A postcard will do.

WASHBURN CROSBY COMPANY, Minneapolis, Minnesota

My Special Offer of Kitchen-tested Recipes

As we test the flour in our kitchen, we are also creating and testing delightful new recipes. We have printed all these Kitchen-tested recipes on cards and filed them in neat wooden boxes. A quick ready index of recipes and cooking suggestions.

These Gold Medal Home Service boxes cost so exactly 70c each. We will send you one for that price. And as fast as we create new recipes we mail them to you free. Just think—new Kitchen-tested recipes constantly!

If you prefer to see first what the recipes are like, just send 10 10c to cover cost of packing and mailing.

Check the coupon for whichever you desire—the sample recipes or the complete Gold Medal Home Service box.

Betty Crocker

MISS BETTY CROCKER, Washburn Crosby Company, Minneapolis, Minnesota

☐ Enclosed find 70c for your Gold Medal Home Service box of Kitchen-tested recipes. (It is understood I receive free all new recipes as they are printed.)

☐ Enclosed find 10c for selected samples of Kitchen-tested recipes.

Name
Address
City   State

GOLD MEDAL FLOUR ~ *Kitchen-tested*

MILLED BY WASHBURN CROSBY COMPANY, MINNEAPOLIS, MINN. ALSO CREATORS OF WASHBURN'S PANCAKE FLOUR, GOLD MEDAL CAKE FLOUR, WHEATIES AND PURIFIED BRAN

Tune in on Gold Medal Radio Station (WCCO—416.4 meters) St. Paul-Minneapolis. Interesting programs daily. Also cooking talks for women. 10:45 Mondays, Wednesdays and Fridays. By Betty Crocker, Gold Medal Flour Home Service Department.

"Service to the Northwest"

4

5

All eyes and ears!

At that time, radio in Europe was undergoing enormous changes and European advertisers were beginning to have another medium at their disposal: the cinema.

1

2

3

The idea of opening an advertising agency first occurred to Marcel Bleustein in 1926, when he was only twenty. The following year, he realised his dream and opened **Publicis** in a miniscule apartment at 17, rue du Faubourg Montmartre in Paris. He found his first clients from among his acquaintances: Comptoir Cardinet, André shoe shops, and Levitan furniture. In a France beginning to equip itself with radio receivers, more and more companies were interested in advertising via the new medium. As early as 1929, Bleustein was using the public radio antenna on the Eiffel Tower on behalf of one of his clients. After a successful campaign he began selling radio time to advertisers on behalf of radio stations, in parallel with developing his advertising agency. He became the sole 'radio broker' for fifteen radio stations spread throughout France, Les Antennes de Publicis. This offered, in particular, the possibility of twinning programmes on several stations and thus of reaching a nation-wide audience. In 1935 he went one step further and bought his own station, which he named Radio-Cité (2). This was located on the boulevard Haussmann in Paris, with studios producing news broadcasts, soap operas, games and variety shows. Most were sponsored programmes and attracted considerable audiences (4). Many, such as "Le music-hall des jeunes" (Youth music-hall), sponsored by Levitan, were very popular and successful (3). This programme was where new French singing stars of the era were discovered, like Charles Trenet and Edith Piaf (1).

4

From the end of the nineteenth century,
Georges Méliès had been creating filmed
advertisements which he called "advertising-views."
These were short, often comic films, projected
onto the fronts of buildings and ending with
"postscripts praising the product." After the First
World War, the number of cinemas grew and in
1924 a special sort of display was born, invented
by an entrepreneur, Jean Mineur, the "advertising
curtain." He sold them to small businesses first
in Valenciennes and then further afield in northern
France. In this way he formed a network of cinemas,
and in 1927 established the Agence générale
de publicité (General Agent for Advertising) to sell
the advertising space. In 1936, he established
Publicité et Films Jean Mineur, an advertising film
production company and in 1950 he chose an
emblem for this company, a little miner figure (5).
These three images are from an animation by
Lortac and Mallet, produced in 1939 by Mineur,
to advertise GMR radio sets (6). At the end of the
1930s Publicis also entered the world of cinema,
owning some Parisian cinemas in its own right (7).
It was also the sole advertising broker for a
network of over a thousand cinemas and owned
an advertising film production company, Cinéma
et Publicité. The broker and production activities
of Jean Mineur and Publicis were to merge in
1970, forming Médiavision.

7

5

6

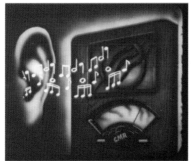

Chapter III

1941-1960

N.W. Ayer & Son

De la Mar

D'Arcy

Elvinger

Publicis

Benton & Bowles

MacManus John & Adams

Compton

Leo Burnett

Dancer Fitzgerald Sample

Masius & Ferguson

Norton

Brose

Cunningham & Walsh

Farner

Modern Times

Piccadilly Circus, London. In 1954, Coca-Cola added its own neon sign to the vibrant, glowing display of advertisements.

This was an era of firsts: the first computer in 1943, the first space satellite, the Sputnik, in 1957. It was an era of inventions that revolutionised everyday life: the transistor in 1948, plastic, chewing gum and nylon stockings. There was an imperative to make up for lost time and leave wartime restrictions behind, to consume and enjoy the new icons of modernity: the refrigerator, the washing machine, the electric razor, the record player and, last but not least, the car. There were many new models: Europeans were beginning to buy their first car when households in the United States were already considering a second. Everywhere, automobile manufacturers were among the biggest investors in advertising.

Modernity also meant television. In 1954, it became the primary advertising medium in the U.S. The television industry completely reshaped the landscape which had been formed by radio twenty years earlier. The major television stations did not want to allow agencies to control programme content, so they produced their own programmes and gathered together commercials into a separate slot.

Finally, modernity saw the arrival in most markets of the big international brands –the arrival of new ways of shopping and eating. New forms of entertainment also arrived in the guise of Disneyland (which opened in California in 1955), Hollywood films, and there was the beginnings of the Nouvelle Vague and Italian cinema. The advertising industry started to use increasingly sophisticated techniques. Ernest Dichter founded the Institute for Motivational Research in 1951 and, in 1957, Roland Barthes applied semiotics to the world of consumption.

During this twenty-year period, the world saw its fair share of drama and crisis –maybe even more than its fair share. Birth rates had picked up in the countries that had been at war, and this demographic regeneration contributed to development which would last. Advertising established its place: it proved it could be effective in assisting growth and particularly the introduction of new products and services.

By the end of the fifties, the scent of youth and optimism was wafting through the air. In 1951, the 23 year-old Vita Alves gave her partner the first kiss in the history of Brazilian television and a certain Elvis Presley, aged 19, made his first record. Another revolution was on the way.

Behind the lines

Advertising helped mobilize enthusiasm and energy everywhere that it appeared.
Its role in stimulating patriotic fervour was especially strong
in the United States.

1

2

3

In the United States, mobilisation *manifested itself in various guises. On the one hand, the U.S. administration introduced specific organisations, to which companies contributed voluntarily; on the other hand, clients and their advertising agencies took initiatives to inform people and sensitize them to all aspects of the conflict. Thus, after the bombing of Pearl Harbor on 7 December 1941, advertisers came together as the War Advertising Council, of which Leo Burnett was one of the very first members. "Are you doing all you can?" asks this poster with the 'pointing finger' reminiscent of Uncle Sam's (1). It formed part of a series, commissioned in 1942 by General Cable, a firm which supplied the undersea pipelines that transported fuel for the allied Normandy landings in June 1944.*
N.W. Ayer & Son *also contributed, delegating its art director Charles T. Coiner to the information division of the Office of Emergency Management in Washington. Here, Coiner's roughs can be seen (3) of the finished poster by Glenn Grohe (2), a call to beware of the enemy listening in, and of another poster by Jean Carlu (4) aimed at stimulating U.S. manufacturing. Both date from 1942.*

4

"My girl's a WOW"

5

6

We Can Do It!

POST FEB. 15 TO FEB. 28

WAR PRODUCTION CO-ORDINATING COMMITTEE

7

Men had gone to fight at the front and women made their contribution to the war effort by keeping the economy running. Primarily, they replaced the men who were away, mainly by making war materials and munitions. These women were iconised by 'Rosie the riveter', a symbol of American womanhood who worked in armaments factories, recognisable by her trademark headscarf. In a poster by Adolf Treidler, a G.I. proudly holds a photo, saying his girl's a 'WOW' –a Woman Ordnance Worker (5). In this 1942 Westinghouse poster, created by J. Walter Thompson and illustrated by J. Howard Miller for the War Production Coordinating Committee, Rosie is proud and resolute (7). On the other side of the pond, a few days before the liberation of Paris, the Resistance slapped a poster by Paul Colin on the walls: the tortured Republic is coming back to life (6). Within a few days, a young French officer, responsible for information under General Koenig, announced the liberation of Paris over the radio of the Resistance from London. After the war, he was granted the privilege of attaching his 'nom de guerre', Blanchet, to his real name. He became Marcel Bleustein-Blanchet.

Brand propaganda

*During the war, the U.S. economy did not stop. Quite the reverse;
manufacturing ran at full throttle and factories and brands were mobilised.
In post-war Europe, reconstruction called for a similar mobilisation.*

2

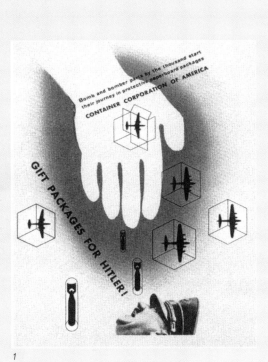

1

All the big companies joined in the civilian war
effort. With their advertising agencies, they drew
up propaganda and public education campaigns
or promoted their products, where these
were appropriate to the circumstances. These
three examples date from 1943. Prior to the
conflict, **N.W. Ayer & Son** had already called on
artists to produce corporate communications
for the Container Corporation of America.
This advertisement by Jean Carlu (1), the French
poster artist who had moved to the United States
in 1939 for the World exhibition in New York,
is characteristic of the time, and illustrates
the active contribution made by the packaging
industry to the war effort. Even Snap, Crackle
and Pop, the three Kellogg's Rice Krispies
mascots, reminded people of the need to save
time, fuel and work so they could concentrate
their energies on the war effort (2). Texaco
emphasised the importance of its products in
equipping armies in this advertisement from
the **Newell-Emmett** agency (3).

From Alice...to Eddie...to Adolf!

The drill whirs in Alice's hands...shaping a
swift new plane...for Eddie to fly.

In Alice's mind is the memory of Eddie looking
handsome as he left to join his squadron...
the sweet sound of his words as he talked of the
home they would some day have together.

They'd have it now if it weren't for Adolf.
Alice and Eddie know why they're fighting.

Such are the human stories that lie behind the
overwhelming production of planes, ships, tanks
and guns that America is now pouring forth to
beat the Axis.

In our fighting industries, millions of loyal
Americans have turned their peacetime skills
into wartime production. Texaco resources are
already producing vast quantities of vitally important 100-octane aviation gasoline...chem-
icals for war explosives...high quality lubri-
cating oils for the Navy, Army and Air Corps
...and a host of other products.

To win, we all willingly drive our cars slower
to save gasoline and tires, buy war bonds and
stamps, conserve our food, clothing, metal.

For this is every American's war...Alice's,
Eddie's, yours, ours. On one point we are all
resolved: *it won't be Adolf's.*

THE TEXAS COMPANY
TEXACO FIRE-CHIEF AND SKY CHIEF GASOLINES
HAVOLINE AND TEXACO MOTOR OILS

3

In the Vanguard of Invasion

In every theater of war, wherever American forces are hitting the enemy—by land, by sea or in the air—Cadillac products are usually in the vanguard of invasion.

Such famous fighter planes as the Airacobra, the Lightning, the P-40 and the Mustang—powered by Allison, America's foremost liquid-cooled aircraft engine—all carry Cadillac-built parts. *For Cadillac builds many parts for Allison.*

In land invasions, Cadillac-built tanks are often among the first to "hit the beach" in the desperate business of overcoming enemy defense positions. And these tanks—powered with Cadillac V-type, eight-cylinder engines, equipped with Hydra-Matic transmissions—are equally busy once the beachhead is won, and land fighting is in progress.

"Craftsmanship a Creed . . . Accuracy a Law" has been a Cadillac principle for more

than forty years. Thus, all the skills we have acquired throughout this long period of peacetime activity are now being devoted to one single end . . . that the finest soldiers in the world shall not lack for anything that it is within our power to produce.

Every Sunday Afternoon . . . GENERAL MOTORS SYMPHONY OF THE AIR—NBC Network

CADILLAC MOTOR CAR DIVISION • GENERAL MOTORS CORPORATION

LET'S ALL
BACK THE ATTACK
BUY WAR BONDS

4

Towards the end of the war Cadillac commissioned MacManus John & Adams for a series of advertisements on the military applications of its civilian know-how. Illustrated by John Vickery, this advertisement appeared in the Wall Street Journal on 6 June 1944, the day the Allies landed on the French coast (4). In 1950, Jean Mineur produced "Le monde à la recherche de la paix" (The world is looking for peace), a two-minute-long animated film for the cinema (5). Created for the Paris department store Printemps and directed by the Dutch artist Joop Geesink, the film shows the trials and tribulations of a figurine representing the world looking for prosperity. The quest took the figurine past the fictitious headquarters of the Marshall Plan. This film was made in Geesink's Dollywood Studios, in the Netherlands.

5

High profile profession

Organised into professional structures, recognised by public bodies – it was time for advertising to settle down and go global. A prestigious address was the tangible proof that advertising had come of age.

1

2

3

4

N.W. Ayer & Son had been one of the first to have specially designed premises. On 1 April 1926, its 60 birthday, the agency moved to a thirteen-storey building that had been built by the architect Ralph B. Bencker in Philadelphia (1). The property on Washington Square was a fine example of Art deco. It encompassed three art galleries, a cafeteria and a relaxation area.
In New York in 1954, **Compton** arrived on the famous Madison Avenue. The agency was welcomed with these words from its neighbour and competitor, **Cunningham & Walsh**: "Hey neighbour, welcome Compton!" (2). Compton responded: "C & W, you satisfy" (3), a reworking of the highly popular slogan created for Chesterfield by Newell-Emmett, which had been bought by Cunningham & Walsh four years earlier. **Leo Burnett**, a relative newcomer, having been around for just eleven years, installed its 650 employees in the Prudential building on 26 October 1956 (4). The agency was the main occupant of this, the first post-war skyscraper in Chicago, which at the time was one of the tallest in the world.

5

From 1948, the Marshall Plan (European Recovery Program) brought four years of substantial assistance to the countries which came together as the Organisation for European Economic Co-operation. "Building work!" is the headline in this advertisement by **De la Mar**, which informs companies that advertising is being reborn and that the agency will transform companies' advertising budget into a profitable investment (7). In December 1957, **Publicis** announced in the New York Times that it was opening its first New York office (5). Several months later, in Paris, the agency moved into 133, avenue des Champs-Élysées, the former Astoria hotel which had temporarily been commandeered as the Supreme Headquarters Allied Powers Europe (SHAPE) between April and July 1951 (6). This new location met the agency's need for expansion as it was to become one of the largest agencies in France. The high profile premises also conferred on the agency a status which reflected on the entire profession. On 1 January 1958, the Treaty of Rome came into force, instituting the European Economic Community. Thus the six signatories, Belgium, France, Germany, Italy, Luxembourg and the Netherlands began the long process of constructing a new Europe. "A market without borders" claimed the German agency **Brose** in the French press (8). Established by Hanns W. Brose in Frankfurt-am-Main in 1947, two years before the creation of the Federal Republic of Germany, this agency played an active role in the communications that accompanied the German economic miracle. Brose merged with Benton & Bowles in 1978.

6

7

8

Wherever, whenever

Back in 1898, Asa Candler, who was at the time president of Coca-Cola, promoted the idea that everyone could take a break and drink a Coke. In the 50's, with people working hard to boost the economy, the occasional break was more than welcome!

1

In the United States, Robert Skemp, a student of Haddon Sundblom, created this poster for **D'Arcy** in 1950, showing a refreshing break from work (1). Other posters conjured up other situations: driving, shopping, relaxing. On the same theme but in a different style, less realistic and more modern, the Swiss graphic artist Herbert Leupin, who had spent two years in Paris with Paul Colin, created a series of posters for the **Farner** agency between 1953 (2) and 1957 (3). Established in Zurich in 1950 by Dr. Rudolf Farner, this agency was to join Publicis in 1973. Another campaign emphasised a related theme: the availability of Coca-Cola, wherever you are –"within arm's reach of desire"– especially in the workplace, thanks to refrigerated dispensers. In 1949, a poster by Arthur Radebaugh, a prolific illustrator who was also a heavy user of the airbrush and a specialist in urban landscapes, invited workers to take a break with a chilled Coca-Cola (4). The drink's price is stated: 5 cents –exactly the same as fifty years earlier, when Asa Candler was promoting the refreshing break a Coca-Cola could provide for that same 5 cents!

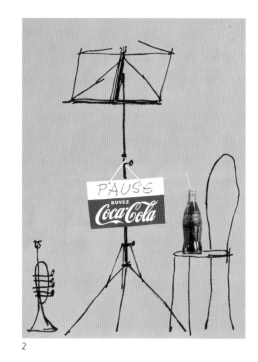

2

3

New shapes and sizes

The period in which illustration dominated advertising was ending.
Photography was polishing its performance and printing processes improved
the quality of reproductions, in black and white and in colour.

we hand it on with pride...

D'ARCY ADVERTISING COMPANY

1

In 1956, D'Arcy said goodbye to Coca-Cola with
this advertisement, published in the Wall Street
Journal (1). It marked the end of a collaboration
which had lasted almost fifty years, but also
meant a certain sort of advertising was no more.
The time for realist illustration was past and
photography was the future. Gil Elvgren, a
disciple of Haddon Sundblom, 'the father of
Father Christmas', was one of the last illustrators
but –and this was a sign of the times– worked
from photos. He was able to bend his drawings
to the requirements of the brand, representing
the good, clean, 'all-American girl' while
remaining the undoubted master of the provocative
calendar 'pin-up'. Once again in this poster,
he glorifies young American womanhood (2),
whose image went with the G.I.s when, at
the request of the U.S. army, Coca-Cola opened
sixty-four bottling plants in Europe and Asia,
"Feel home away" was how the advertising put it.
In 1960, several sizes of bottles were launched
and cans were made available in most places.
Coke (this nick-name first appeared in the 40's)
really became everyone's drink, worldwide.

To play refr

DRINK

Coca-Cola

2

eshed

"We like the way you operate!"

That was what Kellogg Company said during their initial collaboration with Leo Burnett. In four years, the agency was entrusted with all the firm's advertising, first for North America then the rest of the world.

TONY THE TIGER SAYS:

"You bet your life they're Gr-r-reat!"

No wonder Groucho's speechless. What if a tiger stole your microphone and your favorite line. But that's Tony for you. And he's all for you when he tells you to try these big, crackly flakes of corn. Because they're the ones with the secret Kellogg's sugar coating all over. Gr-r-reat? You bet your life.

Kellogg's SUGAR FROSTED FLAKES

1

It all began in Battle Creek, Michigan, *at a sanatorium run by Dr. John Harvey Kellogg. It was there that breakfast cereals were born. Their success was to come later, when Will Kellogg, the doctor's brother, founded the company in 1906. During the 1930's N.W. Ayer & Son was asked to advertise Rice Krispies®. In 1949, Kellogg asked* **Leo Burnett** *to look after two other products. The agency then took an initiative, investigating the use of television to advertise cereals including Rice Krispies which, by then, was being managed by another agency, Kenyon & Eckhardt. Leo Burnett shared the results of their investigations with them, and this generous attitude appealed to Kellogg, who soon gave Leo Burnett the account for the brand. Later on, another study, this time on packaging, led to Leo Burnett becoming Kellogg's preferred partner and launching Sugar Frosted Flakes in 1952 (2). Drawn by Martin Provinsen, an illustrator of children's books, Katy the Kangaroo, Newt the Gnu and George the Giraffe are led by Tony the Tiger®. From 1952, the singer Thurl Ravenscroft lent Tony™ his voice for the launch of the famous rallying cry "They're Gr-r-reat!" and, in 1955, Tony™ was even invited onto Groucho Marx's programme "You bet your life" (1).*

GR-R-REAT NEWS!

about A GREAT NEW CEREAL

Kellogg's

SUGAR FROSTED FLAKES

Imagine the biggest, golden-brown flakes of corn you ever saw in your life. Imagine them sparkled with a shimmering sugar coat.

That's the combination that makes Kellogg's new Sugar Frosted Flakes a deliciously different breakfast treat with a grand new flavor all its own.

It's a have-some-more flavor that makes Sugar Frosted Flakes gr-r-reat for breakfast—gr-r-reat for snacks.

Ask your grocer for a free sample. Then get ready to buy a whole box (featuring Tony, the tiger, or Katy, the kangaroo) because your whole family is going to roar for more!

Sugar frosted flakes of corn... Eat 'em out of the box or out of the bowl

Kellogg's SUGAR FROSTED FLAKES

Sugar Frosted Flakes of Corn

2

"Is this the beginning of a new era in packaging?" asked the trade magazine Tide when it saw Kellogg's® new packets in 1952. These were created in an era when grocery stores kept cereal packets on the top shelf to protect them from the humidity and the front of the packet merely bore the brand and product names. As packets were now being placed at eye level, Leo Burnett decided that a simple masthead (no bigger than a postage stamp, said his detractors!) would be sufficient to convey the brand's message clearly. The space freed up could then be used to communicate with the consumer. This novel idea soon emerged on all Kellogg's packs, beginning with its flagship product, Kellogg's Corn Flakes®, for which Leo Burnett also designed the advertising. After several attempts, the illustration for the packs was entrusted to Norman Rockwell, who had already worked for the Minnesota Valley Canning Company. He produced a whole gallery of portraits of children and adolescents, who gave the packs and the brand a strong personality (3), (4). As a result, the packaging became a key component of the illustration of the advertisements, as this 1955 example by Stevan Dohanos shows (5). Like Rockwell, but with a slightly more caustic view, Dohanos had also created many covers for the Saturday Evening Post.

4

Two "don't forgetters"

New Kellogg's Kids move into your neighborhood

Kellogg's
CORN FLAKES

3

If the lady in charge doesn't turn around soon, she's going to have more corn flakes than Kellogg's. Her son, her pride and joy, has a good thing here, and he doesn't know quite where to stop.

Well any minute now, mother will catch sight of that cart and there'll be some changes made.

Of course, His Nibs has a point. It IS a good idea to have plenty of Kellogg's Corn Flakes. Somebody always seems to wake up and want them. And that big Corn Flakes package has a habit of getting down to the last rustle before you know it.

Even we can't quite describe that appetizing "something" that gives Kellogg's Corn Flakes this disappearing quality and has made them the favorite for 50 years.

Are you going to the store today—with or without a small boy? Why don't you just reach out and pick up a spare package? Tomorrow's breakfast will be here before you know it and you wouldn't want to disappoint anybody, now would you?

REMINDER: Running low at your house? Better get a spare.

5

Ho, Ho, Ho!

Their advertising was so popular and became so established that the Minnesota Valley Canning Company changed its name to the Green Giant Company, becoming synonymous with the character.

2

1

In the Valley of the Green Giant

Why the Green Giant harvests by moonlight

There are people up in Green Giant country who will tell you they've seen the Green Giant adjust the moon so it shines down brighter on the peas he's picking in his valley.

We won't vouch for that. But we do know Green Giant® peas are picked in the moonlight if that happens to be when the fleeting moment of perfect flavor arrives.

You see, from the day the seed is put into the rich soil, these peas are watched over like babies. And whether it's day or night when they reach that one fleeting instant of perfect flavor and tenderness, they're plucked from the vine and rushed into cans without even taking time to shake off the dew.

Even people who usually don't get excited about vegetables love the good things that come from the Green Giant's garden. You get them at your grocer's. With or without moonbeams.

Green Giant *Good things from the garden*

ASPARAGUS • PEAS • PEAS WITH ONIONS • GOLDEN CORN • CORN WITH SWEET PEPPERS • WHITE CORN • BEANS

3

On the recommendation of Leo Burnett, *who had worked with the company throughout its success story, Minnesota Valley Canning renamed itself Green Giant in 1950, almost half a century after the company was created. The company floated on the stock exchange in New York under its new name. For the occasion, the founder's grandson was photographed in the city underneath a statue of the famous giant (1). A new process permitted the company to establish exactly the best time of day or night to harvest its vegetables (3). The Green Giant made his successful television appearance in 1961 as a cartoon character. Len Dresslar, who also provided the voice for Kellogg's Tony the Tiger and the Marlboro cowboy, voiced the popular cry of "Ho, Ho, Ho!" and the song "Good things from the garden". Still in 1961, the company entered the frozen food market with special vegetable recipes which were very successful. The Green Giant was still centre stage but now he needed a cosy red scarf to protect him from his new, chilly environment (2).*

Brightest
idea
in this
whole
corn-lovin'
world...
Quick
Cooking!

The Green Giant quick cooks
his corn to save all the color,
flavor and freshness of
just picked ears. All you do is
raise the lid, heat and serve.
This strikes the Big Green
Man as a pretty bright idea,
too, just as long as the
brand you open is his own
Niblets corn.

P.S. Niblets is vacuum packed.
No excess liquid so you get
as many servings as in
taller liquid packed cans.

GREEN GIANT® Niblets® FRESH CORN VACUUM PACKED QUICK COOKED

GREEN GIANT.

Good Things from the Garden

4

SUPER CREAMY

This advertisement appeared in 1962 proclaiming
"Brightest idea in this whole corn-lovin' world...
Quick Cooking!" (4). In 1972, the brand bore the
Green Giant a companion, Little Green Sprout,
who was to bring freshness and energy to its
communications (5) and the Green Giant stepped
back somewhat, to appear only partially or as
a silhouette. Drawn by Milton Schaffer, who had
worked for twenty years in Walt Disney's studios
as an animator then as a screenwriter and
producer, Little Sprout appeared on television
for the first time asleep in a pea pod (6). Tom
C. Fouts, composer and successful singer of many
advertising jingles, lent Little Sprout his voice.

5

6

Red on red

How do you best present the essential story your product has to tell? Leo Burnett called this factor the product's 'inherent drama' and made this search for truth his agency's golden rule.

2

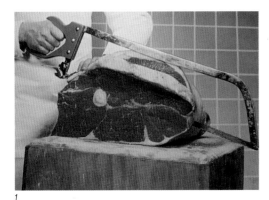

1

The American Meat Institute in Chicago was the first **Leo Burnett** client whose budget reached a million dollars. The agency won the account in 1940, competing against no less than twenty-eight other agencies! Leo Burnett proposed performing their pitch presentation in fifty towns and cities so they could convince all the members of the Institute. Three of the agency's staff criss-crossed the country in a van over a five week period (2). Their campaign was based on a simple observation: their countrymen were forgetting both the nutritional and symbolic value of meat. The campaign tackled this issue head on, demonstrating the 'inherent drama' of the product. "What would happen if you put a piece of red meat on a red background? (…) This was inherent drama (…) It just intensified the red concept and the virility (…) we were trying to express about meat", explained Leo Burnett. That was exactly what the first advertisement would show and tell when it appeared in 1944 (4). The photos were taken in the New York studio of Harney Isham Williams, known as 'Hi', who had been the unrivalled expert in food photography since the end of the 1920's (1). To further increase its impact, the image is in 'full bleed' format, meaning it doesn't have a white frame around it; this was the technique's first outing. The success of this first advertisement provided the impetus for a whole series of others constructed along the same lines. Between 1944 and 1947 these advertisements would put the case for meat's many nutritional properties with the same force (3). Illustrated by a wide variety of cuts, each of the advertisements repeated the same headline almost obsessively: "Meat".

3

This is Life

Standing Rib Roast of Prime Beef
—you may not find it every time you look for it in your store . . . but it's on its way back!

This is not just a piece of meat . . . this is something a man wants to come home to . . . something that helps children to grow . . . something that makes women proud of their meals.

This is a symbol of man's desire, his will to survive. For as old as man's instinct to live is his liking for meat. And to be satisfied in its eating.

Is it any wonder that, as meat moves back to the Home Plate, we look on meat with new regard, not just for its enjoyment, but as a nutritional cornerstone of life?

The protein of all meat (regardless of cut or kind) is complete. It contains all of the amino acids essential to life.

Children must have them for growth. Everyone, young and old, must have them to maintain tissues, regenerate blood, resist infections, rebuild the body after injury or illness.

This Seal means that all nutritional statements made in this advertisement are acceptable to the Council on Foods and Nutrition of the American Medical Association.

AMERICAN MEAT INSTITUTE . . . Headquarters, Chicago . . . Members throughout the U.S.

4

Scandalous!

Savignac, the great French poster artist of the post-war period, said that a successful poster must be 'a visual scandal'.

suivez le bœuf...

In 1957, Publicis, who had the task of promoting Maggi's casserole meat stock, asked Raymond Savignac to create a poster. Savignac, who had been Cassandre's assistant until the latter went to the U.S. in 1938, belonged to the modern poster tradition defined by Jean Carlu as 'the visual expression of ideas'. Savignac used humour and poetry (reminiscent in some respect of Charlie Chaplin) combined with the strength and simplicity of faux-naïf black lines and pure colours which lent his work a 'rugged and primitive' character. This style plus the visual expression of the idea constituted the 'visual scandal' which proved to be the perfect accompaniment to the consumer goods he portrayed: soaps, shampoos, drinks and so on. After an initial draft which was never taken up (1), the poster known as 'the sliced cow' was created in 1959 (4). J. and C. Clerfeuille made an animated cinema film which used Savignac's illustrations: "To make a good casserole, you need carrots, leeks, onions and... beef!" (3). Thus dehydrated products became part of the French culinary repertoire.

3

4

Savignac was to re-use the theme of an animal cut in two for Maggi's chicken stock and then, in 1964, for chicken soup with a tureen shaped like a chicken (5). In 1963, the French economy was overheating, inflation was out of control and De Gaulle appointed a thirty-seven-year-old finance minister, Valéry Giscard d'Estaing. A stabilisation plan was immediately imposed including measures intended to contain rising retail prices. This poster, which Jean Feldman created for Publicis in the spirit of Savignac, encouraged consumers to beware the rises in the price of meat and to select cuts from the 'front quarters' of the animal which were less expensive (2). An attempt was even made to send tax inspectors to check labels in butchers' shops. The phrase "Suivez le bœuf" (Keep your eye on the beef) quickly entered common parlance in France and was still in use years later.

5

What are you looking at?

Could you resist the urge to bite into that cake?
Yes, you! In just a few months, that urge made for a 40%
rise in market share for Pillsbury Cake Mixes.

2

Who...Me?

Yes, Madam, you can make a cake of the very same lush, well-turned-out appearance as the cake you see here. And you do it without raising a single bead on your pretty brow. How do you do it?...

By merely adding milk to either of the two new Pillsbury Mixes ... you triumph, you please, you make everybody very, very happy. How about a Pillsbury Mix Cake tonight? How about...YOU?

Pillsbury CAKE MIXES

1

At the very beginning of 1945, Pillsbury Mills asked **Leo Burnett** to advertise a minor product in their range. Then, in 1947, the agency was asked to launch an innovative product idea: ready-to-use Cake Mixes. The agency stayed true to the principle of finding the product's 'inherent drama', spreading irresistible cakes, in close up, across a full page. It also called upon H.I. Williams, the photographer with whom it had worked on the meat campaign. The humour of the text in the series balances out the extravagance of the image (1), (3), (4). In 1965, Pillsbury turned to Leo Burnett once again for the launch of its refrigerated dough. The agency created a character, Poppin' Fresh: the Pillsbury Doughboy ('Doughboy' was slang in the United States for 'infantry soldier') (2). Originally drawn in two dimensions, Poppin' Fresh ended up in three! He was the hero of innumerable press advertisements and around six hundred TV commercials in which, although only a small and shy pastry chef, he helped children to bake wonderful cakes.

What, this very night?

If it's a reasonable hour of the day when you read this ad and if this cake appeals to you, why don't you go around to your grocer's and get yourself a package or two of these new Pillsbury Cake Mixes. ...(They're the ones in those neat blue and white packages) ... When you get back home you have everything you need right in the package (except milk, which you add) to make a cake just as handsome, just as attention-getting, just as joy-giving as the cake you see here...Why not this very night? You.

Remember –
You and Ann Pillsbury
can make a great team

Pillsbury CAKE MIXES

WHITE AND CHOCOLATE FUDGE

Milk is *all* you add –
No eggs, flavoring, or extras
of any kind required.
These are *complete* mixes.

3

Red, White and You!

Yes, you're the one we mean. Add milk to a package of Pillsbury White Cake Mix (red cherries and whipped cream for filling and topping) and aren't you wonderful? Pillsbury, the best-selling cake mixes, by far. Why don't you get in on a good thing today?

Cherry filling: Combine ⅔ cup sugar, 2 tablespoons corn starch, ¼ teaspoon salt. Stir in 1 cup liquid (juice drained from No. 2 can of red sour cherries plus water). Add ⅛ teaspoon red food coloring, if desired. Boil for 5 minutes, stirring constantly. Add cherries; cool. Spread between cooled, baked layers of Pillsbury White Cake Mix. Top with whipped cream.

Milk is all you add

No eggs to buy. No flavorings or extras of any kind required. These are complete mixes. Finest ingredients money can buy.

Pillsbury Cake Mixes

WHITE...CHOCOLATE FUDGE...GOLDEN YELLOW

4

A real coffee solution

The invention of instant coffee set advertising a challenge: explain that instant coffee is real coffee, really! Different brands took different approaches.

2

AMAZING COFFEE DISCOVERY!

Not a powder! Not a grind! But millions of tiny "FLAVOR BUDS" of real coffee . . . ready to burst instantly into that famous MAXWELL HOUSE FLAVOR!

The only instant coffee with that **GOOD-TO-THE-LAST-DROP** flavor!

1

The Maxwell House brand dates from the late 1900's when it took its name from a big hotel in Nashville, Tennessee. The story goes that Theodore Roosevelt stopped in Nashville in 1907 and was served a delicious coffee. The President greatly appreciated the taste and exclaimed that it was "Good to the Last Drop". The coffee was a blend of various varieties, perfected by Joel Cheek. With his cousin Leslie and their associate James Neal, he set about benefiting from the President's enthusiastic praise. The brand was taken over in 1928 by the Postum Company, later to become General Foods, and the President's expression was still in use when their advertising was entrusted to **Benton & Bowles**. After coffee beans, Maxwell went into instant coffee. Maxwell initially supplied rations of instant coffee for the U.S. army during wartime, then launched it on the market in 1946 (1), adopting the original slogan "Good to the Last Drop" (3). This was the theme on which the agency centred a cinema advertisement the following year, featuring an appreciative Roosevelt (2). Thus instant coffee was launched, relying heavily on the reputation of the original brand in coffee beans.

THE SATURDAY EVENING POST

Everybody knows the sign of good coffee

Early morning on the farm . . . busiest time of all the day. And when the first big chores are done, there's nothing more welcome than good, hearty, refreshing coffee . . . Maxwell House Coffee. There's such *complete* satisfaction in every cup—and there's a very good reason. It's the Maxwell House recipe, the one and *only* recipe for that famous "Good to the Last Drop" flavor. A recipe that demands certain fine coffees, blended a certain way to bring you the *most* coffee-drinking enjoyment. No wonder more people buy and enjoy Maxwell House than any other brand in the world!

WONDERFUL IN INSTANT FORM, TOO!

TUNE IN: *two award-winning hits—"Father Knows Best," starring Robert Young, NBC, Thursday nights, and "Mama," starring Peggy Wood, CBS-TV, Friday nights.*

Products of General Foods

MAXWELL HOUSE . . . the **one** coffee with that "Good to the Last Drop" flavor!

3

4

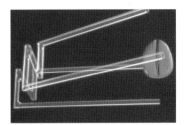
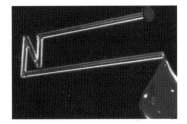

5

At Nestlé, the story of instant coffee started in 1930
when Brazil, faced with massive overproduction
due to a guaranteed price system, turned to the
Nestlé company in Switzerland to find a way of
preserving its coffee. Researchers invented a way of
producing instant coffee cost-effectively but Nestlé
had almost no history in the coffee market.
Thus Nescafé, created in 1938, had to build up
credibility among consumers long used to coffee
beans and the related rituals of preparation
and tasting roast and ground coffee. In the
early 1950's, **Publicis** in France and **Farner** in
Switzerland were commissioned to publicise this
new product and explain that this was still coffee,
and nothing but coffee (4). That was the message
expressed in a 1965 animated cinema
advertisement: "Nothing but coffee" (5) by director
Alexander Alexeieff. In order to fully convince
the consumer, Publicis offered free tastings at
home (6), while Farner organised a competition (7).

6

7

Home on the range

Beginning with a single ad repositioning the brand in 1954,
the Marlboro image was carefully crafted over nearly a decade...
ultimately becoming one of the most successful advertising
campaigns the world has ever known.

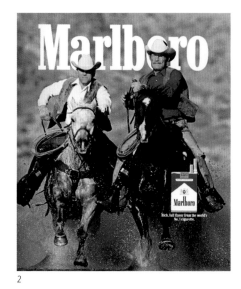

2

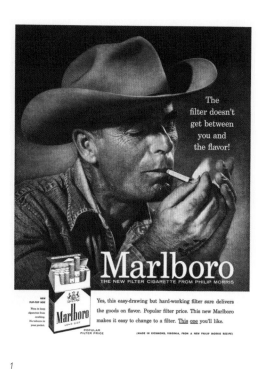

1

Philip Morris began as a tobacconist, with a single
shop on London's famous Bond Street in 1847.
Thirty years later, he introduced the Marlboro brand
in Britain; nearly three decades passed before it
was taken to the United States. Aimed at women,
with a red 'Beauty Tip' and a flavour said to be
"As mild as May", the unfiltered brand enjoyed
very modest success until the early 1950's, when
competitors began offering filter-tipped cigarettes
to men —and the market began to dramatically
shift. In response, Marlboro was repositioned with
a stronger taste, a bolder package design based
on the now-famous 'red roof', a revolutionary
flip-top box... and a Chicago ad agency led by
its namesake, **Leo Burnett**, was brought in to give
the brand a brand-new image. Although the very
first newspaper ad in 1954 featured a cowboy (1),
the advertising went on to include a variety of
masculine images. In 1963, the cowboy was given
a home with dramatic, limitless spaces and
a timeless sense of freedom... Marlboro Country.
The phrases "Come to where the flavor is.
Come to Marlboro Country" followed a year
later —and marketing history began to be made.
In ten years, Marlboro became the world's
best-selling cigarette.

3

Come to
Marlboro Country.

4

The Marlboro cowboy... *the canyons and mountains, the deserts and grasslands of the vast American West... they've been one and the same since 1963 (4). On television in the mid-60's, it was all joined and taken to new levels by composer Elmer Bernstein's theme for the Western classic 'The Magnificent Seven'. Now –it's been a long-standing requirement that any man appearing in Marlboro advertising be an actual cowboy (2). Authenticity has always been a cornerstone of the campaign –though the cowboys' character has subtly evolved over time. First portrayed as a rugged individualist, he's matured, gaining depth and sensitivity (3). Some observers saw this evolution as a reflection of the changing nature of masculinity. Others, spoke of the emergence, at the beginning of the 70's, of the United States' changing self-perspective. However you looked at it, this advertising icon has grown so strong that showing just the slightest suggestion has been enough to conjure up the whole image (5).*

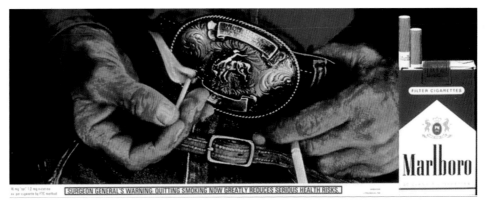

SURGEON GENERAL'S WARNING: QUITTING SMOKING NOW GREATLY REDUCES SERIOUS HEALTH RISKS.

5

Wide open spaces

The imagery of the cowboy and the American West are inextricably linked to the brand...
so much so, that with subtle shifts in color, action and topography, the imagery could be
applied to any Marlboro product. In this case, it was applied to light cigarettes.

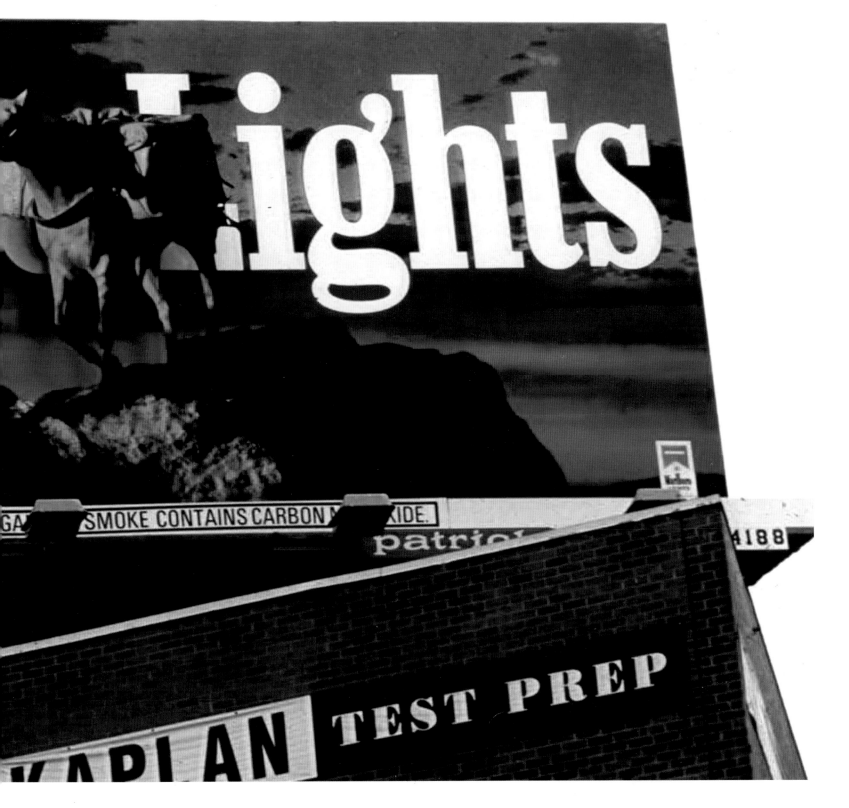

Native territories

Since Santa Fe Railway served the American West it was natural that they should glean inspiration from Native American culture. It was just a question of catching this dream and expressing it in print.

2

1

In 1942, over a period of a few days, thirty-five agencies were asked to submit two pages describing what they could offer Santa Fe, the prestigious railroad company. **Leo Burnett** had entered the fray by chance at the last minute, but surprisingly won the contract. Instead of two pages, the agency had delivered a fifty-page document in the form of a leather-bound album, like a pioneer's log book. Having travelled by train for thirty-nine hours from Chicago to Los Angeles, one of the Leo Burnett team had telegraphed back to the agency his thoughts on the journey for inclusion in its bid. The Atchison, Topeka & Santa Fe Railway Company had, from the 1900's onwards, ordered and bought, for its calendars, paintings representing the cultures and countryside of the south-western United States. Burnett continued this tradition, putting Hernando G. Villa to work for several years. Villa was a painter who had won his reputation for depicting the daily life of the Native American population and the landscapes of Arizona and New Mexico. He created a very strong personality for the company. The trains were called Chiefs (1), (3). Well-known for their luxurious comfort and the efficiency of their services, they imposed new travel standards (2). In 1955, a Zuñi guide on the el Capitan train, introduces his country to a family of admiring travellers (4).

3

He makes exploring the old West fun!

An Indian guide rides with you on El Capitan and Super Chief

There's nothing like it in travel!

You'll meet a Zuni Indian guide on your Santa Fe trip between Chicago and California, westbound on *El Capitan* (all-chair-car streamliner) or eastbound on the *Super Chief* (extra fare, all-room streamliner).

As the train glides across New Mexico, he tells you about the legends of this romantic land.

Traveling Santa Fe is a treat for the entire family. You can roam around the train meeting interesting people, choose delicious meals from a Fred Harvey menu, watch the scenery from the domes, stretch out in reclining chairs, or enjoy the privacy of your Pullman room.

And you can't beat Santa Fe family fares for economy. For instance, a family of four traveling in Santa Fe's modern chair cars, *can save as much as $104.10* on a round trip between Chicago and California.

Why not let your railroad ticket agent or travel agent tell you about it?

Santa Fe

WHEN YOU GET THERE
...RENT A CAR

4

Jet-propelled

To date cars had been heavy and rounded. Suddenly they turned colourful, changed one detail or another every year and, more importantly, became 'aerodynamic.'

Here's the Jet Age *on wheels!* Aerodynamic Plymouth '56

1

Chrysler hired N.W. Ayer & Son *for the launch of its new Plymouth model in 1955. The Plymouth astounded observers with its 'aerodynamic' shape and two-tone bodywork and the agency called on the photographer Irving Penn who had by then begun his brilliant career in the fashion world. His photos of the Plymouth brought the aesthetics of the model to the fore with a look which was characteristic of the period (2). These were the boom years for the designer Raymond Loewy. Functional objects were becoming beautiful. The 1956 model was the most daring yet. Its fins were higher and longer, evoking jet planes which, at the time, had everyone fascinated. In the background of this advertisement, for example, looms the F86 Sabre, which had had a distinguished career during the Korean war (1). A silhouette reminiscent of the 707, Boeing's first jet airliner launched in 1954, flew across the top of another car advertisement (3).*

THE BIGGEST IS THE MOST GLAMOROUS, TOO!

ALL-NEW PLYMOUTH '55

2

The car that's going places with the Young in Heart!

Aerodynamic Plymouth '56

All-new Plymouths in 29 models. Choice of engines—new Hy-Fire V-8 or PowerFlow 6

Driving Takes Wings

Settle yourself behind the Push-Button controls of the all-new Plymouth '56. Look proud, because every eye is turned on this big, beautiful triumph of jet-age design.... Then a gentle toe-touch on the throttle! Feel that forward push against your back ... see how Plymouth leaves other cars behind?

That's Plymouth's magnificent new Hy-Fire V-8 ... plus *90-90 Turbo-Torque* getaway and PowerFlite, for top thrust at take-off ... swift, safe passing. Or, for maximum economy, choose the new, increased-horsepower PowerFlow 6.

Get the news: PLYMOUTH NEWS CARAVAN with John Cameron Swayze, NBC-TV, SHOWER OF STARS and "CLIMAX!" CBS-TV.

PUSH-BUTTON DRIVING

What it means to you. First on Plymouth in the low-price 3! A touch of a button selects your driving range. Easy as pressing a light switch. Then PowerFlite fully automatic transmission takes over. Here's new driving ease!

3

Contains 57 artists!

In the beginning, the well-known adman, David Ogilvy, was critical of it. Forty years later, he hailed it as the best corporate campaign in print. It is a campaign which creates a bold vision of the inter-dependence of art and industry.

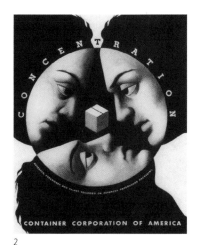

2

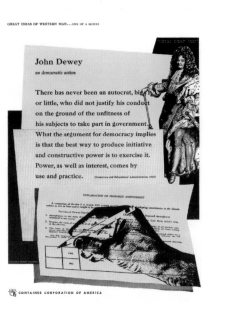

1

Walter P. Paepcke, founder of the Container Corporation of America and creator of the Aspen conferences, and his wife, Elizabeth, were believers in the alliance of art and industry. Paepcke hired a design director, Egbert Jacobsen, to create a visual identity for his corporation and in 1937 the corporate campaign was given to N.W. Ayer & Son. Charles T. Coiner, an agency's art director, asked European artists, including A.M. Cassandre, Herbert Bayer, Toni Zepf, Jean Carlu and Gyorgy Kepes, to contribute to a twelve-part series of black-and-white advertisements each illustrating the values of the packaging industry: concentration (2), harmony, responsibility, diversification and so on. They introduced a new type of advertising expression driven by ideas expressed in an illustration integrating typography (rather than strictly representative of the product). In 1942, a second wave of advertisements, the "United Nations Series", contained works by Henry Moore, Fernand Léger and Willem de Kooning and made reference to the allied nations drawn into the war. In 1946 a third "United States Series" gave U.S. regions and artists pride of place.

No barriers, no masses
of matter however enormous,
can withstand the powers
of the mind; the remotest
corners yield to them;
all things succumb; the very
Heaven itself is laid open.
(Marcus Manilius, Astronomica, 40 B.C.)

CONTAINER CORPORATION OF AMERICA

3

4

In 1949, for the bicentennial of Goethe's birth, Paepcke organised a summer conference in Aspen, Colorado. Mortimer Adler, professor at the University of Chicago, presided over the inaugural conference on the "Great ideas of Western man". These conferences, which Adler held for almost forty years, were to inspire the fourth and final series of corporate advertisements which was launched in 1950. This final wave would be the longest and also the most controversial. It lasted thirty years and involved 57 artists taken from every continent. In 1956, Herbert Bayer, a graduate of the Bauhaus, took over from Jacobsen as head of design at the Container Corporation of America and continued the series with new artists. Each artist offered a visual interpretation of a text with Jacobsen himself illustrating a passage by the North American philosopher John Dewey on democracy and action (1). Charles T. Coiner tackled a text by the Roman poet Marcus Manilius on the power of the mind (3). The North American painter Ben Shahn worked from a statement by the English statesman John Viscount Morley on compromise (4) and René Magritte, the Belgian surrealist, used for his painting a text by the philosopher George Santayana on reason (5). The previous series had retained tenuous links to the world of industry. This series resolutely placed art at the service of philosophy and education.

5

Driving growth

Oil had driven post-war growth. In cars and industrial vehicles, aviation, chemistry and textiles, oil was at the heart of twentieth-century economic growth.

Berliet

T100

le plus grand camion du monde

1

Berliet, established in Lyon at the end of the nineteenth century, introduced the T100, "the largest truck in the world" (1), at the Salon de l'automobile in Paris (Paris Car Show) in 1957 where, over ten days, a million visitors came to see it. With its wheels of over two metres in diameter and its 700 horsepower engine, the T100 was designed for oil prospecting and mining but only four trucks were built. One, the Tulsa, was part of a display by **Publicis** New York at the Oil Trade Fair in Tulsa, Oklahoma, and then at the International fair in Chicago. For that occasion, the company's symbol was updated. This symbol was originally borrowed from the American Locomotive Company in 1905 when that company was working under Berliet's licence. The picture of the locomotive with its cow-catcher was modernised (2) and then used for all the company's vehicles as shown in this 1959 poster by Jean Fortin advertising coaches (3).

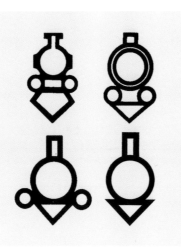

2

cars berliet

3

4

5

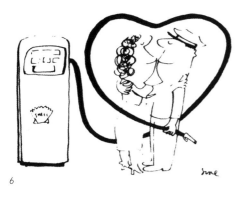

6

The French Shell company emerged in 1948 from Pétroles Jupiter which had been born of the 1922 union of the Royal Dutch/Shell group and the French company Deutsch de la Meurthe, originally a paraffin oil company. In 1954, Shell gave their advertising account to **Publicis**, who created an initial campaign showing the role and activities of the firm as part of the nation's economy and society: "Oil is everywhere in life" (5). This was followed, from 1958 onwards, by a brand image campaign which opened with a series of comic caricatures on the theme "C'est Shell que j'aime" (A play on 'C'est elle que j'aime', 'It's her that I love', replacing 'elle' with 'Shell'). The illustrator Siné provided one caricature (6). The theme would be applied consistently for a decade, as shown in this advertisement for Shell X-100 oil (7). In the early 1960's, engine technology required better-performing fuel and, on 27 April 1967, Elf, a new heavyweight firm, appeared on the French market for petrol distribution. This explains why, in order to meet this fierce competition, communications moved towards a more aggressive style from 1965 with this poster by Jacques Nathan for Supershell fuel, with the additive ICA (4).

7

The phone company

The telephone infrastructure and the equipment for American homes were both originally installed by a private company which was in a quasi-monopoly position. The company behaved like a public service!

Weavers of Speech

Upon the magic looms of the Bell System, tens of millions of telephone messages are daily woven into a marvelous fabric, representing the countless activities of a busy people.

Day and night, invisible hands shift the shuttles to and fro, weaving the thoughts of men and women into a pattern which, if it could be seen as a tapestry, would tell a dramatic story of our business and social life.

In its warp and woof would mingle success and failure, triumph and tragedy, joy and sorrow, sentiment and shop-talk, heart emotions and million-dollar deals.

The weavers are the 70,000 Bell operators. Out of sight of the subscribers,

these weavers of speech sit silently at the switchboards, swiftly and skillfully interlacing the cords which guide the human voice over the country in all directions.

Whether a man wants his neighbor in town, or some one in a far-away state; whether the calls come one or ten a minute, the work of the operators is ever the same—making direct, instant communication everywhere possible.

This is Bell Service. Not only is it necessary to provide the facilities for the weaving of speech, but these facilities must be vitalized with the skill and intelligence which, in the Bell System, have made Universal Service the privilege of the millions.

AMERICAN TELEPHONE AND TELEGRAPH COMPANY
AND ASSOCIATED COMPANIES

One Policy   One System   Universal Service

1

Alexander Graham Bell, who was to invent the 'talking telegraph' in 1876, partnered with Thomas Sanders and Gardiner Hubbard to establish American Telephone and Telegraph Co. in 1875. Patent applications were swiftly submitted and the three men created the Bell Telephone Company in 1877 in order to make the most of the invention. Protected by its patents, the company had a monopoly on telephones in the United States until 1894. Only Bell Telephone and its franchise holders (over which it gradually gained control) were legally permitted to operate a telephone system. This situation, enshrined in various legal agreements, lasted with some adjustments until 1984, when the Bell System was divided into eight companies, the 'Baby Bells'. Throughout its existence, the company aimed to offer the best possible service to its customers and developed a truly mystical devotion to the telephone system. It justified its monopoly position by citing the technical necessity of interconnection between the networks, and demonstrating a keen awareness of a 'higher mission'.

"The Voice with a Smile"

"Hail ye small, sweet courtesies of life, for smooth do ye make the road of it."

Often we hear comments on the courtesy of telephone people and we are mighty glad to have them.

For our part, we would like to say a word about the courtesy of those who use the telephone.

Your co-operation is always a big help in maintaining good telephone service and we want you to know how much we appreciate it.

BELL TELEPHONE SYSTEM

2

"Weavers of Speech"

To you, who each day
Take on anew your tasks
Along the lines that speech will go
Through city streets or far out
Upon some mountainside where you have blazed a trail
And kept it clear;
To you there comes from all who use the wires
A tribute for a job well done.

For these are not just still and idle strands
That stretch across a country vast and wide
But bearers
Of life's friendly words
And messages of high import
To people everywhere.

Not spectacular, your usual day,
Nor in the headlines
Except they be of fire, or storm, or flood.
Then a grateful nation
Knows the full measure of your skill and worth.
And the fine spirit of service
Which puts truth and purpose in this honored creed—
"The message must go through."

BELL TELEPHONE SYSTEM

3

American Telephone and Telegraph Co. (AT&T) entrusted **N.W. Ayer & Son** *with its communications in 1908, at the very moment when the patents protecting the company had expired and thousands of independent telephone companies were being created across the country. For fifty years the agency would express the client's very distinctive culture in its campaigns. The advertisements, always in black and white, explored themes of professionalism, of the company's devoted employees and of the service provided to the community. New examples were found every year and some returned several times in slightly altered forms. Thus the expression "Weavers of Speech" first appeared in 1915 (1), then again in 1947 but with a new visual (3). In contrast, a very similar illustration to the 1947 example was re-used in 1950, this time with a different text (2). The texts were often informative and sometimes poetic, paying homage to telephone operators or linesmen (4). The illustration for this advertisement was by Norman Rockwell and it was re-used in 1974, in another advertisement, this time in colour (5).*

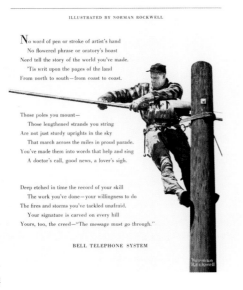

LINES TO A LINEMAN

ILLUSTRATED BY NORMAN ROCKWELL

No word of pen or stroke of artist's hand
 No flowered phrase or oratory's boast
Need tell the story of the world you've made.
 'Tis writ upon the pages of the land
 From north to south—from coast to coast.

Those poles you mount—
 Those lengthened strands you string
Are not just sturdy uprights in the sky
 That march across the miles in proud parade.
You've made them into words that help and sing
 A doctor's call, good news, a lover's sigh.

Deep etched in time the record of your skill
 The work you've done—your willingness to do
The fires and storms you've tackled unafraid.
 Your signature is carved on every hill
Yours, too, the creed—"The message must go through."

BELL TELEPHONE SYSTEM

4

5

Different strokes, different folks

The spread of domestic appliances made daily
life easier, while the arrival of television revolutionised
social and family life.

2

1

In 1939, Philips launched its first electric razor, the
Philishave (in the United States it bore the name
Norelco). In brown bakelite, with a slender shape,
this was one of the first rotating-blade systems. In
1946, a poster by **De la Mar** in the Netherlands
stated that the razor was the most fashionable gift
a modern man could receive (1). Ten years later,
redesigned by Raymond Loewy, the razor had a
second head and was egg-shaped. With an
illustration by Jean Colin, **Elvinger** introduced its
signature statement, which would go hand-in-hand
with the brand's success in France: "Philips, c'est plus
sûr!" (Philips is a safer bet!) (3). The Philips company
later suggested that its two European agencies,
De la Mar and Elvinger, work together on its account
in Europe, or even worldwide. They did indeed join
forces in 1960 under the name Intermarco with the
aim to quickly construct a European network. By
now as the United States had already done, Europe
was gradually dropping illustrations and taking up
photography, as demonstrated in this 1964 poster
by the photographer Paul Facchetti for Philips (2).
The razor continued to evolve; two years later, in
1966, the new Philishave grew a third head.

3

4

PHILIPS *TELEVISION*

5

In 1958, Elvinger commissioned **Geleng,** an expert in movie posters, for this poster promoting Philips televisions (5). With the arrival of television sets, programmes sponsored by brands –'soap operas'– were created as had been the case with radio in the United States twenty-five years earlier. Two examples were created by **Benton & Bowles**. First came "Mama", a series sponsored by Maxwell House Coffee and broadcast between 1949 and 1957 (6). It recounted the life of the Hansens who lived in the United States but originated from Norway. At the end of each episode the whole family comes together to drink a cup of Maxwell House coffee. The second example was created in 1951 for Procter & Gamble (4) with each fifteen-minute episode interrupted by a commercial for the cleaning product Spic & Span.

6

Getting your teeth into a USP

A titanic struggle took place between the two giants, Colgate-Palmolive and
Procter & Gamble over toothpaste! Their toothpaste campaigns illustrate
in different ways what is meant by Rosser Reeves' famous 'Unique Selling Proposition'.

1

2

In his neat 1961 opus "Realism in Advertising",
Rosser Reeves developed the theory of finding
that key argument which differentiates your
product from those of your competitors –your
USP or 'Unique Selling Proposition'– which was
to make him famous throughout the profession.
In his work with **Benton & Bowles** before 1940,
Reeves applied his theory to toothpaste in tubes,
originally launched by Colgate in 1908. Reeves'
unique selling proposition was 'beating bad breath'
and, in this advertisement from 1940, an executive
is given a job because of his sweet-smelling
breath (1). From 1958 onwards, the heroine in a
series of **Publicis** cinema advertisements, Geneviève
Cluny (2), finds her fresh breath helps her escape
sticky situations. One of the protagonists is
amazed: "White teeth, fresh breath?" Smiling
broadly, Geneviève replies: "Super dentifrice
Colgate!" (Colgate toothpaste is great!) (3).

3

TRIUMPH OVER TOOTH DECAY

Crest Toothpaste with Fluoristan
strengthens tooth enamel to lock out decay from within

4

"Look, Mom—no cavities!"

"Look, Mom—no cavities!"

5

Continuing the battle, *Procter & Gamble launched a new toothpaste towards the end of the 1950's: Crest. Procter & Gamble ignored the idea of concentrating on fresh breath. The new USP lay in a fresh promise –the prevention of tooth decay– and the brand was launched in 1956 (4). A demonstration illustrates the story of the advertisement, supplying all the necessary explanation. However, success was slow in coming. It seemed the consumer was not convinced that the benefit was tangible. In order to make the proposition more convincing,* **Benton & Bowles** *turned to the talents of Norman Rockwell for a gallery of portraits of children and adolescents, who return from the dentist's, proudly relaying the same message (5), (6). The argument was strongly presented, but it still wasn't enough. Only in 1960 did Crest find the solution to wresting pole position from Colgate's hands; Crest obtained the support of the American Dental Association. In fact, Procter & Gamble had started its research programme in 1954 to provide the Dental Association with sufficient proof of the effectiveness of fluoride toothpaste. In 1958, Crest's market share was just under 9%; in 1962, it was over 30% and, thirty years later, this USP still spelled success for Crest.*

6

"Look, Mom–no cavities!"

HERE'S HOW TO HELP YOURSELF TO HEALTHY TEETH, AND A BRIGHT, HAPPY SMILE

1. Brush your teeth regularly after eating.

2. Eat foods that keep your teeth strong— such as fresh fruits and vegetables.

3. See your dentist at least twice a year.

To each his own

*A constant desire to construct a particular personality
for each client rather than advocating an agency style proved
to be a source of Publicis' strength and success.*

1

2

3

The shoe chain André, *first established by Albert
Lévy in 1896 in Alsace, began to work with
Publicis in 1932. At that time, a young Marcel
Bleustein invented a slogan for them himself; it is
a slogan every French person still knows by heart:
"André, le chausseur sachant chausser" (André,
the shoemaker who knows how to make shoes) (1).
André used Publicis again after the Second World
War when, in 1952, the agency produced this
poster by Raymond Savignac (3). Around ten
years later, André set up in the emerging
shopping centres and superstores, and developed
an innovative system of franchises to heighten
the presence of their brand name. In addition to
many other French companies which had worked
with the agency before and after the war, like
the furniture manufacturer Levitan, Publicis also
benefited from many new international clients
like Nestlé, Shell and Colgate-Palmolive. This
diverse portfolio of clients formed the foundation
for the company's success and its rise to the top
of French advertising. The 1952 advertisement,
which references the Savignac's poster, illustrates
the company's ambition: "La publicité est l'affaire
de Publicis" (Advertising is Publicis' business) (2).
It was created by Siné, a young, rebellious
cartoonist with a bright future who had just
published his first illustrations in France-Dimanche.*

6

7

4

5

In 1954, Van Cleef & Arpels, *a firm of jewellers based in Paris' exclusive Place Vendôme, needed a boost. Publicis created the slogan: "Il est des signatures auxquelles on tient" (This is one of those signatures you hold on to) (5) and it was these jewellers that Marcel Bleustein-Blanchet turned to in 1966 when he wanted a boost for his most loyal employees. Bleustein-Blanchet's zodiac sign was Leo the lion, so the jeweller created a lion's head set among fourteen sunbeams. This motif was to become the Publicis' logo. The agency had a flair for fashion shown here in two advertisements: one created by Paulin in 1954, for Brunswick furs, "Le fourreur qui fait fureur" (The furrier who creates a frenzy) (4), the other by René Gruau in 1955 for Jacques Fath, a brand established by the flamboyant fashion designer (8). Three animated cinema advertisements also appeared: one by Étienne Raïk, a student of Alexeieff, for Singer (6) in 1956; the other two in 1957 and 1958 for Weill, a ladies' prêt-à-porter label which had been one of Publicis' clients since 1947: "Un vêtement Weill vous va" (A Weill outfit will fit well) (7).*

8

Women get votes, shock!

The importance of women to post-war society was beginning to be expressed in the worlds of retail and the press. This was also a time when women featured a little more widely in the political sphere!

2

1

In the United States, *Procter & Gamble approached* **Leo Burnett** *at the end of 1949 to develop its corporate communications. The agency proposed a campaign in two major national magazines, Time and Life, on the theme of innovation, emphasising the efforts made by the company to keep its customers satisfied. One advertisement took what was, for the period, a provocative stance (3). In fact, this campaign was never to see the light of day and it was not until 1953 that the agency won the account for advertising its first product: Lava soap. In Germany, another major detergent manufacturer, Henkel, commissioned the* **Brose** *agency in 1952 for this poster advertising the multi-purpose cleaning product Fewa: "Hausarbeit in halber Zeit" (Housework in half the time) (2). It marked the return of the brand's mascot, the Waschfrau Johanna (Johanna the Washerwoman). On a very different topic, the Advertising Council led a campaign in 1953 financed by the American Heritage Foundation, which aimed to increase women's participation in the United States' presidential elections. Leo Burnett contributed to this campaign with an advertisement recalling that, in the United States, women obtained the right to vote in 1919! (1).*

3

Never Underestimate the Power of a Woman!

Nor the Power of the Magazine Women believe in!

Authorities agree that more women cast votes than men this month — but then *every* month women alone vote more circulation to this one magazine than men and women combined bring to any other audited magazine.

LADIES' HOME JOURNAL

Largest audited circulation of UNDERLINE ANY magazine

4

Never Underestimate the Power of a Woman!

The following of Ladies' Home Journal is tremendous, too.
More women buy the Journal, issue after issue, than any other magazine

LADIES' HOME JOURNAL
THE MAGAZINE WOMEN BELIEVE IN

5

The Ladies' Home Journal was developed in 1888 by Cyrus H.K. Curtis and his wife Luisa Knapp from a supplement to the Tribune & Farmer. Francis W. Ayer was to bring vital support to this enterprise and, after the Second World War, when competition from television was really beginning to bite, the agency **N.W. Ayer & Son** began a lengthy campaign for the magazine. These two advertisements date from 1952 (4), (5). Around the same time, in France, the daily papers were suffering due to competition from magazines (competition from the audio-visual media would not truly be felt in France until the 1960's). In 1952, **Publicis**, which was already involved in television media brokering, was also promoting the competition –the daily newspaper Le Figaro –with this poster by Savignac (6).

6

Chapter IV

1961-1980

N.W. Ayer & Son

D'Arcy

Publicis

Benton & Bowles

MacManus John & Adams

Compton

Leo Burnett

Dancer Fitzgerald Sample

Norton

Cunningham & Walsh

Masius Wynn Williams

Oscar

BCP

Salles

FCA!

McCormick, Richards

Saatchi & Saatchi

Burrell

Intermarco Farner

Lürzer, Conrad

The Advertising Generation

Ginza, Tokyo. Since the late 1970s, this district has been a focus for all the big name brands and claims to be one of the world's most pricey locations.

It all got off to a strong, even a flying, start. On 12 April 1961 Yuri Gagarin was orbiting our blue planet; eight years later Neil Armstrong took a small leap on the moon. On earth, at Woodstock, thousands of 'hippies' chorused the refrains of Joan Baez and Bob Dylan. There was also the Berlin Wall, built hastily in the early hours of 13 August 1961, cutting a city and its people in half and separating two worlds. There was the Red Guard, operating in a China fired up with Cultural Revolution. And there was the war which, until 1973, offered a whole generation of young Americans a one-way ticket to apocalypse. In 1961 J.K. Galbraith was talking about the 'affluent society' –purchasing power had doubled in ten years, with Europe achieving annual growth rates of 5%, and technological progress was relentlessly making life quicker and easier. The Shinkansen bullet train was introduced in Japan in 1964; motorways, jet planes, telephones, hi-fi and holidays were the order of the day.

A tiny voice, that of a group of experts called the Club of Rome, could be heard to suggest, in 1971, that growth should be curbed. Growth continued –and overheated! On 15 August that year, Nixon suspended the convertibility of the US dollar into gold. Such irony, in an era so full of energy... and in 1973, following the Arab-Israeli war in October, the first oil crisis saw the price of a barrel of oil quadruple in three months. The price was to triple once again in 1979, when a second crisis followed the revolution in Iran.

More than any other, this era was one of 'Youth'. The 'baby boomers', born after the Second World War, invented this idea of 'Youth' and made it their own. This generation was non-conformist in the extreme, resolute hedonists and individualists. They challenged the accepted notion of private life. The questions of contraception, free love and gender relations were now open to public debate.

This was a generation brought up on television. It instinctively knew all about images: how to construct them, how to decode them, how to use them and how to subvert them. This was the advertising generation.

Pop culture

Would the dizzying advances in communications have a tangible effect?
What would be the result of an affluent society?
A fascinated world pulled up a chair, sat back and watched.

1

The critic Lawrence Alloway *is credited with
inventing the term Pop Art in his description of
certain work shown in London in 1956. Brought
to the United Kingdom by the Independent
Group, this movement reached its peak in the
United States in the early 1960s. The divide
between high art and everyday iconography was
happily dissolving: consumer goods, cars, cinema
icons and politicians were all capable of being an
inspiration. Being inspired by the codes of mass
communications, Pop Art often seemed to rejoice
in the 'consumer society'. At the same time,
it kept a supply of scorn waiting in the wings.
In 1958, the critic G.R. Swenson noted that
Pop artists took the world so seriously that they
were making fun about it. The movement was
abundantly fruitful, encompassing Roy Lichtenstein,
who copied cartoon strips, Claes Oldenburg,
who played with everyday objects, and many
others. James Rosenquist, who began his career
in Minneapolis as a painter for General Outdoor
Advertising, juxtaposed advertisements and
magazine photographs (1). He reinterpreted them
in a monumental manner as in this example,
"President Elect", produced for John F. Kennedy's
presidential campaign in 1960 (2). And then, a
sobering announcement one Friday in November
1963: Jacqueline Kennedy was a widow and
America felt orphaned (3).*

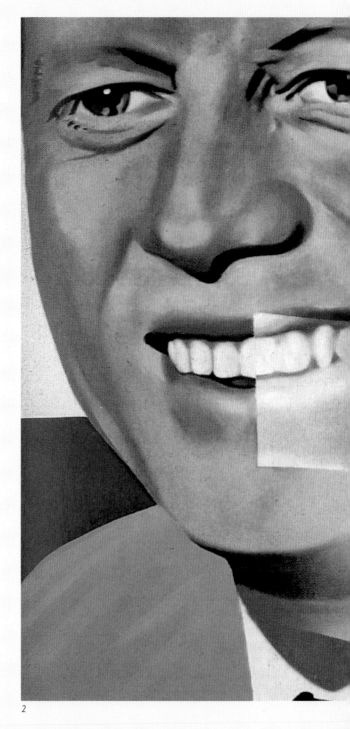

2

3

The art of business

In "The Philosophy of Andy Warhol", the author states his ambition to become a 'business artist'.

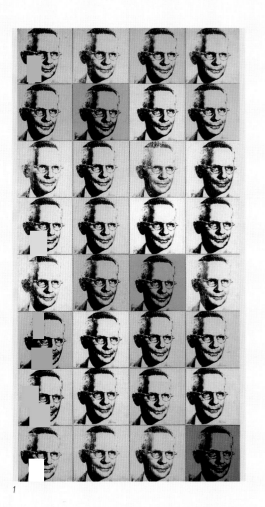

1

2

The process of transferring photographs onto a silk screen allowed Warhol to print repeated images just as the consumer society bred identical items, "210 Coca-Cola Bottles", 1962 (2), for interchangeable consumers, "The American Man –Watson Powell", 1964 (1). "What's great about this country is that America started the tradition where the richest consumers buy essentially the same things as the poorest. You can be watching TV and see Coca-Cola, and you know that the President drinks Coke, Liz Taylor drinks Coke, and just think, you can drink Coke, too. A Coke is a Coke and no amount of money can get you a better Coke than the one the bum on the corner is drinking. All the Cokes are the same and all the Cokes are good. Liz Taylor knows it, the President knows it, the bum knows it, and you know it."

The protest movement

"Make love, not war." A generation of baby-boomers protested vociferously against the war and was heavily affected by it; but at the same time they were making great efforts to implement the rest of their ideals.

LA BEAUTÉ

EST DANS LA RUE

2

Poster and photograph by Richard Avedon

who has a better right to oppose the war?

1

Following France's withdrawal in 1954, Presidents Eisenhower, Kennedy, and then Johnson engaged the United States in the conflict in Vietnam. By 1968, 550,000 soldiers were stationed in Vietnam, and in Paris in 1973 the peace accords were signed by Henry Kissinger on 27 January. The war had caused an unprecedented moral crisis in the United States. Students protested through bodies such as the Student Mobilization Committee to End the War in Vietnam for which the photographer Richard Avedon created this poster in 1969 (1). It was a long way from the fashion subjects he had previously shot for Harper's Bazaar and Vogue. A great gathering of intellectuals and advertisers was organised at Yale in April 1971 and, following this encounter, the Committee to Unsell the War was created for which Steve Horn produced this poster (3). In Paris, during the May 1968 uprising, artists and students at the Atelier Populaire des Beaux-Arts worked feverishly on an enormous quantity of silk-screen-printed posters featuring slogans such as "Il est interdit d'interdire" (Prohibition is prohibited) and "La beauté est dans la rue" (Art on the march) (2).

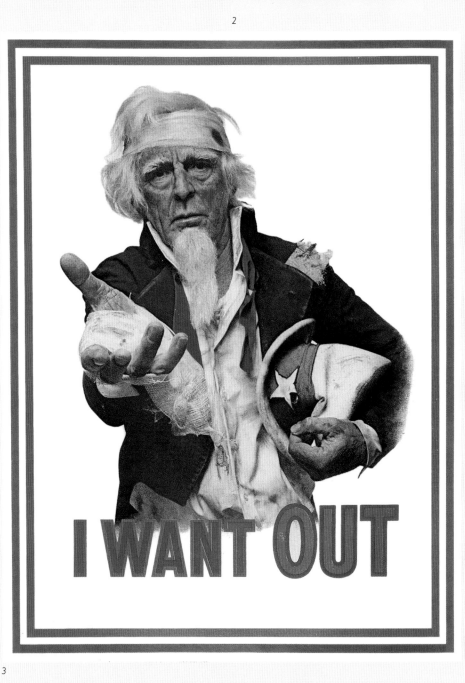

I WANT OUT

3

The upheaval in society was at times dramatic. This was especially true when the civil rights movement in the United States witnessed the assassination of Martin Luther King in April 1968. In Czechoslovakia, as it was then, there was the brutal quashing of the Prague Spring in August 1968. Women were also still fighting for their rights: the women's liberation movement used this poster which was a parody of the very popular advertisement for Virginia Slims cigarettes (4). On a lighter note, in the theatre, the show "Hair" opened on Broadway in April 1968: as much as its nudity, it was the show's defence of counter-culture, flower power and hippies which caused such an outrage. This sign (6), created in Great Britain in 1958 for a march in favour of nuclear disarmament, was quickly adopted by the peace movement. In 1969, in an advertisement to promote the agency, **MacManus John & Adams** explained what it meant to be a citizen of the United States, a country with its fair share both of sorrow and joy (5).

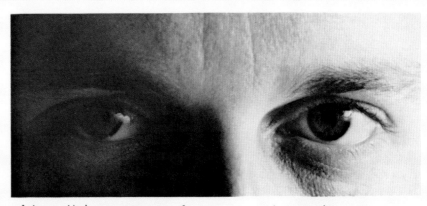

I have died in Viet Nam. But I have walked the face of the moon.

I have befouled the waters and tainted the air of a magnificent land. But I have made it safe from disease.

I have flown through the sky faster than the sun. But I have idled in streets made ugly with traffic.

I have littered the land with garbage. But I have built upon it a hundred million homes.

I have divided schools with my prejudice. But I have sent armies to unite them.

I have beat down my enemies with clubs. But I have built courtrooms to keep them free.

I have built a bomb to destroy the world. But I have used it to light a light.

I have outraged my brothers in the alleys of the ghettos. But I have transplanted a human heart.

I have scribbled out filth and pornography. But I have elevated the philosophy of man.

I have watched children starve from my golden towers. But I have fed half of the earth.

I was raised in a grotesque slum. But I am surfeited by the silver spoon of opulence.

I live in the greatest country in the world in the greatest time in history. But I scorn the ground I stand upon.

I am ashamed.
But I am proud.
I am an American.

MacManus, John & Adams Inc., Advertising: Bloomfield Hills, Michigan • New York • Chicago • Los Angeles • Twin Cities • Toronto • Zurich • London

5

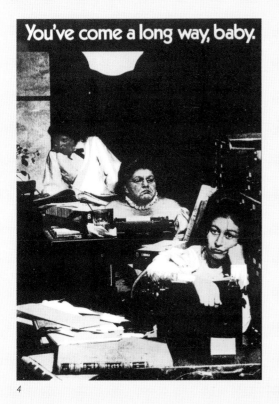

You've come a long way, baby.

4

6

Advertising becomes 'cool'

The communications business had become an industry and advertising was an attractive, even a prestigious, profession. Everywhere, 'admen' were becoming personalities in the public arena.

"A little legwork goes a long way toward bringing advertising ideas down to earth."
The Man from Cunningham & Walsh

Have shoes, will travel. Offices in New York, San Francisco, Los Angeles and Dallas.

1

2

The **Newell-Emmett** agency was born in New York in 1919 and became **Cunningham & Walsh** in 1950 before being merged with N.W. Ayer & Son in 1986. A 1963 advertisement conjures up, with affection and humour, the legwork done by 'The Man from Cunningham and Walsh' (1). In this photograph from the 1960s, almost all **Publicis'** five hundred and eighty staff are gathered at 133, avenue des Champs-Élysées, Paris (2). They are young for the time, with an average age of 32. They are qualified –one in four has a university degree. Marcel Bleustein-Blanchet sought to attract graduates and he gave a lecture at the prestigious Sorbonne University on 10 February 1959 entitled "De la réclame à la publicité" (Giving credibility to advertising). By 1965, **Publicis** was ranked second in the French industry, behind Havas and ahead of Dupuy and Elvinger, and fiftieth in the world. In 1967, Publicis had offices in New York, London, Milan, Barcelona, Frankfurt and Brussels plus a regional presence in eight French provincial cities. France was now ranked tenth in the world in terms of investment in advertising, way behind the United States, the United Kingdom and Germany.

3

SAATCHI & SAATCHI
Nothing Is Impossible

4

On 5 August 1960 in Chicago, Leo Burnett's eight hundred and seventy-five staff celebrated the twenty-fifth anniversary of their agency's creation(4). They are arranged around their founder in the shape of an apple, the symbol of the agency, which was ranked sixth in the United States at that time. By the end of the 1960s, Benton & Bowles, who already had an excellent reputation for marketing thinking, presented its new vision of creativity in the New York Times and the Wall Street Journal (5). On 13 September 1970 in Great Britain, an advertisement appeared in the Sunday Times. It was created by an agency new to the British scene and portrayed an aggressive spirit, closer to American agency style: "Why I think it's time for a new kind of advertising." This fledgling agency was to become the British market leader in under ten years and, by 1982, was one of the world's ten largest. The agency was Saatchi & Saatchi, whose New York teams are featured here, brandishing a banner showing the company's slogan: "Nothing is Impossible"(3).

5

It's not creative unless it sells.

If anything came out of the so-called creative revolution of the 60's and the recessions of the early 70's, it was a clearer understanding of what advertising is and what it isn't.

By the time those years were over, many advertisers and their agencies had been painfully reminded that advertising was not an art form but a serious business tool. And that "creative advertising" really was advertising that created sales and not just attention.

You might say creativity grew up in those years. And one would think that the mistakes made then would never again be repeated.

Yet here we are, a short time later, and like war and politics, advertising seems to be repeating itself. You need only look at television or pick up a magazine to see the frivolities and ambiguities that are passing as creative selling.

It seems such a pity that many advertisers are still learning—the hard way—what some of us have always known:

Not an entertainment medium.

During those crazy 60's, the ambience of television rubbed off on the advertising message and more and more advertising tried to become as entertaining as the programming in which it appeared—very often at the expense of the selling idea. One can still see a rash of imitative commercials

following the advent of popular new television programs and feature films. Extravagant productions featuring everything but a concept are still prevalent. Movie stars and athletes continue to serve as substitutes for selling ideas.

Awards for what.

Awards for creativity conferred by juries of advertising people often have nothing to do with advertising that sells. Certainly, in recent years, the importance of advertising awards has diminished. Their value seems to have decreased in direct proportion to the proliferation of festivals. At the same time, many began to question the worth of honors bestowed out of context of sales results.

But as long as advertising will continue to be written by people, people will continue to give each other awards. And that isn't all bad. George Burns once said of Al Jolson, "It was easy enough to make him happy. You just had to cheer him for breakfast, applaud wildly for lunch, and give him a standing ovation for dinner."

You don't have to be loved.

Criticism of an advertising campaign has little bearing on selling effectiveness. There are many examples of advertising which are disliked by the very people who are reacting to the message.

By the same token, much advertising that is

beloved by the critics and consumers alike fizzles badly.

This is not to suggest that advertising need be grating or irritating or hated to be effective. Wouldn't it be great if we could always write advertising that would win awards, that people would love and talk about, and that would sell the product, too?

But, alas, this magic combination is very elusive. And remember, the main objective is not to win awards, not to get people to love your advertising, but to get them to act upon it. In the process of meeting that objective, you may not endear yourself to some consumers but you may become very popular with your stockholders.

Watch out for distraction.

A selling idea runs a very real risk of being swamped by its execution. It's a cliché of the advertising business, but how many times does someone describe a commercial to you almost verbatim and then fail to remember the product? Humor is most often involved. A good joke, a funny piece of action, a great punch line—all can undermine the strongest selling idea. And yet humor, judiciously used, can uplift a piece of advertising, increasing its chances of being remembered while actually enhancing the selling idea. A good test: Is the humor relevant to the message?

Explore the alternatives.

There is no sure way to sell anything. There are many ways to approach the sale of a product—strategically and executionally. Some ways are better than others and you really don't know for sure which is best until you copy test and market test.

The time is long past when an ad agency can deliver a single advertising campaign to a client without examining and presenting alternatives. Every client has the right to take part in the selection process that an agency goes through in leading up to a creative recommendation.

And the most creative campaign is the one that ultimately proves itself in the market.

Don't overshoot the audience.

A lot of words have been written and spoken about advertising catering to the lowest intelligence level of its prospects. That of course is as untrue as it would be unwise.

But equally ridiculous is advertising that wafts

over the head of the prospect. We still see and hear commercials and ads that are so cleverly obtuse that they reflect no more than the private narrow world of their creators. For every potential customer who reacts to such "sophisticated" advertising, there are countless others who just don't get it.

There is no "soft sell."

The one factor that did more to end the creative revolution and topple the "creative crazies" from power was the recession of 1970. It was a very sobering experience for many high-flying businesses and advertising agencies.

Creative philosophies seemed to change overnight. "These are hard times that call for hard sell" became the watchword.

But the truth of the matter is: All times are hard times and all times call for hard sell. Hard sell meaning the presentation of a cogent, persuasive idea, stripped of any distracting or irrelevant elements, that will convince people to buy a product. Is there any other kind?

There can be no doubt that advertising today must be more intrusive, more imaginative, more innovative than it has ever been. In a business riddled with sameness and clutter, there is a great virtue in being "creative."

Yet, if ever a word was subject to misinterpretation and confusion, it is the word "creative."

To some it means advertising that wins awards. To others it is advertising that makes people laugh. And there are those who think to be creative, advertising must be talked about at cocktail parties and joked about by comedians.

But "creative" can also mean dramatically showing how a product fulfills a consumer need or desire. Or it can be something as simple as casting the appropriate person for a brand. A unique demonstration of product superiority can be creative. So, of course, can a memorable jingle.

There are probably as many opinions of what is creative as there are people who conceive and judge advertising.

But no matter what your interpretation of the word, one thing is irrefutable:

It's not creative unless it sells.

That, in six words, is the philosophy that guides Benton & Bowles.

If you're a major advertiser in need of truly creative advertising, please call or write to Jack Bowen, President, Benton & Bowles, Inc., 909 Third Avenue, New York, New York 10022, (212) 758-6200.

Benton & Bowles

New York, Chicago, Los Angeles, and other major cities worldwide.

Baby-boom

As a result of the population explosion, in France as elsewhere, new companies were bringing a modern response to the expectations of mothers and their children.

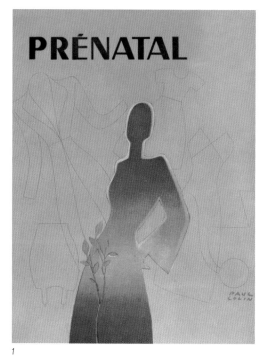

1

In 1947, *a young industrialist* from Limoges, France, Jean-Marie Mazard, launched a business making clothing for pregnant women at a time when nothing of the kind was available in Europe. He opened his first shop in a four-room apartment in Paris and Prénatal was born. It would grow up to be big and strong in partnership with **Publicis**, which had just resumed business and was responsible for the firm's advertising. The advertising began quietly with the agency designing small press advertisements, and then publishing a catalogue every year. Soon, the brand's name had spread throughout France through the medium of the catalogue. Ten years later, Prénatal had more than one hundred outlets in France. In the 1950s, the graphic artist Paul Colin created this poster: a symbolic, poetic image of the mother-to-be (1). Whilst in 1962, the photographer Jeanloup Sieff produced a whole series of black and white advertisements to present a collection specially designed by Pierre Cardin (2). In Europe as in North America, the rise in births was considerable, but the baby boom did not last. Soon, women would begin to marry later and have fewer children.

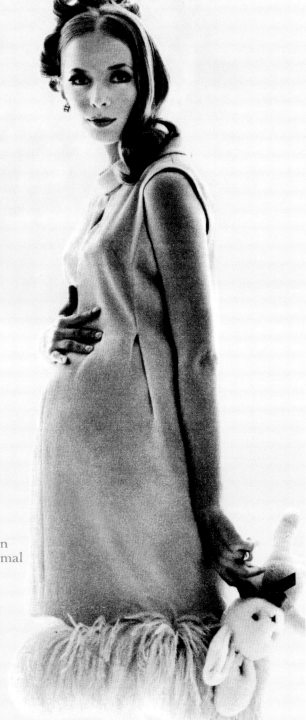

Pierre Cardin connaît bien la femme, Prénatal connaît bien les futures mamans. Il était normal qu'ils se rencontrent, qu'ils s'entendent et qu'ils donnent le jour à une collection de modèles tous plus jolis, plus féminins les uns que les autres.

PRÉNATAL

2

Encouraged by his wife Clementine, Henri Nestlé invented baby milk and founded Nestlé in 1867 in Switzerland. In 1973, Nestlé bought the Guigoz brand and the following year created Ptipo, a range of baby food products. The range was launched in Paris, on the first floor of the Eiffel Tower. Publicis was given the advertising account and the event was publicised by the appropriately named artist Jean Effel. Effel also created a series of humorous illustrations for his book entitled "La création du monde" (The creation of the earth) during the same period (3). The agency then invented the brand's symbol, the little blue bear, in 1978. The bear was later used on all the company's infant food products (4). In 1985, a film made by feature film director Claude Miller brought new life to the advertisements by showing a baby tasting the products and giving its opinion to the whole management board: "Chez Nestlé, le Président, c'est bébé" (At Nestlé, our chairman is a baby) (5). Some years later, when he was asked to produce a documentary on the company, François Reichenbach ended it by putting the same words in the mouth of the (real) chairman, which showed that as far as this company and its products were concerned, the consumer really was the true judge of quality!

5

4

A loving spoonful!

Symbolising the warmth of hearth and home, motherly love
and restorative properties, soup evokes traditional values, which
were perfectly expressed by Campbell's.

We blend the best with careful pains
In skillful combination,
And every single can contains
Our business reputation.

1

"To make the best, begin with the best—then cook with extra care."

Why our soups look as good as they taste
They're color-planned all the way from seed to simmer

2

In Camden, New Jersey, in 1869, *a greengrocer
named Joseph A. Campbell and a refrigerator
manufacturer named Abraham Anderson came
together to establish what would become
the Campbell Soup Company. From 1897, the
company produced tinned soups and, the
following year, adopted their local team's colours,
red and white, to which they added the gold of
the medal they won at the 1900 Great Paris
Exhibition. Much later, in 1953, the company
entrusted its brand advertising to* **Leo Burnett**
*and, in 1960, the agency conducted a campaign
focusing on the quality of its products* (1). *For
several years, one advertisement a month
appeared in the weekly magazine Life, centred
around the theme: "To make the best, begin with
the best." In 1963, a campaign portrayed chefs
selecting the best vegetables* (2) *and in 1967
showed the arrival of the new harvest* (3).

"To make the best, begin with the best—then cook with extra care."

Enjoy the fresh taste of the Campbell Tomato.
Our Big Red Ones are in for '67.

It took fast work and close timing to get
the 1967 crop of Campbell Tomatoes to
our kitchens.

But the real flavor-story began three
years ago when seeds were selected for
this harvest. Much of that time was spent
in research and selection and increasing
the seed yield from which each year's
crop is grown.

Some of these ancestor-proud tomatoes
can brag on family lines that go back
thirty years or more. Each separate strain
brings its own heritage of taste, shape,
color, and flavor.

We call these our "fast" tomatoes.
Because we start picking them wet with
dew, hustle them to our plant to make
sure you get every nuance of vine-fresh,
just-picked flavor.

These tomatoes have to be right. The
Campbell Chefs use tomatoes just the
way you would yourself for Tomato,
Tomato Rice, or Bisque of Tomato Soup.

Our 1967 crop is now on the shelves of
your favorite food store. You'll find the
deep, rich, fresh-picked flavor of the
Campbell Tomato in our soups, tomato
juice, and V-8 Cocktail Vegetable Juice.

We blend the best with careful pains
In skillful combination,
And everything we make contains
Our business reputation.

Campbell's · Swanson · V-8 ·
Franco-American · Bounty
...all made by Campbell

3

4

5

"**When you think about it,** department stores are kind of like museums": Andy Warhol considered that the most ordinary of everyday products were worthy of artistic interpretation, and in March 1962, the critic David Bourdon discovered dozens of canvases showing the Campbell's soup tin in Warhol's studio. They displayed all the varieties on sale at the time: some tins intact, some dented, some tins open, some closed, some tins with torn labels... Then in 1966, for a Warhol exhibition, the Institute of Contemporary Art in Boston drew this bag (4), which would be equally at home in a supermarket or an art gallery. Perhaps Warhol chose Campbell's tins to develop the artistic œuvre he was to pursue with other brands because these soups went to the heart of 'being American'. For generations of mothers, Campbell's concentrated soups were an economical way of feeding their families (at the beginning of the century, a tin cost just 25 cents). This brand symbolised American family values and in 1965, Howard Zieff's film captured this spirit perfectly (5). A child returns home from school with a pot of geraniums for his mother. When he reaches the doorstep, just at the moment his mother opens the door, the pot slips from his fingers and smashes on the ground. Luckily, she knows just how to bring him round: with a bowl of comforting Campbell's soup! While he learns how to smile again in front of his soup plate, she replaces the broken pot.

Sweet and sour

The French don't drink milk –they eat it! Sweet, in the form of dairy specialities such as yoghurt, or savoury as one of the many, beloved varieties of cheese.

C'est comme si on les mangeait à la ferme.

2

Les bons produits de Mamie Nova

1

Nova, a group of dairy cooperatives, was established in 1969 and knocked on **Publicis'** door the following year. The French were consuming more dairy produce, but competition was fierce and the price of milk was falling. In order to position itself, the group had developed products with a high level of added value and had launched new dairy specialities. The company had many assets, but its name, Nova, was not one of them: it conjured up a cold, clinical, lifeless picture which was not in keeping with the type of products it produced. The agency decided to completely redefine the brand's image by emphasising its three strong points: the quality of its products (1) (which truly had a taste reminiscent of products straight from the farm), the variety and inventiveness of its recipes (2), and the constantly changing promotional games offered on its packaging. In order to spread the word about this new brand image, the agency created the character of Mamie Nova (3). While retaining their original logo, the Nova brand turned increasingly to Mamie Nova drawn by the American John Alcorn, and a few years later the company adopted her name as its own.

L'hiver c'est bon.

Yaourts aux fruits de Mamie Nova.
C'est bon. NOVA

3

The cheese created in Croisy-sur-Eure in Normandy by a small-scale industrialist by the name of Boursin, is a savoury speciality flavoured with garlic and fine herbs. It was originally launched by Publicis in 1964 with the agency inventing original, functional packaging for the product, and setting itself two objectives. The first was to give this industrial item the image of a simple rustic cheese: "Du pain, du vin, du Boursin. C'est divin" (Bread, wine and Boursin. Simply divine!) (5). The second was to stimulate an irresistible urge in consumers to eat Boursin every time they saw it or even thought of it. On 1 October 1968, commercials for Boursin appeared on French television (it had taken two years for the permission to advertise on television granted to generic agricultural products to be extended to branded goods). Boursin was up and running right from day one, with a thirty-second black-and-white film showcasing a French comic actor, Jacques Duby (4). He wakes up in the middle of the night, gripped by an irrepressible craving for Boursin. As if in a trance, he heads for the fridge, chanting: "Boursin… Boursin… Boursin."

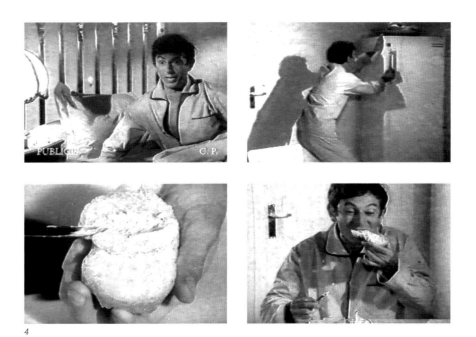

4

du pain, du vin, du boursin   **c'est divin**

5

Brand news

Branding was the answer that mass production had found to the question of guaranteeing the quality of products. Water and wine were, however, not mass-produced. You could have been forgiven for believing that, as natural products, they would not have needed branding, but you would have been wrong...

1

In 1855, a progressive lawyer, Louis Bouloumié, received permission to extract water from the Gérémoy spring, which would later be named Vittel. So that visitors could continue taking their spa treatments after a visit to the spring, the water was sold in bottles to be used at home. From 1875 onwards it was poured into stoneware bottles with a porcelain stopper, and from 1898 into glass bottles. In 1968, **Publicis** designed the first bottles made of PVC (polyvinyl chloride), holding a litre and a half of water (1). The design reflected the shape of the glass bottle, but had pronounced horizontal ridges which allowed the new bottles to be stacked easily. In 1969 Nestlé acquired a stake in Vittel alongside the founding family, and the company developed new ways to market water. In 1978, a spray was launched, followed in 1984 by the first skincare products. Whereas Vittel only comes from the Vittel spring, Schweppes is a mineral water which was invented! In 1783, Jacob Schweppe, a jeweller from Geneva, discovered a process for dissolving carbon dioxide in water, and thus created the first soft drink. Inspired by the habits of the British in India, the Indian tonic water is launched in 1870. Almost two hundred years after its invention, **Intermarco-Elvinger** created this poster with photography by Jean Hoffner (2), and in 1969 Schweppes merged with Cadbury.

2

4

3

Alcoholic beverages were another sort of advertising challenge for **Publicis**. Noilly Prat is a vermouth which is a plant-based apéritif (the French 'vermouth' is adapted from the German 'Wermut', which means wormwood, from which the drink absinthe is made). It was created in 1813 in Marseillan, in the south of France, by Joseph Noilly and his son-in-law Claudius Prat, from light and fruity blanc de blancs wine from the Languedoc region, with the addition of plants and spices from around the world. The image of the apéritif was in need of modernisation and Pascalini produced an illustration on this bottle which was used in a 1968 advertisement (3). Champagne was perfected much earlier at the end of the seventeenth century by the monk Dom Pérignon from the abbey of Hautvillers, in the Champagne region. Wine merchants Eugène Mercier, established in 1858, used mainly a combination of pinot noir and pinot meunier grapes in their champagnes. Port, from the Douro region of Portugal, also dates back to the end of the seventeenth century. The company Sandeman was founded in London in 1790 by the trader George Sandeman who, in 1805, was the first to use a brand to make his mark on wine barrels –giving birth to the idea of a distinctive 'brand'. Mercier's image needed fine tuning (4) and Sandeman's needed new life (5). This was what the photographer Philippe Quidor tried to achieve in these two 1970 advertisements.

5

Famous for what?

Big brands tend to base their communications on simple things:
a single shape, colour, name or style. These become the crucial signs
and symbols the consumers recognise.

72 out of 100 men recognized this shape. Do you?

The brown shape above is called a rhomboid. We showed it to men just as you see it here and said, "What trademark is this?"

72 per cent of them said, "Schlitz?"

Those men recognize the mark of a great beer.

When you taste the beer behind this famous shape you'll recognize the *taste* of a great beer, and that's a lot more important.

How about a Schlitz?

1

Jos. Schlitz Brewing Co. entrusted Leo Burnett
with its advertising in 1961. Over the previous five
years, the market had grown by 5% yet Schlitz's
sales had fallen by 7%. Schlitz was certainly a
well-known name, but it did not have strong
meaning to beer drinkers. Awareness was not an
issue. People knew the slogan: "The beer that
made Milwaukee famous". The brand had assets,
but these needed recharging. Firstly, the brand
name needed to be linked once again to warmth
and feeling. Yes, it had a strange name, but that
was no obstacle; indeed, 'strangeness' proved the
key. Burnett retold the story of the founder, a
man who had consciously followed the legacy of
his wife's first husband (2). The label was also
slightly odd, but everyone recognised the logo,
which merited a mention in this advertisement (1).
The ordinary-looking brown bottle was also
worthy of comment; its (now widely copied)
coloured glass had light-protective properties,
which were described in another advertisement (3).

His first name was Joe... Schlitz

The above is a Milwaukee engraver's version of the way Joseph Schlitz signed his name.

Jos. Schlitz did not actually found the Jos. Schlitz Brewing Company. He married the widow of the man who did. But before he drowned in the Irish Sea his name had been put on a beer so good that it has endured and prospered for 112 years.

All this time the same family that founded the company has directed the patient, prideful brewing of Schlitz beer.

And the beer has become such a familiar friend that no one thinks of the name as odd at all any more.

2

The Brown Bottle

Why did it make the beer taste better?

Today, most beer comes in brown bottles that look pretty much like this one.

Fifty years ago practically all beer came in clear glass bottles. What changed things?

Well, the Schlitz people up in Milwaukee put up a beer that they were particularly proud of, and they wanted it to taste as good when people drank it as it did when it left the brewery.

This wasn't possible with a clear glass bottle because just a little exposure to sunlight would cloud the beer and ruin the flavor. So Schlitz set out to find a bottle that would protect the beer from light.

The brown bottle did it and more and more people began to drink Schlitz.

Since that time most other breweries have copied the Schlitz brown bottle, but no one has ever been able to copy the taste of the good Schlitz beer inside.

How about a Schlitz?

The Beer that made Milwaukee Famous

© 1961 Jos. Schlitz Brewing Co., Milwaukee, Wis., Brooklyn, N.Y.
Los Angeles, Cal., Kansas City, Mo., Tampa, Fla.

3

real gusto

in a great light beer

If the beer you're drinking now leaves you with a vague feeling that there's something missing, try the beer brewed specifically for the head of the house—Schlitz!

Schlitz knows that a great beer begins with character. Schlitz brings that character to lighthearted life with just the kiss of the hops.

So Schlitz gives you the gusto a man wants in a great light beer. Schlitz tastes bright, sits light. Settle on Schlitz, the Beer that made Milwaukee Famous—simply because it tastes so good.

Schlitz

The Beer that made Milwaukee Famous

4

Besides aspiring to be well-known, brands must also try to stimulate desire. For Schlitz Beer the Latin American connotations of the word 'gusto' conjure up vitality, movement and relaxed socialising (4). Between 1961 and 1965, sales of Schlitz increased by 24% in a market which only grew by 13%. However, that was not enough to oust the leading beer, Budweiser, which developed even more rapidly. In 1966, Leo Burnett tried a new campaign, showing Schlitz as the only 'real' beer, implicitly dismissing all its competitors (5). Four years later, sales of Schlitz were up 62% in a market expanding by only 16%. What was more, the brand could pride itself on being the most attractive: consumers switching beers turned most often to Schlitz.

"When you're out of Schlitz, you're out of beer."

5

First lady

The women's liberation movements were taking action and delivering speeches which were creating a lot of debate about women's status. And then there was a campaign for Virginia Slims that also dealt with the status of women, but in its own rather more conservative way.

1

At the end of the 1960s, women made up over a third of the market for cigarettes. Having created for Marlboro (originally a female-oriented brand) a new masculine image, Philip Morris and its agency **Leo Burnett** decided to launch a new cigarette in 1968 especially for women. The tobacco came from Virginia and the cigarette was slim: hence the name Virginia Slims. The campaign used humour to dimensionalize the progress made for the status of women. On this poster, a woman has emerged in the National Memorial at Mount Rushmore to take her place among the four prominent past presidents of the United States, George Washington, Thomas Jefferson, Theodore Roosevelt and Abraham Lincoln, who were sculpted by Gutzon Borglum in 1927 (2). In 1908, the Sullivan Ordinance had banned women from smoking in public in New York, but in the 1960s, to paraphrase Bob Dylan, the times they were a changin'. However, this 1968 advertisement was prophetic in suggesting that women still had some way to go –perhaps a woman could run for the presidency? (1). Something we still ask today!

Warning: The Surgeon General Has Determined That Cigarette Smoking Is Dangerous to Your Health.

Regular: 16 mg. "tar," 1.0 mg. nicotine—Menthol: 15 mg. "tar," 1.0 mg. nicotine av. per cigarette, FTC Report Oct. '74

2

Virginia Slims reminds you that Founding Fathers couldn't have been Founding Fathers without Founding Mothers.

YOU'VE COME A LONG WAY, BABY.

Say no

French companies approached corporate and financial communications with a timidity not felt by US corporations, which were quite happy to use the same techniques they applied to brands.

At the end of 1957, Publicis opened a department specialising in financial communications, called 'Information industrielle' (Information for Industry) (1). Besides conventional advertisements, this department created 'advertorials'. These pages, designed by the agency, were presented as ordinary pages of a newspaper, containing articles, exposés, reports and items on public opinion. Only the words 'Information for Industry' set them apart from the editorial (4). In December 1968, BSN issued a hostile takeover bid for Saint-Gobain (2). This was not the first such bid to be made in France but, thus far, the bids had generally been friendly. BSN's approach to Saint-Gobain caused a significant stir. BSN (Boussois-Souchon-Neuvesel) was born in 1966 when the glass firms Glaces de Boussois and Souchon-Neuvesel merged. In comparison Saint-Gobain had deep roots, which went back to the reign of Louis XIV, and whereas BSN's main strength lay in hollow container glass, Saint-Gobain was the market leader in plate glass, predominantly used in the construction and automobile industries. Saint-Gobain, which was owned in large part by small private shareholders, asked Publicis to convince its shareholders not to sell their shares. The agency responded by producing this advertorial: "Dites non" (Say no) (3). The Publicis campaign went beyond this one advertorial, with the agency organising an open day at the factory and a shareholders meeting. The bid was unsuccessful yet the impact on the companies was significant and lasting. BSN moved away from glass containers into the agri-foods they contained, merged with Gervais Danone and, in 1994, became Danone. Saint-Gobain joined forces with a metallurgy company, Pont-à-Mousson, and became a major player in materials. Takeover bids, which had been generally badly thought-of, became a normal means of achieving external growth in the 1980s.

United States Steel Corporation was established in Pittsburgh in 1901 by the biggest names in the US economy: J.P. Morgan, Andrew Carnegie, Charles Schwab and Elbert H. Gary; Gary was the group's first chairman. While the railways and automobile industries were developing, U.S. Steel was one of the country's main drivers of economic growth. One of its divisions, American Bridge, was famous for the construction of skyscrapers and bridges, as shown in this 1970s advertisement by **Compton** (5). Later as the 1980s began, U.S. Steel was to undergo a dramatic transition in order to adapt to international competition, with this advertisement demonstrating the company's iron will to "(...) Rebuild the American Dream"(6). They diversified into energy with the acquisitions of first Marathon Oil Company and then, at the beginning of 1986, Texas Oil & Gas Corp.

Many of America's mightiest structures were built by people wearing our hard hats.

There are many U.S. Steel people who have spent their working lives on the "high iron" — putting up most of the great bridges in this country and dozens of the buildings that are landmarks across the nation.

Our American Bridge Division, U.S. Steel's construction arm, has fabricated and erected the San Francisco-Oakland Bridge, the Mackinac Bridge in Michigan and the New River Gorge Bridge in West Virginia—to name a few.

The steel work for Chicago's Sears Tower, the world's tallest building, is theirs as is New Orleans' Superdome. And the United Nations Complex in New York.

They also fabricate less famous but vital structures, such as towers for long-distance electrical transmission, giant storage tanks—even barges for bulk cargoes.

For their remarkable courage, know-how and technical accomplishments, the people in our American Bridge Division are hard to beat. They do big things with our steel.

Capability. It's one of our strengths.

5

You are looking at one of the largest steelworks in America.

U.S. Steel's Gary Works in Gary, Indiana. Five years ago many industry analysts were convinced that the 70-year old plant could never again compete in the marketplace.

From laborers to the general super-intendent... from pipe fitters and iron-workers to foremen... our people had a different dream for Gary. They believed in Gary. They believed it could compete successfully, given an honest chance. And, above all, they believed in themselves.

Everyone pitched in to improve productivity, throwing out old methods of operating in favor of newer, more efficient systems. U.S. Steel invested heavily in modernizing the plant to upgrade the quality of its products as well as its oper-ating efficiency, with more to be invested in the next few years.

The task of rebuilding our industry is far from completed. But at the Gary Works our goal is no empty dream. Thanks to the believers, its a dream coming true.

Helping to Rebuild the American Dream.

United States Steel, 600 Grant St., Pittsburgh PA 15230

6

Ethical acts

A manufacturer's reputation is a priceless ingredient that can distinguish one product from all others. Good quality research can also bring real added value to a brand.

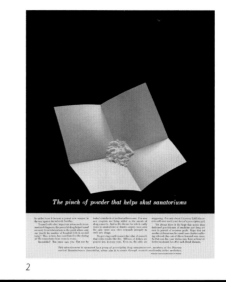

The pinch of powder that helps shut sanatoriums

2

1

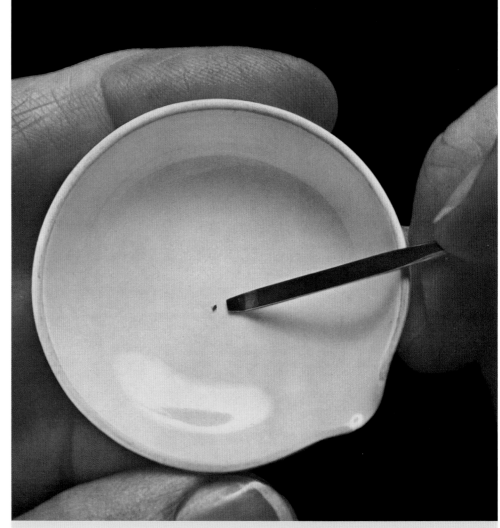

This tiny crystal means someone will live

The tiny crystal weighs only 25 millionths of an ounce. Yet it is so powerful that it provides enough doses to control pernicious anemia in a patient for about two years.

It is vitamin B₁₂.

It was developed through the efforts and faith of American drug company scientists. After almost ten years of continuous experimentation and seemingly insurmountable obstacles.

And their work was sustained by a philosophy characteristic of the drug industry: a principle that says research must go on even though it will result in a drug which helps only those who suffer from a comparatively rare disease.

Pernicious anemia is incurable but it can be controlled. Not too long ago 6000 Americans died of it every year. Today, minute doses of vitamin B₁₂, prescribed by a physician, restore the sufferer to an active life at moderate cost.

This is the value of modern drugs—protecting health and reducing the cost of illness.

This advertisement is sponsored by a group of prescription drug manufacturers*, members of the Pharmaceutical Manufacturers Association, whose aim is to create through research continually better medicines.

3

The scene for this advertisement is in Baghdad and begins with a tale full of eastern promise. "Tell me, Wise One, what shall I do to receive the most for that which I spend?" a young man asks. "A thing that is bought or sold has no value unless it contains that which cannot be, bought or sold. Look for the Priceless Ingredient", the wise man answers. "But, what is the Priceless Ingredient?" "(…) The Honor and Integrity of him who makes it." (1). The advertisement, created by **N.W. Ayer & Son** in 1921, is an authoritative statement of the decisive role brands play. The laboratory in question was founded in 1858 by Edward Robinson Squibb, who had decided it was his duty to produce medicines as safe and free from impurities as possible. In 1906, six years after his death, his sons sold the company at the time of the adoption by the United States Congress of the Pure Food and Drug Act. This ethical concern with the honour and integrity of the manufacturer would remain this company's fundamental credo. In 1989, it merged with Bristol-Myers (a laboratory founded in 1898) and to continue the long tradition, in 1997, Bristol-Myers Squibb opened a major research centre in New Jersey, proving that innovation is a necessity in this industry.

5

Today's child has a stronger grip on life

May good health keep me independent

4

In 1962, N.W. Ayer & Son *was approached by the Pharmaceutical Manufacturers Association, a group of nine laboratories. They chose to address the public through the national press, as this would reach two-thirds of all families. Over three years, in the context of the Pharmaceutical Industry Advertising Program, the agency made the public aware of the importance of research and the significant sums the association's members were investing in research. Among the thirty advertisements illustrating the various facets of the programme there was one on the fight against tuberculosis (2), one on anaemia (3), one on infirmity (4), one on pneumonia (5) and another on infections (6). The association would later become known as the Pharmaceutical Research and Manufacturers of America (PhRMA) and today represents almost the entire pharmaceutical industry in the United States. Similar associations exist in many countries, especially those with strong pharmaceutical manufacturing sectors. They play a key role in the development of public health policy and intellectual property issues relating to medicines.*

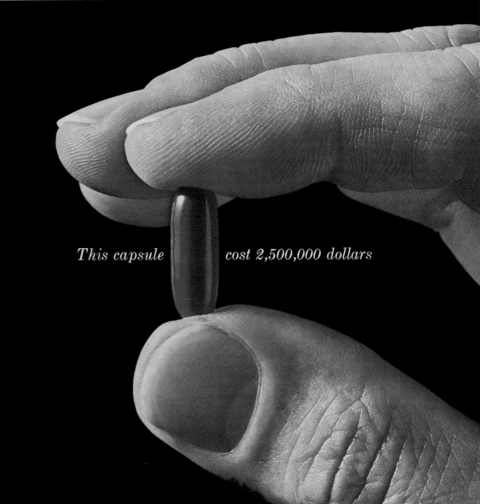

This capsule cost 2,500,000 dollars

6

On the road

For oil, these were the last decades of plenty before the times of crisis, and from the 50's onwards motorway interchanges were the cathedrals of the developed world. Jack Kerouac even went on the road to exorcise his angst.

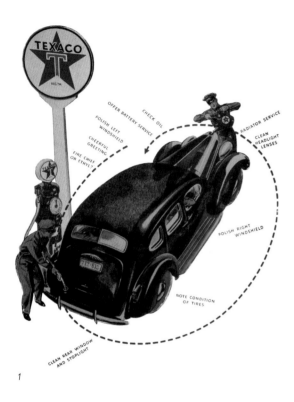

2

Up ahead: more desert. Can you make the next gasoline stop? Here you realize how important gasoline mileage can be. Add more miles to every gallon with Sky Chief—because of Texaco's extra steps to quality. Fact: Texaco buys tons of a rare chemical at $9 a pound—to use in refining Sky Chief. Result: Texaco blends in more extra-mileage components. Extras like this make Sky Chief the nearest thing yet to a perfect gasoline. It pays you to say Sky Chief.

Trust your car
to the man who
wears the star

3

The first drilling for oil occurred in Pennsylvania in 1859. By buying small, local businesses, Standard Oil, created in 1868, quickly gained control of much of the oil production, transport, refining and marketing on American soil. Service stations took off and from a standing start of 15,000 stations in 1920, they sped past the 120,000 barrier in only ten years. In 1911, the Supreme Court ordered that the Standard Oil trust be dismantled. A large number of oil companies emerged from this demolition, reestablishing the names that had been erased during their absorption into Standard Oil. This was the case with the Atlantic Refining Company which had been established in 1866 and which would later become Arco. It was relaunched in 1952 with a large-scale poster campaign designed by **N.W. Ayer & Son** (2). In 1936, another oil company, The Texas Company, established in 1902, partnered with Standard Oil Company of California to create the California Texas Oil Co., known as Caltex. The Texas Company became Texaco in 1959 and first used **Dancer Fitzgerald Sample** for its advertising (1). In 1961, with this advertisement shot by Jay Maisel, **Benton & Bowles** introduced a slogan directly linked to the brand symbol, which became burnt into the public's consciousness (3).

1

4

In France, Publicis developed a highly emotional image for Shell and built a very strong bridge between the brand and the consumer.
The campaign idea was "C'est Shell que j'aime" (It's Shell's that I love), which sounds memorably like "C'est celle que j'aime" (It's her that I love). This illustrates a favourite theme of advertising agencies —using easily memorable soundbites. The brand gained great renown and that slogan became symbolised by a heart to represent love and the brand's namesake shell emblem to represent the company (4). The brand symbol, created in 1904, has often been redesigned and the version shown here was the seventh, the work of the great designer Raymond Loewy. With a daring which was rare at the time, he judged that the public knew the brand's name so well he no longer needed to mention it. In 1976, **Norton**, a major Brazilian agency established in São Paulo in 1947, which would join Publicis in 1996, made the first film for Tropical tyres, directed by Carlos Manga (5). This brand had been created in 1975 by J. Macêdo, the industrial group from Brazilian Nordeste, whose relationship with the agency was to last some thirty-five years.

5

Cartoon lifestyle

The partnership between Renault and Publicis has lasted over forty years. It began in France, expanded into Europe in the 1970s, and then went global.

1

2

The French engineer Louis Renault established Renault-Frères in 1898 with his brother Marcel. By the 1960s, the company was the world's eighth-largest automobile manufacturer and the advertising account for all the models was awarded to **Publicis** in 1963. The attractions of the Renault 5, launched in 1972, were manifold: the innovative hatchback for loading convenience; at the same time, it had an elegant shape, and was comfortable to boot. The agency launched it as an anthropomorphic cartoon character, 'Supercar'. In a break from automobile advertising tradition, no reference was made to the technical aspects of the vehicle. Instead, posters and films showed how much fun this car was in town (1) and on the open road (2). When production stopped in the 1980s, its departure was announced in the same tongue-in-cheek vein: "Goodbye, cruel world!" (3).

3

Project 115 *was the code name for the Renault 16, a top-of-the-range car, launched in 1965. Communications embodied company values by showing the entire top tier of management together giving "the green light for Project 115" (4). From a technological viewpoint, this car marked Renault's definitive decision in favour of front-wheel drive and showcased various technical improvements: "16 patents for this revolutionary structure" (5). But the main breakthrough came with the design of the car as a whole: it had a 'fifth door' and a back seat that could be folded down. Experts would describe this type of car as a 'two-box' (typical saloons of the time were 'three-box'): one 'box' for the engine and one 'box' for the passengers and the luggage. Renault's concern for comfort and its modular approach to the interior spaces became characteristic of the company's vehicles, and was expressed between 1985 and 2000 by the slogan "Les voitures à vivre" (Cars for a new style of life).*

feu vert pour le projet "115"

Projet "115": c'était le nom de code de la future Renault 16. Et ces chercheurs, ces "cerveaux" de la Régie Renault avaient mission de lui donner la vie.

Point de départ: sondages et études de marché donnant un portrait-robot de la voiture: 5 places grand standing - confort supérieur - performances brillantes sécurité exceptionnelle et un intérieur totalement repensé, rompant avec les conceptions actuelles démodées.

A partir de là, feu vert...
Des mois durant, seuls ou en équipe, ils ont cherché, imaginé, calculé. Jusqu'à l'heure décisive du choix.

Alors, il se passa une chose exceptionnelle: parmi ces maquettes qui toutes répondaient aux exigences du cahier des charges, l'unanimité se fit sur un modèle: parce que le coup de foudre existe, même chez des techniciens. C'est le jour J... La Renault 16 est née.

4

16 brevets pour cette structure révolutionnaire

Si la ligne de la Renault 16 a étonné les spécialistes automobiles, c'est parce qu'elle est réellement... étonnante. On peut même dire que sa structure est tout simplement révolutionnaire.

Elle l'est tellement qu'elle a fait l'objet de seize brevets. Car Renault a conçu la caisse de la Renault 16 à la façon d'une cellule d'avion, aussi solide, aussi rigide, et la fabrique avec la même rigoureuse précision.

En imaginant ces poutrelles fermées (c'est pour cela qu'elles sont en saillie), en créant ces flancs à double paroi, en fixant le tout sur une plate-forme d'acier, les techniciens Renault ont doté la Renault 16 d'une incroyable robustesse, tout en diminuant le poids de la voiture. Vous y gagnez en outre une accessibilité exceptionnelle.

Révolutionnaire dès le «gros œuvre», la Renault 16 se devait de l'être jusqu'au bout. Et elle l'a été.

Renault 16 «voiture de l'année»

5

Small is big

Renault's reputation was built on big-selling smaller cars. This image, which ensured its commercial success and guaranteed public sympathy, provided a firm foundation for its development of larger cars in the years ahead.

1

2

Since its launch eight years earlier, three million Renault 5's had been sold. In 1980, after the second oil crisis, Renault had to emphasise how economical the car was in terms of fuel consumption (1) and how generous it was in terms of space (as shown here with reference to the five-door model (2), which had been out for some time). **Publicis** developed a campaign on a Lilliput theme, with photographs by Jean Larivière. After a brilliant sales career, the original Renault 5 was replaced in October 1985 by the new 'Super 5' and Renault began major expansion in the rest of Europe. Renault had long been a feature on the Belgian and Spanish landscapes, but was beginning to significantly reorganise its commercial presence in most other major European markets. To illustrate the drop in prices resulting from increases in productivity, an economist, Jean Fourastié, calculated the price of Renault's popular vehicles in terms of the number of hours it would take a factory worker to make them. In 1950, a popular model 'cost' over 3,000 hours; in 1998, the Renault Twingo only 'cost' 887 hours. The Renault 5 could have been dubbed the French 'people's car' like the German VW Beetle, immortalised by Bill Bernbach.

Fly guys

One of the top North American airlines went through an entire century with only three advertising agencies. This continuity allowed its image to slowly evolve from solid foundations to a major world player.

Hardnose

Don't let the Captain fool you. His middle name is "No Nonsense."

He spent a lot of years getting to be a United jet Captain. Four years as a Second Officer. Three as a First Officer. Four years as a Captain on United propeller planes.

Then—jet Captain.

He knows the skies like you know your backyard. He should. He has spent more than three million miles "upstairs."

Maybe you've flown with him, for more people fly United every day, every month, every year, than any other airline.

He's smart. Expert. Dedicated. Extra careful. All business.

Except about that son of his.

He's a *nut* about that kid.

"Today is my kid's birthday"

fly the friendly skies of United.

1

*United Airlines was created in 1926 out of the merger of four small air-mail carriers who, between them, linked the east and west coasts of the United States, from New York to San Francisco via Chicago and Salt Lake City. In 1930, United became the first airline to put a hostess in the air, and in 1936 was the first to serve a hot meal on board. In 1939, it entrusted its advertising to **N.W. Ayer & Son**, who built a brand personality around the idea of 'extra care': everything the company did, it did with extra care. This concept was first applied to the quality of service and, in 1957, it was also applied to safety. The airline's planes possessed a new piece of equipment: an on-board weather radar to spot atmospheric disturbances and thus avoid them.*

***Leo Burnett**, in charge of communications from 1965, kept the emphasis on service and safety, but updated the way the message was expressed. From the idea of the famous radar, located in the nose of the plane, which made for safer, more comfortable flights, the agency created the signature slogan: "Fly the friendly skies of United". This was soon applied to all aspects of the airline, including the competent cabin crew (1), the extensive network of routes (2) or the quality of service (5).*

He's the only one who flies more places than we do.

When it comes to air travel, Santa Claus is Mr. Big. United Air Lines is second.

We say, "If you can't beat him, join him."

So while he's busy flying presents to people, we help out by flying people to people.

Students coming home for the holidays.

Servicemen on Christmas leave.

Children and grandchildren. Uncles and aunts.

Cousins by the dozens.

And so, Merry Christmas to all, and to all a good flight.

"Yes, Virginia, there is a Santa Claus."

fly the friendly skies of United.

2

4

3

Business travellers *were almost exclusively men and airlines courted them assiduously. United was very attentive to frequent flyers (4) and in 1967, the airline offered them an exciting new benefit. They could be accompanied by their wives and obtain a significant reduction in the price of the second ticket. It was a big hit, as it gave part of the population that would otherwise not have had the opportunity, a chance to sample the delights of air travel. When they returned home, the businessmen's wives received a letter of thanks from the airline. To promote this, United created the first televised commercial for an airline. It took the form of a ballet, in which women sang: "Take me along!" (3), a line borrowed from the musical of that name, showing on Broadway in 1959 and itself inspired by "Ah! Wilderness", a 1933 play by the Nobel Prize winner Eugene O'Neill. At this time, allowing the wives to experience airline travel was an innovative breakthrough in the airline sector leading, later on, to frequent flyer point schemes.*

5

The former Miss Butterfingers.

Two months ago Sheri Woodruff couldn't even balance a cup of coffee.

But she was friendly, intelligent, and attractive. And wanted more than anything else to be a great stewardess.

So we put her to the test. (We take only one out of thirty applicants.) Five and a half weeks at United's Stewardess School.

We taught Sheri how to serve a gourmet dinner, how to soothe a first-flyer, how to apply everything from make-up to first-aid. Along with courses like aviation principles and geography.

Today she can warm a baby's formula with one hand and pour four cups of coffee with the other.

But more than that.

She's still the same Sheri Woodruff. Friendly, intelligent, attractive. And wants more than anything else to be a great stewardess.

She is.

"This is what I call a balanced meal."

fly the friendly skies of United.

Money talks

Banks attempted to seduce the public with subtle pleas and metaphors. Then, they finally tackled, head-on, a taboo that no one would talk about —nest eggs!

2

For a better way to protect your nest egg
talk to the people at Chase Manhattan

THE
CHASE
MANHATTAN
BANK

1

The Chase Manhattan Bank emerged from the 1955 merger of the Chase National Bank, (established in 1877 and controlled by the Rockefeller family since 1933) with the Bank of the Manhattan Company, which had been dedicated to banking since 1840. Chermayeff & Geismar, a New York design office that had opened in 1960, created the logo for the new bank in 1961 (2). The bank's reputation in business-to-business was well established, but it wanted to expand its provision of banking services to individuals and so **Compton** created a campaign that played on the idea of a 'nest egg', as illustrated by this 1956 advertisement (1). From the 1960s onwards, the photographs to illustrate this campaign were taken by Mark Shaw and the campaign popularised the slogan "You have a friend at Chase Manhattan" (3). It was deployed through a variety of advertisements, in which a range of characters are shown, shackled to their nest eggs. In 1996, the Chemical Bank of New York acquired control of the Chase Manhattan Bank, and in 2000, J.P. Morgan.

Chesapeake Eagle photo by Mark Shaw

Unshackle yourself. You have a friend at Chase Manhattan to help you care for your nest egg and act as your trustee. Delegate us at your convenience.

THE CHASE MANHATTAN BANK
NATIONAL ASSOCIATION
Head Office: 1 Chase Manhattan Plaza, New York, New York 10015

3

– Pour parler franchement, votre argent m'intéresse.

B BNP

4

The Banque Nationale de Paris (BNP) was born in 1966 from the union between the Comptoir National d'Escompte de Paris, established in 1848, and the Banque Nationale pour le Commerce et l'Industrie, which emerged in 1932 from the former Banque Nationale de Crédit. In 1972, when **Publicis** took charge of its advertising, the BNP was still largely unknown among the public at large. The agency redesigned the brand's logo: the 'B' for bank was writ large, in the spirit of such key urban icons as 'P' for parking or 'M' for the Paris metro. The logo was intended to be a sign to identify the bank's branches, with each dot on the logo's grid made up of a coin. In the spring of 1973, in the press, on walls, on the radio and on television, a character with a shy smile, photographed by Jean-François Bauret, confided in the French public that he was interested in their money (4). This campaign, aimed at private customers who did not yet use banking services, emphasised the mutual interest bank and its customers share. The feature film director Constantin Costa-Gavras made a film using the same character (5) and the campaign was later expanded to specifically target young people and women: "The bank where women count" (6).

5

C'EST MOI QUI COMPTE.

Aujourd'hui les femmes comptent. Elles paient l'école et choisissent les cartables, elles règlent les comptes et achètent les cadeaux, elles travaillent souvent et décident des vacances, elles dépensent ce qu'il faut et s'investissent beaucoup... les femmes ont un beau métier.
Alors les femmes ont besoin d'autonomie et d'un carnet de chèques.
Ouvrir un compte à la BNP, c'est simple, c'est bien.

BNP. UNE BANQUE OÙ LES FEMMES COMPTENT.

6

I just called

The advertising approach of Bell System had originally
put the firm's staff in the spotlight but slowly changed to show
the emotional and practical advantages of the telephone.

2

Long Distance is the next best thing to being there

It's pleasant... satisfactory... reassurance... love. Wouldn't you enjoy a visit by telephone right now?

BELL TELEPHONE SYSTEM

1

The advertising agency for The Bell System for
over eighty years between 1908 and 1994,
N.W. Ayer & Son introduced the company's
signature in 1966 (1). In 1974, the United States
Department of Justice brought an antitrust lawsuit,
which ended with a ruling in 1982 resulting in
the company being effectively dismantled in
1984. Prior to this, and despite continuous
threats to the company's future, The Bell System
was a consistent advertiser. In 1969, the famous
bell logo was redesigned, and in 1978 the slogan
changed to "Reach out and touch someone", as
shown in this advertisement, which appeared the
following year and which plays on the words
'halo' and 'hello' (3). In 1980, this television
commercial was to take an even more emotional
tack: a woman tells her husband that their son
has called. The father is concerned and the
mother reassures him. The man asks why the boy
called. The woman bursts into tears: "He just
called to say he loves his mother" (2). By the end
of 1978, there were 133 million telephones in the
United States. Having equipped and connected
a whole country, The Bell System now faced
a new challenge: long-distance communications.
This was the focus of AT&T's activity post-1984,
when it chose to leave behind all its regional
telephone companies.

"Halo everybody, halo?"

Reach out.
Reach out and touch someone.

Wherever you are, you're never too far to spend a few moments with someone
special, someone who's waiting to hear from you. You can make your day
by sharing it with faraway family and friends. Call to express your care, even
if it's just to say hi. It means so much to keep in touch. So reach out. Reach out
to those who make you feel good. You'll both feel good. With a phone call. Bell System

3

In 1878, the first telephone directory contained fifty names and no numbers —the operator was there to connect the calls. Very soon a printer named Reuben H. Donnelley, who printed the first paperback books as well as the Encyclopaedia Britannica in 1910 and also the magazine Time some while later, began to specialise in telephone directories. In the 1920s, he was the Bell System's largest independent directory sales agent. In the post-war period, his classified 'Yellow Pages' telephone directories and the sale of space in those directories became a truly important activity. In 1961, R.H. Donnelley became a subsidiary of Dun & Bradstreet and in the 1980s began to grow internationally. Yellow Pages commissioned **Cunningham & Walsh** for their advertising and, in 1962, they launched the now-famous slogan "Let your fingers do the walking!" (4). The pictorial version of this advice was adapted to fit everyone, including Father Christmas (5)! In 1965, the New-Yorker cartoonist Henry Syverson produced a poster for Pacific Telephone that gave his own take on the slogan (6). The image of two fingers walking through the Yellow Pages in search of good advice was used again in a 1975 television commercial. But why yellow pages? Because the original printer had run out of white paper.

Let your fingers do the walking! Any gift worth giving is easy to find when you...shop the Yellow Pages way!

5

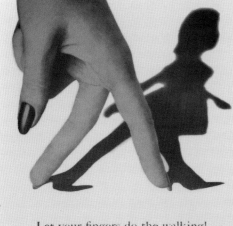

Let your fingers do the walking!

Shop the Yellow Pages way!

4

find Picnic Grounds fast in the YELLOW PAGES

6

IBM, Made In Britain

There are times when advertising must shed its seductive clothing and baldly state its message. This was the stance IBM took with an explanatory campaign which attacked received wisdom and irrational fears.

The trouble with the British worker is he works too hard.

Too many British workers are toiling away on dull, repetitive work that a machine, controlled by a computer, could do instead.

The result is that they are having to work long hours, in unpleasant conditions, without doing as much as modern technology would let them. And, because they are producing a lot less, they get paid a lot less.

Compared with the average German worker, the average British worker works 5 longer hours. Yet he produces 35 less and earns 45 less. Is this his fault? Or the fault of his management? Yet both sides seem intent on ignoring what's happening in the outside world.

No wonder that the heavily automated factories overseas are capturing markets that used to belong to Britain.

No wonder that the standard of living in the rest of Europe is rising far faster than in Britain.

Yet IBM invested £136 million in Britain last year alone to provide businesses of every size with the automated systems they need.

Systems that can speed up office work. Cut manufacturing costs. Improve productivity. And hasten delivery times.

But automation has further benefits too. For instance, other countries may start admiring us for working so little.

IBM

1

The prestigious company International Business Machines (IBM) was born in 1924 from the Computing-Tabulating-Recording Company (CTR), whose origins went back as far as 1886. IBM soon came to set the standards for data processing. It all began with punched cards but, from the Second World War onwards, IBM responded to the US army's requirements and came up with the first calculators. By the end of the 1950s, electronics had arrived on the back of the transistor –invented in Bell's laboratories in 1947. Electronics increased these machines' power considerably·and consequently reduced the size of their footprints. Computers were still extremely large machines and remained the preserve of specialist users. After an initial foray in 1975, IBM produced its first personal computer in 1981. It was equipped with an Intel processor and a Microsoft operating system (two suppliers destined to become world famous). On the personal computing market, the battle between Macintosh –whose Apple II came out in 1977– and IBM and its clones (compatible computers) was soon raging. In 1961, IBM launched the Selectric, the first electric golfball typewriter (all the characters were arranged on a golf-ball-sized typeball). Much more equipment was to follow (photocopiers, dictaphones, etc.) revolutionizing the world of 'the office'.

Two men were watching a mechanical excavator on a building site. "If it wasn't for that machine," said one, "twelve men with shovels could be doing that job." "Yes," replied the other, "and if it wasn't for your twelve shovels, two hundred men with teaspoons could be doing that job."

There are two ways to regard technological development. As a threat. Or as a promise.

Every invention from the wheel to the steam engine created the same dilemma.

But it's only by exploiting the promise of each that man has managed to improve his lot.

Computer technology has given man more time to create, and released him from the day-to-day tasks that limit his self-fulfilment.

We ourselves are very heavy users of this technology, ranging from golf-ball typewriters to ink-jet printers to small and large computers, so we're more aware than most of that age-old dilemma: threat or promise.

Yet during 27 years in the UK our workforce has increased from six to 15,000. And during those 27 years not a single person has been laid off, not a single day has been lost through strikes.

Throughout Britain, electronic technology has shortened queues. Streamlined efficiency. Boosted exports.

And kept British products competitive in an international market.

To treat technology as a threat would halt progress. As a promise, it makes tomorrow look a lot brighter.

IBM

IBM United Kingdom Limited P.O. Box 41, North Harbour, Portsmouth PO6 3AU

2

How patriotic is it to buy a computer from IBM?

from six when we started in 1951, to 15,000 British people working in Britain and for Britain.

They're working at Hursley, in IBM's biggest research and development laboratory in Europe.

At Greenock and Havant, manufacturing machines that help keep British products competitive in an international market and at the same time building our exports.

Every year we're increasing our investment in laboratories, plants, offices and training centres, in developing know-how and expertise.

Or an electric typewriter? Or a photocopier? A dictation system? Or even a typewriter ribbon?

There's only one way to answer questions like these. Not with persuasively worded opinions but with cold, hard facts.

Last year alone, our capital investment in Britain amounted to £90 million. We've increased our staff

The fact that we've already invested over £490 million should speak volumes about our commitment to Britain.

And a lot more about our faith in Britain's future.

IBM

IBM United Kingdom Limited, P.O. Box 41, North Harbour, Portsmouth PO6 3AU.

3

IBM set up in the United Kingdom in 1951 and, by the end of 1970, was working with Saatchi & Saatchi. The UK economy began to falter in 1973 and by 1976 the government had asked for a loan from the International Monetary Fund. Public expenditure had fallen, and both unemployment and prices were rising and, in 1978, it all culminated in the 'winter of discontent'. Saatchi & Saatchi's fine typographic campaign was launched against this backdrop: IBM sought acceptance although it was a foreign company (3) that was introducing a technology perceived to be destroying jobs (2), (4). In short, IBM sought to restore the public's confidence (1).

Find out more about computerised broking. Send off the coupon before someone else does.

4

Boring, boring, boring

Nowadays many people believe that using the theme of 'reliability' in advertising is 'old hat' but not when it came to household appliances and Leo Burnett's creative resources.

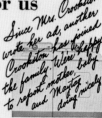

2

1

Maytag initially produced agricultural equipment: in 1902, it was the world's top manufacturer of threshing machines. The company then moved into domestic appliances, building its first washing machine in 1907. Twenty years on, one in five US citizens owned a Maytag washing machine. In 1948, the first automatic washing machines arrived on the scene, and in 1955 Maytag wanted a new advertising agency. It approached seventy-two, sixty responded, six were selected and three were invited to give a presentation. One was retained and that agency was **Leo Burnett**, who busied itself building a distinct brand personality. It began by emphasising Maytag's reputation, as illustrated in floods of letters from satisfied customers. The honesty and simplicity of these testimonials to the machines' reliability was a great success, as in this 1961 advertisement (1). Other examples featured large families (2), (3)!

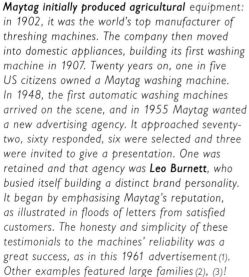

3

One Maytag and 1,088 babies later...

MAYTAG *the dependable automatics*

4

Just how robust Maytag's washing machines are is
clear from this advertisement (4). In 1967, still on
the subject of reliability, the Leo Burnett agency
launched Maytag on television and invented
the solitary, ageing repair man (6). The poor guy
had nothing to do, since Maytag machines never
needed fixing. So he waited, read the newspaper
and ate alone in his office, until one day
he dropped off to sleep. A voice off-screen
commented on a new washing machine model
with a built-in drier. The word 'new' woke him up,
then he exclaimed: "New?... Perfect!" and went
back to sleep (5). Having been trained to respond
to calls that never came, he adopted a dog he
named Newton (after the city where Maytag was
created in 1893) to keep him company and even
ended up training his assistant to learn how to
handle boredom. In the United States, the repair
man was played by a succession of three actors
(Jesse White, Gordon Jump and Hardy Rawls).
He became a living legend and an integral part
of popular US culture.

6

The more things at Maytag change, the more they stay the same.

Squeeze it, touch it, feel it!

Demonstrating a particular product's performance or quality in a clever way is a whole advertising genre in itself. In the 1970s, toiletries and detergent manufacturers made extensive use of this genre.

Charmin toilet paper, which Procter & Gamble acquired in 1957, is very soft to the touch. In 1964, the team at **Benton & Bowles** gathered around a table covered in packets of Charmin and asked themselves how best to convey this quality. Every now and then, without thinking, they would each pick up a packet, squeeze it, then put it down. Finally, someone got sick of this and cried "Stop squeezing the Charmin!" That was it –a campaign was born. The agency invented a character called Mr. Whipple, a grocer played by Dick Wilson, who kept his eye on customers who were tempted to touch the packets of Charmin (1). He even put up a notice to warn them off yet Mr. Whipple himself could hardly stop touching it! (2). The name, George Whipple, came from the agency's directory: he was the head of public relations. The first commercial was filmed at Flushing in Queens, New York, and for the next twenty-one years five hundred and four others followed, all featuring Mr. Whipple and his famous warning. From 1970 onwards, the brand was nearing the top spot and, in 1978, our hero actually became the third best-known character in the United States after President Nixon and preacher Billy Graham.

3

Camay, the soap launched by Procter & Gamble in 1926, entered a new phase of development in 1969 with a richer formula, which produced more lather. The **Leo Burnett** agency, which had managed the brand's advertising since 1954, produced three new commercials to demonstrate the qualities of this soap. In appearance, they reflect the realistic conventions of traditional demonstrations yet they lead the viewer into a fantasy world. The scenario is a constant throughout the three commercials: the salesman and his customer are irresistibly drawn to each other by the power of Camay. To prove the new soap's creamy smoothness, he takes her hands in his which, by some miracle, are already smothered in luscious lather. Absorbed in his demonstration, which the customer watches closely, the salesman caresses her hands to the sound of the opening bars of Tchaikovsky's Romeo and Juliet Overture. The first commercial portrays the enthusiasm of a young Camay researcher, who excitedly shares his discovery with a female colleague. The second is set in a supermarket (3). The third shows Mr. Rogers, a traditional grocer of an advanced age, offering his loyal customer, Mrs. Becker (herself no spring chicken), a sample of the new Camay, while the voice-over explains: "Twice the lather, twice the cream. To believe it, you've got to feel it." (4)

4

Smile, please!

Just a touch of colour makes the lips come to life. In all their various brands and through all their various retail environments, beauty products offer women the chance to sparkle.

2

1

A network of 'ambassadors' who sold products to their friends and neighbours is what made Avon cosmetics such a success in the United States and in hundreds of other countries during the '60s and '70s. **N.W. Ayer & Son** created this 1978 campaign to accompany the brand's success (1). In Germany, Margaret Astor, a brand from the Coty group, entrusted **Lürzer, Conrad** with its advertising. The agency was established in 1975 in Frankfurt-am-Main and would join **Leo Burnett** in 1980. This 1978 campaign emphasises the colour of the nail varnish and lipstick: "Der Favorit des Monats" (This month's favourite: Red Champagne) (2). Other exotically named colours followed, including Green Panther, Havana Harvest and Barbados Brown. Mrs. Ayer, the founder of Harriet Hubbard Ayer, had claimed in the 1880s that a French pharmacist had given her the formula for the cream used by the famous literary figure and beauty Madame de Récamier. The **FCA!** agency, established in 1966 and part of Publicis from 1993, created advertisements for the company in collaboration with the American photographer Bill King (3).

3

4

6

5

7

Jesse Boot's father owned a small pharmacy in Nottingham, England, and following his father's death in 1860, Jesse and his mother ran the medicinal herbalist's shop. His highly aggressive trading policy soon turned the small business into an empire: Boots the Chemist is now the United Kingdom's largest chain of chemists, with 1,400 shops selling healthcare and beauty products. Its N°7 cosmetics brand was created in 1935 and targeted young, working-class women who wanted fashionable colours at affordable prices. This product line was regularly relaunched with different communications and the packaging was constantly redesigned with the latest trends in mind. The agency **McCormick, Richards** –which joined Publicis' European network in 1978– worked on just such a relaunch, producing one campaign for skincare products (6), (7) and another for cosmetics (4), (5). Another commercial featured a young woman pulling the faces only women see while applying their makeup (8).

8

Movers and shakers

L'Oréal's success stemmed from its capacity to combine research with sensitivity to women's beauty expectations. Beyond the products, the company sells the idea of beauty and well-being.

1

In 1907, **Eugène Schueller,** a young French chemist, perfected a harmless hair dye called Auréole and this is where the name of the global cosmetics giant L'Oréal came from. The first hair lacquers emerged in the early 1960s and promised to set women's hairdos perfectly, but this effect went hand in hand with a loss of flexibility in the hair and, crucially, the spray was difficult to remove. L'Oréal finalised a new formula for its Elnett hairspray, which made it remarkably easy to brush out and the agency **Oscar**, which joined Publicis in 1980, took the golden colour of the packaging and the idea that it could be brushed out. This was illustrated by blonde hair, spread out and photographed with the light behind it, alongside the slogan: "The only hairspray that can be gently brushed out" (1). The idea of movement in hair that has been sprayed, was then conveyed in this 1971 commercial (2).

2

In the days of strong economic growth in Europe, lifestyles and mentalities underwent many transformations. Of these, the move towards hedonism was surely the most remarkable. For example, in personal hygiene, clean was no longer enough; one also had to take pleasure in personal grooming. This was the context in which bath foams were introduced in the 1960s. In 1963, L'Oréal created O.BA.O and commissioned **Publicis** for the launch. The brand built up a portfolio of exotically refined images, evoking the sophisticated and erotic world Westerners readily associate with the Japanese geisha tradition. The sound of its name contributed to this idea, as did the harmoniously-proportioned blue bottle. Thus the product was launched as "The Japanese foam bath experience" (3). The illustrations, inspired by Japanese prints, are by Alain Le Foll. Here is an original document for a double-page spread in a magazine with the finished illustration and hand-written technical notes (4). The **FCA!** agency, which had the account, hit on a strong, original expression of O.BA.O hedonism, with commercials filmed by Helmut Newton, among others. A woman can be seen through a gap in a bamboo screen whilst we hear the traditional tune 'Sakura-sakura'.

3

4

Now you see it, now you don't

A naked woman and a naked man appear: the woman in 1962, the man in 1967.
She was not the first woman, but he was the first man. The boldness was
embodied not in the nudity, but in the absence of a product.

1

Here are two of Publicis' campaigns in which the product is conspicuous by its absence. The first advertises Rosy lingerie, a brand established by the hosier Leon Josephson in 1936. Josephson turned to Publicis for his advertising in 1947. Inspired by a phrase from the English poet John Ruskin, "The path of a good woman is indeed strewn with flowers (…) Her feet have touched the meadows, and left the daisies rosy", Publicis invented a symbol comprising a woman and a rose. This was captured magnificently in Jeanloup Sieff's 1963 photograph (1), which portrayed not the product but the reasons to buy it: luxury, elegance and seduction. Publicis was using inspiration from Ernest Dichter's "Strategy of Desire" which had been published in Paris in 1961. However, for men it was a totally different matter. When Selimaille came to Publicis for the launch of its men's underwear in 1967, it had registered the name of a type of white underpants with a 'black belt' intended to conjure up the idea of martial arts. Just as the advertisement showing the underpants was about to be aired there was a ruling that prevented the product from being shown, as one of the firm's competitors had already registered underwear with a waistband in a contrasting colour. What was Selimaille to do? The advertising had intended to show the first designer underwear for men. Now there was nothing for it but to choose between showing the Greek model Frank Protopapa, clothed (2) or unclothed (3). Thus the photographer, Jean-François Bauret, took the first advertising picture of a naked man.

2

Selimaille

3

Sixy

France has been hearing the six notes that make up the Dim brand's signature since 1970. Since then, the melody has been arranged over many rhythms and adapted for the introduction of new products.

Showing your knickers!

Since DuPont's invention of nylon in 1938 and Lycra® in 1959, hosiery has become a unique blend of highly sophisticated materials and an extremely intimate expression of the way women view themselves.

2

1

Stocking manufacturer **Les Bas Dimanche** was marketed by Bégy, established by Bernard Giberstein in France in 1953, and moved to **Publicis** in 1963. The agency immediately suggested that it simplify its name and Dimanche became Dim. More innovations were to follow, including seamless stockings, stockings sold in singles and unfolded stockings, wrapped in a cube. With the advent of the mini-skirt came tights. Dim proved that a fashion item could also be a mass-market product: its products were easily and widely available yet highly desirable. The advertisements had positioned them at the pinnacle of the latest fashion and lifestyle trends. While its competitors only showed women's legs, Dim showed a woman who moved freely, naturally and happily, even cheekily. Major directors, including William Klein (the illustration on the previous page comes from one of his commercials), Hugh Hudson, Adryan Lyne, Ridley and Tony Scott, Bertrand Tavernier and Luc Besson went on to portray Dim's products to the soundtrack of Lalo Schifrin's tune from the film "The Night of the Fox". Major photographers also worked for the brand: in 1972, Nadia Rein produced this picture (1) and in 1975 Jeanloup Sieff created these images (2), (3), (5).

Le Dim Voile est très fin sur les jambes, pour aller avec tout ce qui est beau, raffiné, sophistiqué les soirs de fête, avec tout ce qui est léger, souple et gai, les jours d'été.

3

Dim's new label-shaped logo was created in 1977 (6) and in 1986, when stockings came back into fashion, Dim launched Dim'Up, stockings that held themselves up, featured in this 1987 poster by Eddy Kholi "Take your Dim and run" (4). In the United States, the Hanes Hosiery brand turned to **Dancer Fitzgerald Sample** in 1969 for the launch of its mass-market women's hosiery products. The market was huge, but very fragmented: none of the six hundred brands present held more than 4% of the market. In the face of this diverse competition, the task was to build a strong brand that could use its name, packaging and presence at points of sale to demonstrate that it was different and of superior quality to brands sold in superstores. The aim was also to produce an advertisement that would really persuade customers to try the product and thereby put the distributors at ease. The L'eggs brand resolved these issues and achieved the highest sales in the United States. The original, egg-shaped packaging and the display units represented a bright new solution. The brand name says it all: "Our L'eggs fit your legs" (7).

4

6

5

7

Emotional commitment

When advertising hit television screens across the
United Kingdom and then the rest of Europe, Publicis
was the first agency to have a regular policy of
using big-name film directors to make TV commercials.

1

2

The pleasure gained through taste is highlighted
in this 1976 commercial by Robert Enrico (1),
which states: "I like its subtlety". In 1982,
Alain Franchet evoked convivial pleasure in his
advertisement for "The beer that makes you like
beer" (6). The Renault 18 Diesel was portrayed as
edgy in Sergio Leone's 1981 commercial for
Publicis. "Diesel unleashed" had all the emotional
impact of his œuvre, with the car throwing off its
chains like a latter-day Spartacus (2). To promote
lobster from Cuba, Jean-Jacques Annaud's 1975
commercial plays very effectively on innocent
sincerity: a chorus of real-life housewives sing
a somewhat naive refrain against a shabby
backdrop (3). O-cedar also chose to use humour
to polish up its image for furniture polish in this
1981 film by Manuel Otero, showing a wooden
doll dancing (4). Dim, in this gently teasing film
by Ridley Scott for Dim bras in 1977, features
a mother and daughter and egg cups (5).

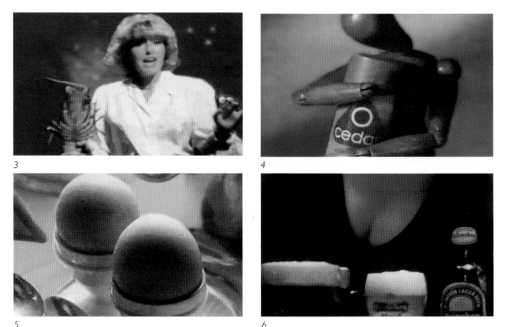

3

4

5

6

Crunch appeared in France in 1960. A milk chocolate bar containing crunchy grains of puffed rice and making a characteristic noise when bitten which, when amplified, suggested the effect of a powerful force. This provided the starting point for the commercials which were to give Crunch its strong personality. In 1984, Jean-Paul Goude created a little gem for **Leo Burnett** (7) when, by biting into her bar, a mischievous young woman destroys the studio where the commercial is being filmed. In 1976, the same agency made a commercial for Nestlé Dessert, the cooking chocolate launched in France in 1971. Directed by Lester Bookbinder, the commercial showed a sensual couple sharing an appetising-looking, chocolate-covered pear (8). This commercial strongly stimulated the classic 'appetite appeal' that is so sought after in advertising food products. In 1974, **Publicis** asked Sergio Leone to produce a commercial for Gervais' ice creams and Leone, inventor of the spaghetti western, dreamed up a parody of the film "Lawrence of Arabia". The script only contained one character, the Tuareg tribesman tasting his ice cream in the middle of the desert but Sergio Leone gave him a wife, wearing a veil, who guides the dromedary of her lord and master on foot, by the sweat of her brow and the whole scene is set to the thundering "Ride of the Valkyries" as arranged by Ennio Morricone, Leone's regular composer (9). An amusing idea by Publicis for the client Lactel on the possibilities of how to get fresh milk: either keep a cow at home or buy Lactel. The commercial, produced by Jean-Jacques Annaud in 1981, is based on the first, absurd alternative; it pictures cows on the streets and in people's apartments (10).

Shabby chic

The advertising generation were questioning received wisdoms and social codes and this led to a shift in thinking, new courses of action and new styles: alternative behaviour was the new distinction.

Dieu soit loué, ils vont faire leur tunnel ailleurs.

✿ **Irlande**
Allez loin sans aller loin.

2

Racontez l'Irlande en une photo.

✿ **Irlande**

1

How do you persuade people to think black is white? At the height of the swinging 60's Ireland was a tourist destination with no sun, no well-known sites and no accessibility. At the instigation of the Irish Tourist Board in 1968, **Intermarco-Elvinger** came up with a way of making this an attraction: "Go to Ireland, no one else does." Although never released in this exact form, it spawned more than 400 advertisements. These turned a country where no one goes into a destination for people who seek authenticity and who shun the herd mentality. On the theme: "Go far without going far" (3), these campaigns offered the former student protesters of the sixties a whiff of a cheap, chic anticonformism as an antidote to their new adult, executive existence. The advertisements followed current affairs as illustrated by this example from 12 February 1986, "Thank God they're building their tunnel somewhere else" (2). This refers to the signature by the United Kingdom and France of the Treaty of Canterbury, thereby agreeing to the construction of a Channel tunnel. The usual protocols are subverted, as in this advertisement which asks readers of the photographic journal in which it appeared to send in illustrations of Ireland, citing the Board's own lack of funds as an explanation (1). In twenty-five years, the number of French visitors rose from 25,000 to 250,000.

Imaginez l'homme qui a bâti sa maison ici.

Vous avez gagné : il s'appelait Sean, ou tout comme. Mais vous avez perdu : ce n'était pas un misanthrope mais le plus grand bavard du monde.

La mémoire locale raconte que si Sean (ou tout comme) s'en alla construire sa maison au bout de la falaise, c'était pour s'obliger à travailler un peu entre deux histoires, loin de tout auditeur.

Mais peut-être tout ceci n'est-il qu'invention, que Sean n'a jamais existé et que personne ne peut répondre à cette question que posent tous les étrangers, ces gens bizarres.

Allez explorer vous-même le sujet : pour 1525 F* par personne environ (si vous êtes quatre), vous aurez l'aller et retour en ferry direct pour vous et votre voiture.

Et peut-être trouverez-vous que tout ceci n'a pas de sens, qu'il était évident qu'il fallait construire sa maison là, avec toutes les collines d'Irlande derrière soi, l'océan juste devant, des lapins gambadant partout pour se distraire et, de temps en temps, une vague venant laver le rez-de-chaussée.

Comment imaginer l'homme qui n'aurait *pas* bâti sa maison ici ?

Aer Lingus, la compagnie nationale aérienne irlandaise assure toute l'année des vols journaliers Paris-Dublin ainsi que des vols vers Cork et Shannon. De juin à septembre, vol Rennes-Cork le dimanche.

Irish Continental Line, la compagnie maritime irlandaise relie toute l'année la France à l'Irlande. Du 23.05 au 15.09, départs quotidiens du Havre ou de Cherbourg pour Rosslare (pour Cork le jeudi en été).
*Prix haute saison.

Tous les prix de vos vacances figurent dans la brochure "L'Irlande en Kit". Pour la recevoir avec une documentation générale remplissez ce coupon.

Nom

Adresse

Et envoyez-le (en joignant 4 timbres à 2,10 F pour frais d'envoi) au Mailing Express, Irlande, BP 591, 75830 Paris Cedex 17, ou venez nous voir, 9, bd de la Madeleine, 75001 Paris, Tél. 260.10.42

✿ **Irlande**
Allez loin sans aller loin.

3

Woolmark ● La laine est vraie.

4

Established in 1937 by Australian, New Zealand and South African producers to promote wool, the International Wool Secretariat arrived in France in 1947. The Woolmark label was created in 1964, using a symbol designed by Francesco Saroglia, a graphic artist from Milan. The war with synthetic fabrics was in full swing and the first washing machines with wool cycles appeared in Europe in 1969. French executives at the International Wool Secretariat turned to **FCA!** in 1974. They focussed on the natural, authentic quality of wool and created the slogan "Wool is true" –this was to be the brand's signature for many years. The photographer Daniel Aron produced this poster, featuring over two hundred sheeps, which all had to be attached to individual stakes, one by one (4). Other posters promoted specific products with this photograph by Jacques-Henri Lartigue being the first: "Sim, me, Charly, Nanik and Rico, Manzat Bridge, 24 September 1913" (5).

5

De-luxe!

Watches and fountain pens had always been status symbols. Even before they became disposable, ballpoint pens made writing a more relaxed affair; watches, previously very special accessories, became fashion items.

2

1

The principle of the ballpoint pen was discovered in 1888 by the American John J. Loud, who used it to mark leather. Improvements were made by the Hungarian József László Bíró in Argentina in 1938, but the pen still wasn't perfect, as it leaked. Marcel Bich, who had set up in business in 1945, launched an hexagonal pen in France in 1950. The pen was made of transparent plastic, which showed the level of ink, and he called it Cristal. Available in black, red, blue and green inks, it guaranteed three kilometres of writing. In 1953, Marcel Bich adapted his family name and called his company Bic and a new way of writing was born. True success came in 1961, with a technical innovation: the tungsten carbide ball, which stopped the ink running. The ballpoint pen was initially rejected by schools, which stayed faithful to the calligraphy involved in using fountain pens. It was eventually permitted in France from 3 September 1965, following an original communication campaign during which pupils were given desk blotters illustrated by Savignac and Effel. The **Masius-Landault** agency built up the brand's reputation by launching a campaign with a ball-point head pupil: "Real Bics are branded Bic" (1); "Back to school with Bic" (2). Savignac's pupil held the pen behind his back and appeared on all the advertisements: "New ballpoint" (3). On the strength of this success, the company launched disposable lighters in 1973 and disposable razors in 1975. These new, non-rechargeable products complemented a lifestyle and consumption pattern that prioritised everything that was easy, light and ephemeral.

3

A **stopwatch** made by Emmanuel Lipmann was presented to Napoleon in 1807. In 1867, Lipman's grandson Ernest opened a workshop in the city of Besançon, and in 1896, the word Lip was first used to designate a stopwatch. Fred Lip, Ernest's descendant, entrusted **Publicis** with the advertising in 1962, but the market situation was difficult: he had many competitors and relations with jewellery and watchmaking retailers were tense. Although brand awareness was 98%, market share was a mere 20% so Publicis decided to change the rules of the game completely. In 1963, buying a watch was a once-in-a-lifetime event and watch manufacturers still had a traditional image, so the agency constructed a different, more modern image for Lip. In fact, this image did reflect a company reality –the average age of Lip's employees was around 35. All the characteristics associated with the brand were linked to the name Fred Lip: youth, photography by Michel Certain –"Fred Lip is young" (6), an obsession with detail –"Fred Lip is a stickler" (4), modernity, eclecticism and passion. The following year, a young boy, Nicolas Matton –nick-named Mathieu and photographed by Marc Hispard– became the spokesperson for the brand "Fred Lip told me it's robust" (5).

4

5

6

Diamonds are forever

*It takes a long time for carbon to crystallise and form a diamond.
It also takes a lot of passion to love for a lifetime.
But you need to abolish the whole idea of time when you're
talking about precious stones!*

2

1

At the end of the 1930s, *after the Great
Depression, the traditional diamond engagement
ring was no longer in vogue and sales were
feeling the impact. In 1939, the South African
mining company De Beers gave its advertising
account to* **N.W. Ayer & Son**. *The agency
established a link between paintings and diamonds,
and indicated that diamonds had all the advantages
of works of art, including significant investment
value. Major artists such as Dufy, Derain, Dalí
and Marie Laurencin, were asked to contribute to
what would become known as the De Beers
collection. In 1940, Picasso himself designed an
advertisement for the series* (2). *The campaign was
informative, explaining the '4 Cs': cut, carat,
clarity and colour. As with art, so with diamonds:
a knowledgeable customer is an appreciative
customer. In 1949, the slogan "A diamond is
forever" was born. In the United States in 1951,
a diamond was the choice for 80% of marrying
couples but times were changing and campaigns
needed to keep pace. The greatest photographers
of the day, such as Irving Penn and Richard
Avedon, took up where painters had left off and
the slogan became "Diamonds are for now"* (1).
*Diamonds became more popular and were no
longer only the preserve of the rich* (3), *and in
1969, De Beers devoted an advertisement to
man's first steps on the moon* (4).

Frog pins by David Webb. Your jeweler can show you many exciting diamond pieces priced from about $200.

A surprise look at what once was strictly a grande dame gem.
No more. Diamonds can be kicky as frog's eyes, classic as
ear drops or anything your pleasure or purse desires.
The one thing that hasn't changed is the thrill you get from wearing them.
A diamond is for now.

3

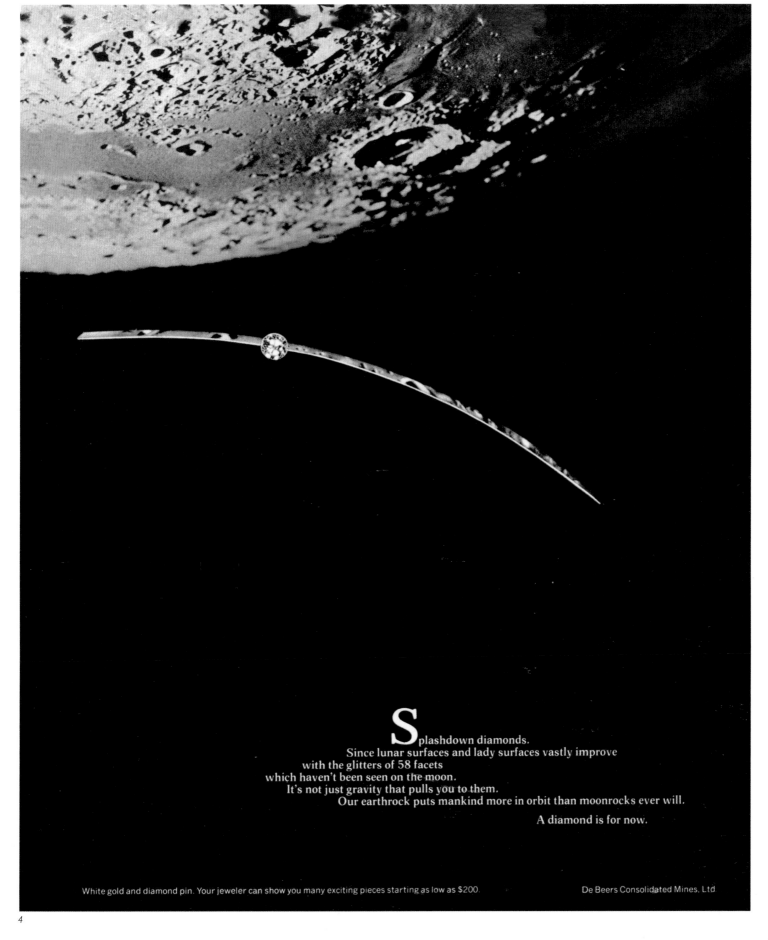

Splashdown diamonds.
Since lunar surfaces and lady surfaces vastly improve
with the glitters of 58 facets
which haven't been seen on the moon.
It's not just gravity that pulls you to them.
Our earthrock puts mankind more in orbit than moonrocks ever will.

A diamond is for now.

White gold and diamond pin. Your jeweler can show you many exciting pieces starting as low as $200.   De Beers Consolidated Mines, Ltd

4

The Iron Lady

"Marvellous!" Margaret Thatcher is said to have exclaimed on seeing this campaign. It was the first time a UK political party had turned to a major advertising agency for its election material.

1

After Edward Heath's Conservative party victory in 1970, Margaret Thatcher was appointed Education Secretary. After the Conservative defeat in the March 1974 general election, they chose Mrs. Thatcher as party leader in 1975. She decided to call on an advertising agency to help with the party's next election campaign. The agency would have to be British and not too big or too small and most importantly, it needed to be highly creative. Although *Masius Wynn Williams* and *Saatchi & Saatchi* were neck and neck, Saatchi & Saatchi was finally chosen. The agency was convinced of one thing: as far as public opinion is concerned, oppositions don't win elections, governments lose them. In spring 1978 they put together a campaign which was fiercely critical of the Labour incumbents: "Britain is going backward. Don't just hope for a better life. Vote for one." In August, this classic poster was unveiled (2). Labour's arms policy was viewed in the same vein (1). The Conservatives came to power in May 1979, and stayed there until 1997.

2

The price of the press

'Scripta manent': the spoken word disappears, but the written word remains. However, in the face of developments in television, the press had to convince the public of its credibility and also to attract advertisers.

2

1

Advertising agencies have never forgotten that their roots lie in the press and **N.W. Ayer & Son**, in the United States, provides an excellent example of these special ties. At a time when sixty-second television commercials were absorbing an ever-greater share of advertising budgets, the agency was approached by the Magazine Publishers Association. In 1968, it created a campaign to promote magazines, 'the involving medium.' In order to illustrate the special rapport between readers and magazines, the advertisements focused on emotionally-charged events (3) such as the story of the German boxer Max Schmeling who fought american Joe Louis in 1936 and 1938. From 1965 onwards, the agency also promoted the magazine Newsweek. The campaign emphasised the magazine's credibility: "Quote Newsweek, the newsweekly that separates fact from opinion." At the beginning of the 1970s, the agency created a series of advertisements about the quality of the magazine's investigative reporting. The examples shown here are a report on counter-culture (1) and a young man's bad experience with the legal system (2).

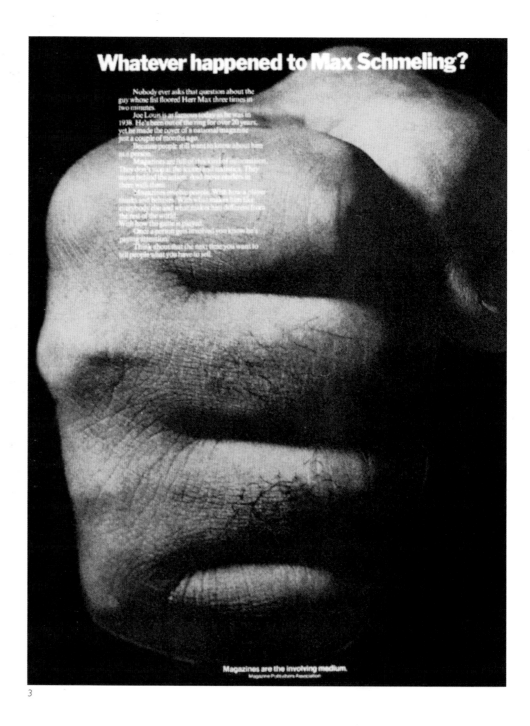

3

In fact, all print media was reacting to the advance of television. In France, in 1974, the union of regional daily newspapers conducted a vigorous campaign that challenged the supremacy of electronic communications. **FCA!** and the photographer Michel Meunier were employed (4). Gutenberg, inventor of the printing press, responds to Herbert Marshall MacLuhan, a contemporary Canadian sociologist famous for his analysis of the media and the effect of technology on mass communications. This full-page colour advertisement in the daily papers was aimed at advertisers, and showed that the press is an essential counterpart to television. It quotes figures to support this idea and explains that, whereas television arouses people's interest, the press provides detailed explanations. The campaign's clear objective was to remind advertisers not to forget the regional daily press when considering their advertising budgets. The prestigious British newspaper The Times, established in the eighteenth century, also emphasised the quality of the information it supplied, as shown in this 1978 advertisement created by **Leo Burnett's** London office (5). The newspaper, alongside its weekend version The Sunday Times, which was launched in 1962, belonged to the Canadian Roy Thomson. From December 1978 to November 1979 a lengthy industrial dispute prevented the paper from being published, and in February 1981 both editions were bought by Rupert Murdoch's News Corporation group.

4

5

Unselling sex

The late 1960s saw an increase in advertisements aimed at raising the public's awareness of problems in society. These were attempts to provide support during a period in which cultural change was now taking place increasingly rapidly.

1

Birth control was gradually becoming part of life in Europe and family planning associations played a crucial role in providing information on the various methods available for contraception as well as lobbying for changes to enable the legalisation of abortion. The real turning point was the arrival of the contraceptive pill and, in 1967, abortion was legalised in England, Scotland and Wales for women over the age of 21, which was then the age of majority. In 1969, the British Family Planning Association used an advertisement, photographed by Alan Brooking, which was to become famous in the industry to explain to men that birth control wasn't all down to women (2). **Saatchi & Saatchi** ran another campaign on the theme of shared responsibilities in 1971 for the Health Education Council, an organisation that had been created alongside the social security system in 1948. Ron Mather was the illustrator (1). With the start of the AIDS pandemic in the 1980s, there would be many more battles in a fight against the risks associated with sex.

2

Now is the time for all good men to come to the aid of their planet.

What we don't know about this earth we live on not only can hurt us–it can kill us.

What we don't know–or refuse to recognize–is that modern man has been altering his total environment so swiftly and suddenly that the whole "great chain of life" on this planet is endangered.

All of us live on a tiny space-ship which is hurtling through the universe at a speed 600 times faster than the fastest jet plane–carrying with it its own limited resources for sustaining life.

What we have now is all we will ever have to keep us alive. Having already set foot on the lifeless moon, we shall presumably find that we are the only creatures in our solar system. As lonely astronauts on our own ceaseless journey through space, what do we have as our basic equipment for survival?

Above us, a narrow band of usable atmosphere, no more than seven miles high, with no "new" air available to us.
Beneath us, a thin crust of land, with only one-eighth of the surface fit for human life.
And around us, a finite supply of "usable" water that we must eternally cleanse and re-use.

These are the elements of man's physical environment. This is the "envelope" in which our planet is perpetually sealed.

Together, and left alone, land, air, and water work well as an "ecosystem" to maintain the great chain of life, and the delicate balance of nature, from ocean depth to mountain top.

But man, since he first rose up on two legs, has been tampering with this system. He cannot help it. Everything we do alters our environment: the ways we grow food and build shelter and create what we call "culture" and "civilization."

Now, entering the last three decades of the 20th Century, we face the shocking realization that we have gone too far too fast and too heedlessly–and now we are forced to cope with some of the consequences of our "progress" as a species.

For, increasingly, all over the world scientists and statesmen and specialists in every field are coming to agree on the pressing paradoxes of our modern age:

–that, as societies grow richer, their environments grow poorer.
–that, as the array of objects expands, the vigor of life declines.
–that, as we acquire more leisure to enjoy our surroundings, we find less around us to enjoy.

It is nobody's fault, and it is everybody's fault.

The real culprits are the three main currents of the 20th Century–Population, Industrialization, and Urbanization.

Together, these three swift and mighty currents of history have acted to foul the air, contaminate the land, pollute the waters–and to accelerate our mounting loss of beauty and privacy, quiet and recreation.

WORLD population is growing at a rate that will double by the year 2000–only a brief three decades away–when nearly seven billion people will inhabit the earth.

Already, the poverty-stricken countries of Asia, the Near East, Africa, and Latin America contain 70 percent of the world's adults and 80 percent of its children. The most people are concentrated where the least food and goods are available.

INDUSTRIALIZATION has added its own burden to the population pressure. The more we produce and consume, the more waste products we discharge into the air and water and land around us, where they do not "disappear," but last forever in one form or another.

Our natural resources–both renewable and non-renewable–are taxed to the utmost by industrialization. The U.S. water supply, for instance, remains at the same fixed level, but we are using four times as much per person as in 1900.

Yet, at the same time, the volume of waste waters discharged into our lakes, rivers, and streams has risen 600 percent so far in this century. Less than one-tenth of one percent of contaminating materials can kill fish life by consuming oxygen in the waters. (The de-salting of sea water for household and agricultural use on a large scale is a long way off.)

We now spew 150 million tons of pollutants into the atmosphere annually, and 90 percent of this consists of largely invisible but potentially lethal gases. This may reduce solar radiation, and raise the temperature at the earth's surface. Some predict that this could conceivably melt the polar ice cap, thus flooding the coastal cities of the world. Moreover, these contaminants are global in their effects; as the Bible tersely reminds us, "The wind bloweth where it listeth."

From the plains in Russia to the mountains of Switzerland, from the blue waters of the Pacific to the smokestacks of Chicago, the air is hazier, the smog is thicker, the sun dimmer. Throughout the world, the statistics are uniformly appalling–but the figures speak less vividly than the sad bewilderment of California school children who are now excused from outdoor games on those days when the atmosphere chokes their lungs.

Industrialization plagues the land as well as the air and waters. Our rise in synthetic technology has given us innumerable conveniences–but the roadsides are strewn with cans, bottles, and cartons, the dumps overflow, and in some cities it costs three times more to get rid of a ton of junk than to ship in a ton of coal.

URBANIZATION is perhaps the most menacing of the three converging trends that threaten our planet today.

In the U.S., land is being urbanized at the rate of 3,000 acres a day. One million Americans a year leave the rural areas for cities. Seventy percent of all Americans now live on 10 percent of the land; by the year 2000, some 85 percent will live in urban areas. And the same is happening all over the world. By the end of this century, most human beings–for the first time in history–will be born, live, reproduce, and die within the confines of an urban setting.

Each time we build a new highway, bulldoze a woods into a shopping center, or turn farmland into housing developments, we decrease the acreage that will grow food. Great progress is being made in the productivity of our soil, yet agriculture is now taking three to four million tons more nutrients from it than are being replaced each year.

The word "ecology" was devised exactly a hundred years ago–in 1869 –to signify the study of the relationship between life systems and their environment. "Ecology" is what everybody on this planet must start thinking about–and quickly–if we are to avoid irreversible changes within the closed system of our space-ship.

For everything around us is tied together in a system of mutual interdependence. The plants help renew our air; the air helps purify our water; the water irrigates the plants. Man, as a part of nature, cannot "master" it; he must learn to work with it–and with his fellows everywhere–to ensure that we do not alter the environment so drastically that we perish before we can adjust to it.

MANKIND as a species needs esthetic as well as physical values–sweet rivers to walk by in solitude and serenity, and pleasant prospects even in the midst of industrial affluence. The constant din of urban life assails the ears relentlessly, and noise contributes its own ugly obligato to the disharmony of our surroundings.

"The world is too much with us, late and soon," as Wordsworth prophetically put it more than a century ago, "Getting and spending, we lay waste our powers."

We have laid waste our powers for too long, not merely by ignoring the warnings of dead lakes and noxious air and ravaged countrysides, but also by periodically killing off our bravest and our best in senseless warfare.

Now is the time for all good men to come to the aid of their planet.

We have the technical skill and resources. We have a common cause worth fighting for: a new kind of war to make the world safe for humanity against its own worst instincts.

Perhaps this mighty global struggle to restore the quality of our human environment may provide an effective and inspired substitute for national conflict and bloodshed.

Perhaps only a planetary view of man can guarantee our survival.

We have the weapons that enable us all to die together; can we not forge the tools that enable us all to live together?

3

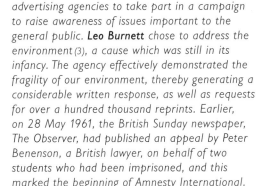

*In 1969, the US magazine Time invited advertising agencies to take part in a campaign to raise awareness of issues important to the general public. **Leo Burnett** chose to address the environment (3), a cause which was still in its infancy. The agency effectively demonstrated the fragility of our environment, thereby generating a considerable written response, as well as requests for over a hundred thousand reprints. Earlier, on 28 May 1961, the British Sunday newspaper, The Observer, had published an appeal by Peter Benenson, a British lawyer, on behalf of two students who had been imprisoned, and this marked the beginning of Amnesty International. **Publicis Brussels** office created this advertisement in 1983: "You have a weapon to fight torture" (4).*

Contre la torture, vous avez une arme.

Amnesty International

AMNESTY MOUVEMENT IMPARTIAL D'INTERVENTION DIRECTE POUR LA DEFENSE DES DROITS DE L'HOMME ET LA LIBERATION DES PRISONNIERS D'OPINION DANS LE MONDE. CONTRE LA TORTURE ET LA PEINE DE MORT. PRIX NOBEL DE LA PAIX 1977.

4

Chapter V

1981-2006

Ayer	Casadevall Pedreño
DMB&B	Burrell
Publicis	Bromley
Leo Burnett	BBH
Saatchi & Saatchi	Ambience
Norton	Arc Worldwide
Salles	Basic
Nazca	Freud
BMZ	Publicis Consultants
Fallon	Starcom MediaVest Group
Hal Riney	Kaplan Thaler Group
Manning Selvage & Lee	Publicis Dialog
Frankel	Médias & Régies Europe
Medicus	Publicis Events
Mojo	ZenithOptimedia
Vitruvio	Prakit
Wet Desert	Beacon Communications
Welcomm	

New Frontiers

The Bund, Shanghai. Situated on the banks of the Huangpu river, this metropolis is a global cultural and economic driving force of the early 21st century.

Did the turn of the century actually begin in the early '80s? That was certainly when signs began to appear that new forces were at work: Japanese investors buying the famous Rockefeller Center in New York and millions of American households driving around in Japanese cars. The balance of power was also shifting in Europe: the Berlin Wall falling in the winter of 1989 and the euro introduced a decade later. The impression of a constantly expanding world was confirmed when China, manufacturer of half of all computers and televisions across the globe, became a member of the World Trade Organisation in November 2001 while India became a force to be reckoned with in the generic medicine market. The world was becoming more open and its focus was shifting.

Communications kept pace with this change. Most major brands gained a global dimension, and both advertisers and agencies were on the lookout for an ideal way to link the effectiveness of national campaigns with the coherence of international strategies. Major cultural icons emerged from the wings and went global such as glamour goddesses like Maggie Cheung or virtual vixens like Lara Croft! From music to cuisine, everything has become "world". This is the era of globalisation.

Yet at the same time, individualism was on the rise. In the early '80s, the video cassette and remote control freed up the television viewer; computers became personal, then portable. All these innovations in communication channels gave the individual greater choice. The relationship with television changed: faced with a cornucopia of channels, all viewers can choose their favourite offering and when they watch it. Convergence between images, telephones and computers contributed to an explosion in the way information and entertainment can be accessed. You can send text messages, take photographs and film with your mobile phone —you can even consult your emails. The Internet rode out the turbulence surrounding the "dotcom" boom that began in 1998 and the storm of panic surrounding the millennium bug, to finally deliver what it had promised: to revolutionise communication and consumption patterns.

And now, at the onset of the third millennium, the individual is at the centre of an ever-expanding communication universe.

Not quiet on the Eastern front

*Democratic ideals romped through Central and Eastern Europe,
bringing with them a thirst for consumption. In China, freedom to be a consumer
has outpaced democratic freedom.*

1

The Berlin Wall fell on 9 November 1989.
Saatchi & Saatchi *UK immediately claimed to be
the "First over the Wall" (1). Originally designed
for a client, the poster made the front page of all
the papers. In 2003,* **Leo Burnett** *Prague created
this poster for the opening of a museum of
communism in the Czech Republic (2). In 1985,
Mikhail Gorbachev initiated the policy of 'glasnost'
(transparency) and 'perestroika' (reform) in the
Soviet Union. Encouraged by this new climate of
openness, Procter & Gamble established a
foundation which organised four concerts in
Moscow and Leningrad in 1990. The conductor
was the head of the United States' Washington-
based National Symphony Orchestra, Mstislav
Rostropovich, who had returned from twenty-six
years of exile. Raïsa Gorbacheva, the president's
wife attended the first concert, which was broadcast
to a Soviet viewing public of 160 million. Before
the concert, viewers were treated to a twelve-
minute documentary on Procter & Gamble (3)
produced by the Düsseldorf agency from the*
DMB&B *network, which was born in 1985 of the
union between D'Arcy and Benton & Bowles.*

2

3

On the first anniversary of the 11 September 2001 attacks, *Propaganda & Marketing*, the Brazilian advertising journal, asked five agencies to show their feelings. **Neogama**, in which BBH bought a minority share in 2003 thereby creating Neogama BBH São Paulo, used the famous "I love New York" slogan commissioned by the New York State Department of Commerce, and conceived by the graphic artist Milton Glaser in 1976 to promote tourism in the city. The missing legs of the N reflect the void created by the destruction of the World Trade Center's Twin Towers: "They hit the towers, but missed the heart" (4). Since 1966, an Asian advertising and communications congress, AdASIA, has been held at regular intervals by the Asian Federation of Advertising Associations, which spans twelve of the region's countries. The 22nd Congress in November 2001 was the first to be held in Taipei. **D'Arcy** Taiwan took this opportunity to focus on the success of its client, Coca-Cola, and of advertising in general: "Advertising. It's a principle" (5).

4

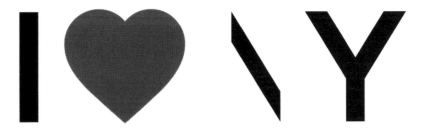

They hit the towers, but missed the heart.

廣告，是硬道理

從 60 年代到公元 2000 年，從人人手中一本紅小書變成人人手中一瓶紅小瓶。今天，每年有超過 10 億瓶的可樂在紅色中國流通，演化成了一個新象徵。人們高舉著它，為的絕不只是其中的碳酸水和焦糖，更多是為了它代表的自由感受、歡樂氣氛、開放精神⋯，讓一罐軟料真正引人入勝的這些感性原料，你認為來自哪裏？
就是廣告。改變人對生活的想像，讓實經及貨反物質的一元化社會過渡到充滿選擇的新世界。一個可樂化的社會主義，只是 20 世紀廣告展現它力量的一個例子！
廣告讓不同的意識形態和文化可以更從容的對話，事實上，有廣告的世界是一個更多元化的世界。最可貴的是，你還大可以選擇不喜歡它，不服從它。
在這個世紀，繼續讓廣告和文明一起成長吧！廣大的消費群界！前進吧！全球的廣告份子！前進吧！
11. 18 ~ 21 2001 年亞洲廣告會議台北大會，讓廣告繼續推動文明，從演進到飛躍！

AdASIA
2001 TAIPEI
www.adasia2001.org.tw

The art of advertising

Advertising and art tend to endlessly mirror one another.
Art borrows brand images and, in return, advertising is happy
to tip a wink to art.

1

Andy Warhol produced a series of pieces on the
theme of the Last Supper in 1986. Principle among
these is the monumental canvas "The Last Supper" (1)
(118 in. by 252 in.). This work was clearly inspired
by Leonardo da Vinci's "Last Supper", and
associates several symbolic elements of consumer
culture with this iconic image. The Unilever soap
brand Dove, the General Electric company logo
and a price ticket all appear. The choice of this
genre, painting of Jesus' last meal with his disciples,
at which communion and betrayal sit side by side,
is no coincidence. And the choice of the name
Dove resonates with the image of a bird, which
Christians associate with the Holy Spirit. This
underscores the artist's view of consumption as
communion. Another work by Andy Warhol, his
famous reproduction of the Campbell's tomato
soup can, achieved the nice price of 34,000 pounds
sterling (more than 50,000 euros) at a New York
auction by Sotheby's in the '80s. In 1984, on the
eve of its one hundredth supermarket opening,
the major British supermarket chain Tesco and
its advertising agency **Saatchi & Saatchi** UK could
not resist telling their customers that 26 pence
could buy them an original (2).

THIS COPY SOLD AT
SOTHEBY'S NEW YORK
RECENTLY
FOR ALMOST £34,000.
YOU CAN
BUY THE ORIGINAL AT
TESCO FOR 26P.

2

The artist Arman, one of the founders of New Realism, used the idea of parking at airports when he christened the 19.5 by 6 metre column he created in 1982 "Long Term Parking" (4). Fifty-nine cars in bright colours were drowned in one thousand six hundred tons of concrete to form this monument to the consumer society, built at the Domaine du Montcel near Paris, formerly home to the contemporary art promoters Fondation Cartier. The two French artists behind the collective IFP (Information Fiction Publicité) (Information Fiction Advertising) used this installation to hold a mirror up to reality. Entitled "Image (fatalement) publique" (Image (inevitably) public) (3), it was installed on the Lombardsbrücke in Hamburg in 1989. In 1990, straight after the Wall had been torn down, Hans Haacke used one of the remaining observation towers on Potsdamerplatz in Berlin as part of the exhibition: "The finite nature of freedom". He fitted a Mercedes-Benz logo on one side, which symbolised the strength of the companies which had begun to rebuild the city. On another side, the artist affixed a quotation from the great Johann Wolfgang von Goethe: "Kunst bleibt Kunst" (Art is always art) (5).

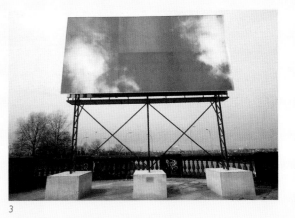

3

4

5

Star signs

The major advertising networks built brands for their clients that were both globally consistent and adapted to national culture. They applied the same principles to their own communications.

1

2

3

D'Arcy Masius Benton & Bowles Advertising. Telephone us today on (09) 520-4499.

4

5

Inspired by a passage in Virgil's Aeneid, "Sic itur ad astra" (book IX, line 641: "Thus to the stars"), **Leo Burnett** adopted a highly evocative graphic for its own launch in 1935. A stylised white hand reaches towards six stars, picked out against a black background. This symbol, created by Walter Dorwin Teague, a friend of Leo Burnett, was used until 1997, when the agency adopted the founder's signature in green ink as a logo. In 2002, the hand and stars graphic made a comeback (1), interpreted differently for different cultures. Among the countries to have their own interpretations were Mexico (2) and Malaysia (3). In 1993, **DMB&B** Auckland (New Zealand) created a poster to fix a rather long name in our minds: D'Arcy, Masius, Benton & Bowles. The agency's initials are written on the musical scale (4). In Brazil, the **Publicis Norton** name had been around since 1996 but in the year 2000 the agency decided it was not sufficiently well-known and ran a campaign to boost recognition. This was planned to coincide with the launch of the network's new global identity, and ensured that the Publicis lion would leave a symbolic pawprint on the Amazon rainforest ("The difference") (5).

Can an advertising agency change the world?

TWENTY FOUR YEARS AGO, two brothers set up an advertising agency in London. All they had was a pencil and a desire to produce a new kind of advertising. One that was based totally on the power of creativity.

This simple philosophy proved very attractive. And on the strength of it, in 1979, Saatchi & Saatchi became the first agency to be appointed by a British political party to mastermind their election campaign.

It was universally acknowledged that the agency played an instrumental role in the election of Margaret Thatcher: the woman who was popularly, yet sometimes grudgingly, held to be responsible for transforming Britain from a sluggish socialist state with moribund industry into a competitive, successful, trading nation.

MANY HAPPY RETURNS.

Saatchi & Saatchi subsequently went on to play a major (pun intended) part in helping the Conservative Party win a record breaking four consecutive elections. This included the election of 1991, when the party went to the polls with the lowest support rating of any incumbent in British history.

Saatchi & Saatchi mounted a campaign to convince the public of the benefits that Conservatism had brought and, in spite of everything, managed to get the Tories re-elected. (We could talk about market research at this point, but that's another advertisement.)

Mrs. Thatcher's success led other political figures, from around the world, to request Saatchi's expertise.

Take Boris Yeltsin. He was the first democratically elected President of

Russia to benefit from the skills of an advertising agency. Borrowing an executive Aeroflot jet to do an intensive, if whistle-stop, research programme Saatchi arrived at the slogan, "A strong leader for a strong Russia". The rest, as they say, is history.

Saatchi & Saatchi was also involved in three crucial events that changed attitudes towards apartheid in South Africa: the 1983 referendum that allowed non-whites to enter into parliament, the 1992 referendum on power sharing and the 1994 fully democratic election. These events without any doubt contributed to a peaceful and successful transition from minority to majority rule in that country.

Success led to more success and we were also called upon to assist in political campaigns in Austria, Greece, Italy, Norway and Poland to name but a few.

SPACE: TICKETS STILL AVAILABLE.

Not all change has to be political.

For instance, fourteen days after the Gulf War the skies were empty; no one was flying. How to get people to change their minds? Saatchi's solution was "The World's Biggest Offer"; 50,000 free trips on British Airways.

The campaign appeared on one day, in 26 languages, in 69 countries and in 290 publications. It was seen by over one billion people and received a world record of over six million responses. (Which just goes to show, the right incentive can have quite an extraordinary effect.)

Or, how do you get the first Briton into space? This time we were giving away seats on the Anglo-Soviet space mission. The advertisement elicited 15,000 applications and yards of news coverage. Several months, and many weightless hours later, Ms. Helen Sharman went into space aboard Soyuz TM12.

Another perhaps even more unlikely partner was the Roman Catholic Church. New Italian tax laws meant the church stood to lose a considerable amount in donations. Working with our Rome office they were able to persuade over half the tax paying public to donate part of their income to the church. (Anywhere else in the world this would have been considered a miracle.)

On a yet more serious note the Clinton Administration wanted to alter people's attitudes towards violent crimes against children. Saatchi developed a campaign featuring the President and a Washington teenager called Alicia Brown. Response was outstanding. In just two months over 30,000 calls were received, three times more than any of the previous commercials.

And when it was all change in Eastern Europe, Saatchi was the first agency over the Berlin Wall, an event which made front page news around the world. We could go on, and indeed will.

ASIA: THE WORLD'S FASTEST GROWING MARKETS.

With Asia's household incomes currently growing 14 times faster than those of the rest of the world, it is not

surprising that we have invested significantly in developing our growing Asian network.

In China for example, where advertising is still in its infancy, we have spent a considerable amount developing the best media buying and planning capabilities.

Where no media information existed, we set up our own systems and quality checks. For instance, there was no media research outside major cities. Saatchi's solution was to set up a group of independent monitors, through the Chinese Disabled People's Association to provide the confirmation that paid-for advertisements actually appeared. It also provided a welcome income for the disabled.

As a result of this and other unique media initiatives, like setting up our own advertising breaks, we are now the largest buyer of media in China. In fact, according to a recent survey in Advertising Age magazine, we have now become the largest agency in this huge market.

Moving into Pakistan, Saatchi & Saatchi worked with the Investment Board to attract funds by communicating the new economic reforms. The campaign attracted a massive 5,000 responses.

As a whole, Saatchi & Saatchi Advertising works with 70 of the top 100 companies in the Fortune 500. That includes five of the world's brand leaders. Selling more goods, to more people, in more places, than any other agency in the world. Gosh.

Even now Saatchi has 19 offices in 12 Asian countries, handling US$409,000,000 in billings for international clients such as: Bayer, British Airways, Cadbury Schweppes, Danone, DHL, Du Pont, Guess?, Hewlett-Packard, Johnson & Johnson, Lexus, Nestle, Procter & Gamble, Qantas, Seiko, Toyota and Whirlpool.

Just as importantly we handle a wide range of locally-based accounts including: Indian Oil Corporation, Tata Tea, Malaysia National Insurance, Philippine National Bank, The Peninsula Group, The Republic of Singapore Navy, Samsung, San Miguel, The Singapore Tourist Promotion Board, Tiger Beer, Wharf Holdings, Wheelock and Xian-Janssen.

IMPOSSIBILITIES BECOME POSSIBILITIES.

Saatchi & Saatchi is also creating a history of changes throughout Asia.

It used to be held that this region was a creative backwater. Not any more. Last year's anti-drink-drive commercial, produced by Saatchi in Singapore, was the first advertisement in history to win every significant creative award in the world (and quite a few insignificant ones to boot). More importantly it helped save a great many lives at the same time.

In Hong Kong they said you couldn't launch a luxury car that wasn't European. We said you could. And we did. The Lexus launch took the car straight to number one, making it Asia's most celebrated car launch ever.

Our media "firsts" are becoming

legendary too. They said you couldn't buy every advertisement in a newspaper. But that's exactly what we did for Panasonic in the Sunday edition of the Straits Times. And very successful it was too, increasing recognition of the brand name by 33%.

"Get Hong Kong magazines to audit? No way." Our independent survey created an uproar, but it persuaded certain media owners to do just that. Now our clients know exactly how many readers they're getting.

In Jakarta there was no control over positions in breaks or within programmes. Not any more. Saatchi persuaded the stations to place Bank Artha Graha's commercials exactly where they wanted them, in order to tell a three part story in one break. Unprecedented, revolutionary and 100% effective.

No wonder we've been voted International Advertising Agency of the year by the IAA for a record breaking four years running.

We refuse point blank to be limited by the norm, the ordinary, the mundane.

Because you can change attitudes, prejudices and sacred cows.

That's why our philosophy is, and always will be: "Nothing is impossible".

Even handing out our business card to 32,000 people in one day.

NOTHING IS IMPOSSIBLE.
SAATCHI & SAATCHI ADVERTISING

"Can an advertising agency change the world?" asks **Saatchi & Saatchi** *Hong Kong in this 1994 advertisement showing its major successes and intended to spread the word about the agency. This British colony was due to be handed back to the People's Republic of China on 1 July 1997. The change in status could have been a cause for concern about an uncertain future. Yet the agency remained optimistic, applying the slogan used by Saatchi & Saatchi the world over: "Nothing is impossible" (6). In 1998,* **Leo Burnett** *Milan was the only member of the Italian Association of Advertising Agencies to obtain ISO 9001 accreditation for its quality management system, issued by DNV (Det Norske Veritas). This success inspired a four-part campaign, encouraging its competitors to follow suit (7). Because it improves the quality of service provided for clients, certification would benefit the overall level of services provided throughout the profession.*

IMITATIONS ARE WELCOME.

So far, only one Assap (Association of Italian Advertising Agencies) Agency has been awarded the ISO 9001 Quality System Certificate: Leo Burnett Italy. We hope that other agencies will follow in our footsteps. Because as the concept of quality spreads, so will clients be ever more able to reap the rewards of creative excellence.

Leo Burnett

Eau dear!

Renewal and continuity. Despite a change of ownership and of agency, Perrier's advertisements remained the same. This continuity was probably one factor in the brand's sparkling success.

2

1

The first reference to the Perrier spring *goes back as far as the time of Hannibal, 218 BC. Closer to the present day, the nineteenth-century doctor Louis Perrier became the first to own the spring, located near Pont-du-Gard in the Languedoc region of France. The doctor created the Société des Eaux et Boissons Hygiéniques de Vergèze, a water and health drink company named after the neighbouring village. A wealthy young Englishman, John Harmsworth, bought the company in 1903 and three years later named the spring after its first owner. The Englishman also invented the slogan "The champagne of bottled waters" and popularised the little bottle which was shaped like the Indian clubs he used for his physical therapy. Perrier became the number one natural sparkling mineral water in the world. Although it had been launched by an Englishman, it was hard to sell any French mineral water in the United Kingdom of the '70s. Britain had its own health spa tradition and its own bottled waters and it was in this context that* **Leo Burnett** *UK won the account for this brand's advertising in 1974.*

3

Leo Burnett's campaign employs all the puns it can muster on the French word "eau" (water). In 1978, "Eau-la-la." bubbled up like a throaty laugh (1). In 1979 the tone was scientific, with "H$_2$ Eau." (2). In 1982, the advertisements turned cubist with "Picasseau." as photographed by John Turner (3). **Publicis** London then took over the series when Perrier entered the Nestlé fold in 1992. The same ingredients were used – the word 'eau', a gallon of humour and a splash of sophistication. They were transformed into "Aphreaudisiac" in 1996 (4) (that's what they say about oysters) and "Heaume James" (5) (that's what you say to your chauffeur). The first advertisement was photographed by Adrian Burke, the second by Paul Bevitt. As official supplier to the Wimbledon tennis tournament, Perrier greeted the beginning of the fortnight on 21 June 1998 with a special advertisement: "Wimbubbledon". Eau dear!

4

5

Coca-Cola. A legend refreshed

By the late 20th century, after trying to build highly homogenous images across the world using identical communications, many major advertisers began to attach more importance to specific national characteristics.

2

1

3

For the Moscow Olympics in 1980, *Coca-Cola designed a can with the brand logo in Cyrillic script (2). The cans, made in Baltimore, were intended for the Olympic Village but never reached their destination. US President Jimmy Carter decided to boycott the Games and, with the United States' athletes missing, the sponsors also withdrew. In the '90s, the Atlanta company decided that the cola brand should emphasise its closeness to the customer in a stronger way and avoid becoming a somewhat distant international icon. This meant advertisements designed for the United States would have to be adapted to reflect other national realities. Different advertisements might even need to be created. It was at this point that* **Publicis** *began working with Coca-Cola and took responsibility for brand communications across almost twenty European countries. These two 1996 posters were locally created by* **Publicis** *Poland for the Atlanta Olympics (1) and by* **D'Arcy** *Poland (3). Publicis also worked on international communications for Diet Coke and caffeine-free Diet Coke.*

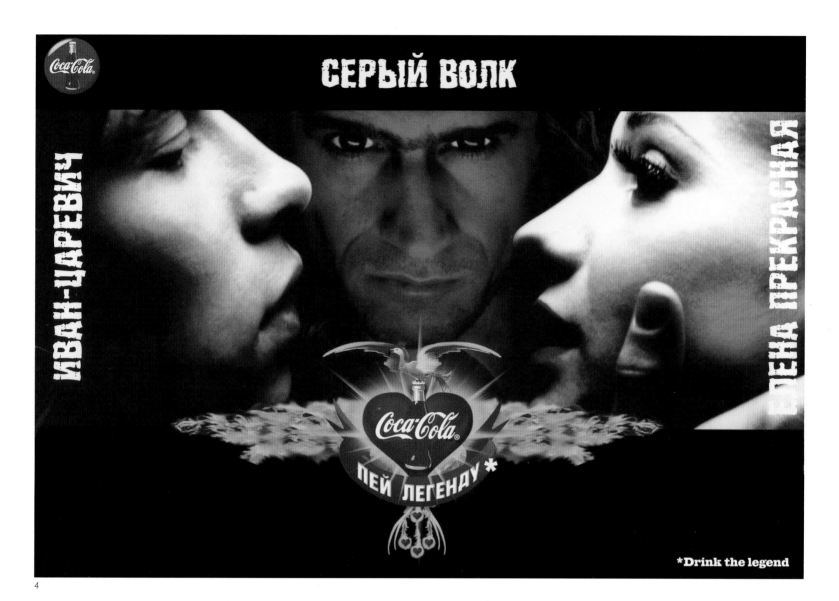

СЕРЫЙ ВОЛК

ИВАН-ЦАРЕВИЧ

ЕЛЕНА ПРЕКРАСНАЯ

Coca-Cola

ПЕЙ ЛЕГЕНДУ*

*Drink the legend

4

In Russia more than anywhere else, Coca-Cola wanted to get closer to its customers. On 1 January 1997, Russian television viewers discovered an advertisement that left them astonished and deeply moved: Ivan sets off to chase the firebird which plucked the golden apples from a garden belonging to his father, the Tsar. Everyone could recognise the story of the popular folk tale "The Firebird". Four more advertisements followed: viewers witnessed the hero confronting his two brothers, Dimitri and Vassili, meeting the Grey wolf and then discovering the Horse with the golden mane, before finally falling hopelessly in love with the lovely Elena (5). These films were produced in Moscow by Paul Weiland and set to music from Craig Armstrong. They were trailed with posters inviting the public to "Drink the legend" (4). This campaign was the result of close collaboration between **Publicis'** Russian and British teams. It took an essential feature from the Russian cultural landscape and handled it in a contemporary way.

5

A tale of two tastes

A Dutch beer with a light lager flavour that's popular the world over and an English beer with a distinctly bitter taste: two distinctive approaches to marketing and communications.

1

2

In 1864, the twenty-two-year-old Gerard Adriaan Heineken bought "The Haystack" (De Hooiberg), a prestigious brewery in the heart of Amsterdam. The beer that now bears his name is a "lager" (from the German "lagern", to store), which undergoes a secondary fermentation stage at low temperatures and a period of cold storage. From the '80s onwards, Heineken used modern techniques to guarantee beer of consistent quality which travelled well. Yet for some of the markets, the beer was produced in-situ rather than imported. Heineken began working with **Publicis** in France in 1976; the agency launched the "spirit of beer" theme in the late 1990s. This 2003 advert by Blaise Arnold illustrates that theme (1). In 2005, Publicis launched the "For a fresher world" campaign, illustrated here with an advertisement by Bruno Contesse (3). In 2002, the agency began working with Heineken in the United States; it retained D'Arcy's signature creation for Heineken, "It's all about the beer" and in 2004, David Shane made a commercial along those very same lines (2). A man finds that the best way of drinking his beer in peace is to tell the sleeping woman lying alongside him "I love you". She cosies up to him, and he can finally bend his arm to drink!

3

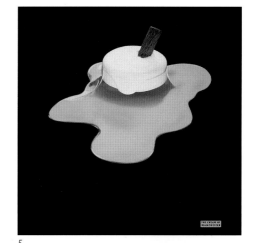

5

BODDINGTONS. THE CREAM OF MANCHESTER.
Boddingtons Draught Bitter. Brewed at the Strangeways Brewery since 1778.

4

Boddingtons in Manchester has been brewing beer since 1778. This "bitter" is a beer that is made from malt, with the addition of hops to give it a certain 'bitterness' and fine water from wells 200 feet underground. Bitter is normally stronger in terms of colour and taste than lager. In 1989, this local brewery was bought by Whitbread, a major brewing company. In 1991, the latter turned to **BBH** London who launched the nation-wide campaign 'The Cream of Manchester'. BBH was founded in 1982 by John Bartle, Nigel Bogle and John Hegarty. In 1997 BBH entered into an equity-based partnership with Leo Burnett who acquired a significant minority stake in the agency. In 2002 Leo Burnett became part of the Publicis Groupe. A national magazine advertising campaign began in 1992 (4), (6), with photographs by Tif Hunter. The glamorous Melanie Sykes appeared on television in 1996, serving a creamy pint yet announcing cheekily, in a broad Manchester accent 'Ere Tarquin, are your trollies on the wrong way round?' ('trollies' being colloquial Mancunian for boxer shorts). The campaign became so readily identifiable with the brand that subsequent executions ran without the Boddingtons logo. The black, gold and cream were enough to symbolise the brand, as in David Gill's example shown here (5). In three years, sales tripled and Boddingtons became Britain's favourite bitter. In 2000, Whitbread sold its beer business to the Belgian company Interbrew.

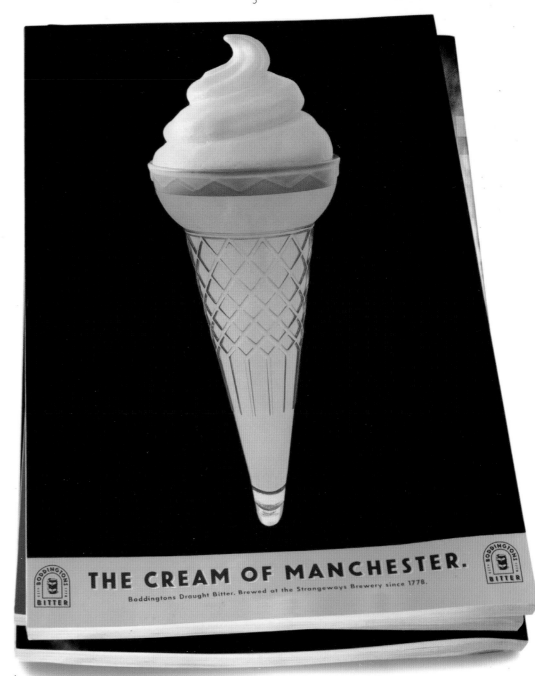

THE CREAM OF MANCHESTER.
Boddingtons Draught Bitter. Brewed at the Strangeways Brewery since 1778.

6

Down under style

The end goal of all beer communication is to appeal to people's taste for, and enjoyment of, beer. It's the advertisers job to find a style of communication which is unique to the brand: that's what makes all the difference.

1

Three British brewers joined forces in 1961 to form Allied Breweries. In 1984, Allied planned to launch Castlemaine XXXX, one of the "light bitters" that are popular in Australia. **Saatchi & Saatchi** UK won the advertising account, and drew on the stereotype of an 'Aussie' as a rough diamond with a great fondness for beer. The first of the six commercials was filmed in Australia for the launch, with Australian actors and an Australian director, and tells the story of two rugged types on an isolated farm (2). One is ill, and the flying doctor has said, by radio to give him a cold drink, the coolest thing in the house. All that's left in the fridge is a can of XXXX. When the anguished patient asks his companion what the doctor said, he replies that he's gonna get 'real bad'. The companion then drinks the beer. The launch was also accompanied by 48 sheet posters on a single theme "The Australians wouldn't give a XXXX for anything else" (1). Allied Breweries ended up leaving its brewing activities behind and united with the Spanish company Pedro Domecq in 1994, forming Allied Domecq, which specialises in wines and spirits. The XXXX brand went to Interbrew in 2003.

2

Two New Zealand companies merged in 1988 to become Lion Nathan. These were LD Nathan & Co and Lion Breweries (one of Auckland's oldest breweries, dating from the mid-19th century). Lion had created the Steinlager brand in 1958 in response to the threat of an import ban on foreign beers. Initially called Steinecker, the beer was renamed Steinlager in 1962 and found a warm welcome on its home turf. From 1973 onwards, Steinlager set off for new pastures in the guise of several foreign markets. **Saatchi & Saatchi** New Zealand was responsible for advertising the 'Steinie' brand. In 2001, they created a campaign using photographs by Eryk Fitkau: "A crisp clean bite" (3), (4). This expression is usually used to describe strong spirits like vodka, and coupled with the equally strong image of an aggressive 'biting' bottle top, the campaign gave Steinlager a distinctive personality in the world of beer.

3

4

Ed, Frank and Johnnie

*Advertising can sometimes give a brand exactly what it may have lacked.
It can give a new product roots in tradition or give an age-old product
a novel image.*

Some products are just like this. Very successful, but only for a short time. Sitting somewhere between a punch and a sangria, the refreshing "wine cooler" drink was one of these products. It came into fashion in the United States in the '80s on the back of the overproduction of grapes which had occurred in the '70s. Around 461 million litres of wine coolers were consumed there in 1987. When it came to selling its Bartles & Jaymes Wine Cooler in 1986, Ernest & Julio Gallo Winery, one of the major producers, turned to **Hal Riney & Partners**, a San Francisco agency which had just opened its doors and would join forces with **Publicis** in 1998. The agency invented the story of Frank Bartles and Ed Jaymes, which played out over four commercials directed by Joe Pytka. In the first one (1), they introduce themselves: "Hello there. My name is Frank Bartles, and this is Ed Jaymes. You know, it occurred to Ed the other day that between his fruit orchard and my premium wine vineyard, we could make a truly superior, premium grade wine cooler. It sounded good to me, so Ed took a second mortgage on his house (...). Thank you very much for your support." In the second (2), Frank is holding a bottle and addresses the viewer again. "Hello again. (...) We have selected a bottle for our new premium wine cooler, and we were about to print up a label when Ed drew my attention to the fact that we did not have a name for our product. (...) So if you have any good ideas for a wine cooler name, we'd really appreciate your sending them along. Thank you again for your support. "By the third commercial (3), they have received answers. "We want to thank you for all the name suggestions for our new wine cooler. There were some really clever ones. But we decided just to call it 'The Bartles and Jaymes Wine Cooler' because my name is Bartles and Ed's is Jaymes. If you don't like the name, please don't tell us because we have already printed up our labels. Anyway, you could always just call it Bartles and skip the Jaymes all together. Ed says that is okay with him. Thanks for your continued support." The fourth instalment informs the viewer: "Well, the new Bartles and Jaymes premium wine cooler is finally in the bottle (...). Please, buy some, because frankly from our point of view there's no other wine cooler anywhere that's nearly as good at any price. It would also be a personal favour to Ed, because he took out that second mortgage on his house and pretty soon he's got a big balloon payment coming up. Thank you (...)."

1

2

3

IMPOSSIBLE

4

KEEP WALKING™

JOHNNIE WALKER.

5

John Walker opened a grocery shop in Kilmarnock, Scotland in 1820 and created a very popular blend of malt and grain whisky. Tom Browne, the cartoonist, created Johnnie, the Striding Man, for the brand in 1909. This was also the year when Red and Black Labels were created. Johnnie was a constant source of inspiration for publicity. This was certainly the case when, in 1999, to rekindle consumers' interest and consolidate the brand's leadership position, **BBH** London created the "Keep walking" campaign. The commercial shows countless humanoid creatures swimming in the sea (6). Then, as if skipping an evolutionary step, one of these sea creatures approaches the shore, stops swimming, starts walking and leaves the sea behind. This commercial, filmed in 2002 by Daniel Kleinman, was accompanied by a print campaign on the same 'progress' theme. It has run all over the world and includes these examples of 2002 (5) and 2004 (4). At 120 million bottles a year, Johnnie Walker is one of the best-selling whiskies in the world. Some products are just like that. They are successful straight away and, with a little help from great communications, they stay that way.

6

Truth in disguise

How to say what can't be said? Brand communications for some alcoholic beverages build up whole worlds of poetic imagery, characterising these products with a fundamental, intrinsic truth.

1

Take two coffee liqueurs promoted by **Publicis Dialog**. First, there was the British brand Tia Maria: the agency constructed a feminine, enigmatic and deceptively soft image for the liqueur in this advertisement from illustrator Andy Dymock (1). Second, for the US brand Kahlúa –which uses Mexican coffee beans– the agency emphasised the drink's power to transport its drinker with the slogan "The everyday exotic". A commercial (2) filmed in South Africa by Christian Loubek illustrates the drink's exotic promise but with a humorous twist: a giraffe passes tools to a worker who's climbed a pylon, a woman walks round town with an alligator on a lead and a tiger plays the part of a pet. This exoticism stands in stark contrast to the visuals for the vodka account won by **Publicis** New York. In Simon Harsent's campaign, the bottle of Stolichnaya, a truly strong alcohol, dominates a frosty scene. After all, vodka is "best chilled", as the red stamp suggests (3). All three campaigns date from 2004 and the brands are from the stable of the Allied Domecq Group, today part of the Pernod Ricard Group.

2

3

The world's restaurant

McDonald's leadership position was won with a series of great ideas impeccably executed, ranging from the McDonald's burger recipe to the variety of menus, or from the franchising system to the delivery service. And, last but not least, enduring communications.

1

The McDonald brothers opened a small restaurant in 1937 in San Bernardino that offered only hamburgers, French fries and drinks. It was quick and cheap to eat there and, from 1948 onwards, you could buy a meal without leaving your car. This establishment attracted the attention of one Ray Kroc, interested in who had bought eight 'Multimixers' from him, each of which was able to prepare six milkshakes at once. Kroc saw that the efficiency of the organisation was an excellent means of selling his machines and imagined furthering this formula across a chain of franchises. In 1955, he opened the first McDonald's in Des Plaines, Illinois, and in 1960 he bought the company from the brothers. This was the beginning of a meteoric rise: four years later, McDonald's counted 100 restaurants and, in 1967, the company began its international expansion. Ronald McDonald, created in 1963, soon became one of the most famous brand icons (3). In 1980, **Leo Burnett** was assigned the advertising for McDonald's in Europe and, in 1982, in the United States. **Leo Burnett** Mumbai created this advertisement for home delivery service in 2004, photography by Sanjeev Angne (2). In 2005, in Japan, **Beacon Communications** rekindled young adults' interest for the brand by introducing the McGrand, photography by Akira Sakamoto (1).

2

3

HOME DELIVERY CALL 1600-22-00-99

Specials of the day

McDonald's global expansion goes hand in hand with an exceptional diversification of their products. Besides the original hamburger, the brand develops a long list of other products and services to answer today's new ways of living and eating.

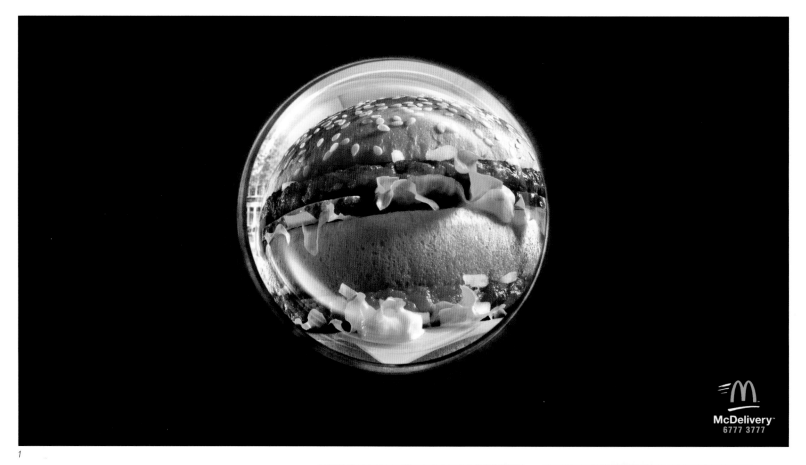

1

McDonald's is synonymous with an informal and inexpensive way of eating, as this commercial directed in 2001 by Kwanghyun Park for **Leo Burnett** Korea shows (2). Two young men are seated at the back of a bus: a larger one who is asleep holding a carton of french fries, a small one who would very much like to take one. When at last he succeeds in doing so, the bus brakes, the larger one bends forward and the french fries fall. The larger one wakes up and stares angrily at the empty carton and then at the small one who shamefacedly handles a fry. A voice concludes: "Don't risk your life. McDonald's now offers tasty fries at only 500 won!" The brand also engages new services, such as home delivery. In most Southeast Asian countries, this was left to each individual restaurant. From 2005, a single call centre was put in place in each market. **Leo Burnett** Singapore was assigned the re-launch of this upgraded service (1).

2

3

As McDonald's prospered all over the world, some restaurant openings became genuine symbols, like the one in Moscow, close to Pouchkine square, on 31 January 1990 or, the same year, the one in Beijing. The company also paid attention to certain categories of customers who were previously neglected and, to do so, it called **Burrell**. This agency, created in 1971 in Chicago by Thomas J. Burrell to reach out to African-Americans, created the first commercial of the brand specially geared towards this clientele in 1978. McDonald's constantly launched innovative products: the Big Mac was created in 1968, the Happy Meal in 1979, followed by the McMorning. Moreover, the brand addressed nutritional preoccupations by including salads in its range. In 2005, Jeb Milne directed for Burrell a commercial about the new fruit and walnut salad (3). A young African-American woman is heading to a backyard garden where three female friends are having a very animated conversation. When one sees the three women on the screen, they appear as 3-D characters —animated! From this, the four friends start chatting about the nutritional values of the new recipe. In 2005, again in the US, **Leo Burnett** presented the creaminess of the new McDonald's milkshake in a very spectacular way: "Triple thick milkshakes" (4). The poster carried the global brand signature launched in the beginning of 2003: "I'm lovin' it".

4

Restaurants of distinction

Some contenders will always challenge the market leader's position head on.
These challengers, however, highlighted variations of their recipes based
on local cuisine or competitive position.

1

2

3

Miami, Florida, *was where James McLamore*
and David Edgerton created Burger King in 1954
and where they launched their landmark
Whopper in 1957. Their first "drive-thru" was
opened in 1975. As early as 1967, the company
had been sold to Pillsbury, based in Minneapolis.
Pillsbury was later sold to a British conglomerate,
which became Diageo in 1997 after a merger
with Guinness. Diageo sold Burger King in 2002,
and it is now controlled by a private American
consortium. Burger King's 11,000 establishments
are now spread across over 60 different
markets. The chain moved into Asia in 1982
and developed various recipes designed to please
the palates of their potential new customers.
Saatchi & Saatchi *Singapore ran a campaign in*
1998 –this sample was photographed by
Shaun Pettigrew (4). A short while later, the
Burger King logo was redesigned and the slogan
changed to: "It just tastes better" (2). In 2002,
the agency conducted another campaign. This
poster, highlighting the 'gerkin', with an
illustration by Weng Foong, was part of the
campaign displayed in Burger King restaurants (1)
and, in 2003, Edward Loh cleverly photographed
a pepper mill to encapsulate the latest
burger recipe (3).

Fiery Fries. BURGER KING

4

Dave Thomas opened his first restaurant in 1969 in Columbus, Ohio: it was called Wendy's Old Fashioned Hamburgers. By February 1985, the chain had three thousand restaurants across the United States and in fourteen other countries. Although the quality of its burgers was excellent, public perception of the brand image had not always been so great. In 1980, **Dancer Fitzgerald Sample** was appointed to take charge of advertising; they believed the problem lay with the company's flagship product, the Single. Its name conjured up an image of a less generous portion than those of its competitors. But Dave Thomas noticed that the competition was mainly generous with bread buns, much less so with meat. From this contrast emerged a commercial produced by Joe Sedelmaïer in 1984. Three rather prim old ladies are in an imaginary fast-food restaurant, the Home of the Big Bun. One lady, played by Clara Peler, peels apart two halves of a huge bun and asks: "But where's the beef?" (5) The media budget for the commercial was tiny —eight million dollars, barely a tenth of the budgets employed by some of its big competitors— yet it enjoyed considerable success and the slogan became a popular American expression.

5

Slow is also good

Thirty years' success attests to two things. First, that the company is acutely aware of the product's selling points and value for the consumer. Second, that this awareness has been used skilfully in the company's communications.

1

In 1869, twenty five year-old Henry John Heinz of Pittsburgh, Pennsylvania, founded the company which bears his name. Its first products were pickles packed in transparent glass jars to show the quality of the product. Ketchup was added in 1876 and over time numerous other pickles were added to the range. In 1896, in order to promote his range, Heinz launched the celebrated slogan "57 varieties". The brand had many more varieties but this particular phrase pleased him the most. In the 1970s, this quality brand had to face a stagnant market and cheaper competitors and so Heinz decided to award its advertising to **Leo Burnett** USA in 1974. In 1983, the squeezable plastic bottle is launched, besides the glass one. The brand turned to young people in oder to sustain its appeal. In 1999, the advertising agency launched "Ketchup with Karisma" bottles, a.k.a. "Heinz Talking Labels" or "Say Something Ketchuppy". The label texts supply a youthful riot of colourful language (1), (2), (3).

2

3

By hook or by cook

It's not every day that a fisherman gets to fight a bear or that workers stand and sing the national anthem. But the tall stories concocted in advertising tell important truths about products. And advertising uses humour partly to keep the bears and the workers sweet.

nothing but fish

1

Emergency! When John West turned to Leo Burnett UK for its advertising, sales had already dropped significantly and the brand's position on the supermarket shelves was under threat. John West had been producing excellent tinned fish for more than one hundred years. Lifestyles were changing and tinned fish seemed less attractive when fresh or frozen fish was also readily available. The brand needed to capture the public's imagination, and quickly! The "Nothing but Fish" poster, which appeared in 2000 with photography by Andy Roberts, is a brilliant expression of the idea that this product stays as fresh as the day it was caught (1). The commercial produced by Daniel Kleinman in 2001 went one step further towards making an impression. It shows a fisherman in a kung-fu fight with a grizzly bear: the fisherman wants to steal the animal's salmon, so he fights for dear life, and ultimately wins (2). This hilarious film was forwarded all around the world by email. Sales rose by more than 23% over the previous year, and John West's market share reached 72%.

2

The Le Creuset story begins with 14th century cannon balls and continues into cookware. The brand entered the UK market in the '60s and, in 1989, Le Creuset distributor Kitchenware Merchants asked **Saatchi & Saatchi** UK to advertise it. The aim was to attract a new customer base by emphasising the authenticity of this cult brand. In 1990, the agency produced a series of illustrated black and white advertisements showing Le Creuset employees at work. The photographs were taken by Sebastião Salgado, a Brazilian artist renowned for this type of work. The campaign presented the manufacturing process as if it were a recipe: "French country cooking: can't you just smell it?", "Our speciality: pot au feu", "Casserole Provencale" (4). In 1991, Saatchi & Saatchi made a commercial featuring the factory workers singing the French national anthem. They are standing up, accompanied initially by a small village orchestra, then by an impressive army of musicians. An orange screen, symbolising the brand, is interspersed between the black and white shots in time with the music (3).

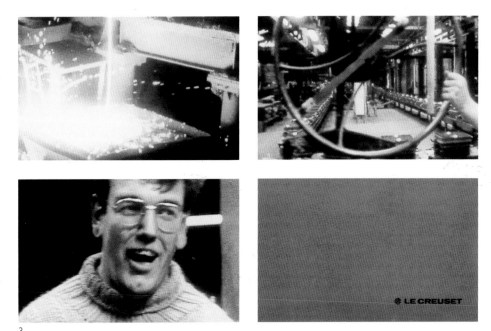

3

4

CASSEROLE PROVENCALE:

8 lbs Pig Iron,
2 lbs Sand,
2 lbs Coke,
1 lb Enamel.

Cook in factory for 30 mins at 800°C (or Gas Mark 24). Glaze, then enamel. Re-heat. Leave for three days. Serve.

@ LE CREUSET

Welcome to Altoidia

Altoidia is a country where the mints are curiously strong. The advertisements are in dubious taste, but –curiously– they are another of the country's strengths.

1

PARENTAL GUIDANCE ADVISED.

THE CURIOUSLY STRONG MINTS

2

In the very early part of the 19th century, during the reign of George III, Smith & Company of London invented mint lozenges for the relief of intestinal discomfort. They called these mints Altoids and by the end of the '20s they were being touted as an antidote to stomach upsets. This was when the slogan: "The mint with the curiously strong taste" first appeared on the packaging. The mints had previously been sold in cardboard packets but were now being sold in tins. The slogan really took off when it was promoted by **Leo Burnett** USA, who began advertising the brand in 1995 (4). The agency took the "curiously strong" idea and applied the theme to all the brand's communications. In 1999, the advertisements harked back to the mints' original medical claims (5), (6). That same year, a new Altoids Wintergreen variety was launched (containing a mixture of oil of wintergreen, extracted from gaultheria, and oils from other ericaceous plants such as the blueberry) (1), (7). The brand was relaunched in 2003 (3). **Leo Burnett** Toronto continued very much in the off-beat spirit, as this 2001 advertisement shows (2). Tony D'Orio, who was the photographer for many of these advertisements, created a deliciously nostalgic '50s aesthetic.

ALTOIDS WINTERGREEN

THE CURIOUSLY STRONG MINTS

curious? altoids.com

3

'NICE ALTOIDS'
THE CURIOUSLY STRONG MINTS

4

PLEASURE
IN PAIN
THE CURIOUSLY STRONG MINTS

5

NOW THIS
WON'T HURT A BIT.
THE CURIOUSLY STRONG MINTS

6

THEY APPEAR
TO BE DIVIDING!
THE CURIOUSLY STRONG MINTS

7

Steamy ice cream

We all know that people eat ice cream for pleasure.
The challenge was to take this pleasure motivation to its ultimate
extreme and make an empty ice cream tub synonymous
with the satisfaction of desire.

2

1

The small family ice cream business based in the Bronx had already been created a long time ago, when the son, Reuben Mattus, invented the Häagen Dazs brand in 1961. The logo and Scandinavian-sounding name conjured up an aura of mystery. The company was sold to Pillsbury in 1983 and, in 1990, turned to **BBH** London for its advertising. The agency created the "Dedicated to pleasure" campaign which rapidly became famous across the globe. The communication uses a very sophisticated code so that it is clear what sort of people it talks to —smart adults who grasp the understated comparison between two people's sensuality and the pleasure of sharing a top-of-the-range ice cream (2). The photographs for these advertisements were taken by Barry Lategan, Nadav Kander (1) and other well known names in photography.

3

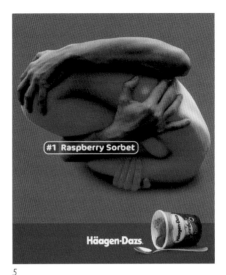

#1 Raspberry Sorbet

Häagen-Dazs

5

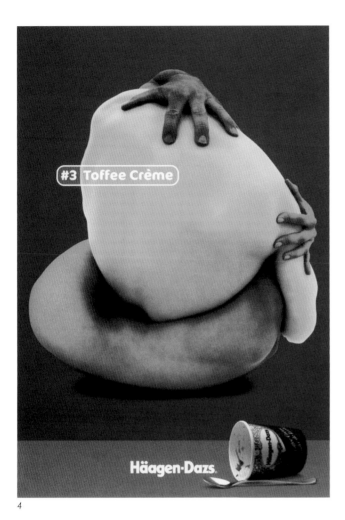

#3 Toffee Crème

Häagen-Dazs

4

In 1995, Chris Palmer made, also for BBH, a steamy commercial in which ice cream becomes a lovers' toy. The scene is portrayed in a highly sophisticated way, filmed with a thermal imaging device so the hottest areas appear in red (3). Sales rose dramatically! Five years later, several thousand miles away, Häagen-Dazs was still managing to send a shiver down the spine. In Australia in 2000, **Leo Burnett** Melbourne was in charge of brand communications. Its mission was to launch individual Häagen-Dazs tubs, at a very expensive eight Australian dollars, onto a market already full of apparently similar products. The campaign targeted the young trendsetting urban adults and it took up where the landmark BBH campaign had left off. It featured each of the ice cream's flavours: toffee crème (4), raspberry sorbet (5) and cookies and cream (6). The photography was by Howard Schatz.

#8 Cookies & Cream

Häagen-Dazs

6

Four arguments and a coffee

Developments had made filter coffee-making equipment easier to use and the emergence of ground coffee had thus begun to erode the advantages of instant. But convenience is not the only reason why people drink coffee.

1

Instant is still real coffee *and there were two arguments you can use to remind people of this. The first is to emphasise where the coffee comes from, which was the approach taken by* **Publicis** *Paris, in 1981, when it created a campaign around the South American origins of Nescafé, Nestlé's instant coffee brand. The commercial was directed by Alain Franchet and showed a train passing through the Andean Altiplano in South America, to the soundtrack of "La Colegiala", a song the crew had discovered while they were filming on location (2). The same spirit imbued this 1989 poster which suggests that the brand's varieties allow consumers freedom of choice: "Destination freedom" (1). The second approach is to allow consumers to recognise the product's inherent value themselves (3). This was the argument* **Leo Burnett** *USA used to promote Taster's Choice in 1971, which had been launched in the United States in 1965. In this case, the quality lay not in the coffee's origins but in the process of lyophilisation, a new way of keeping more of the coffee's original flavour.*

2

3

In Australia, a third argument was developed by **Publicis Mojo** Sydney. In 2004, they picked out a quality commonly associated with coffee, namely the kick-start people need to start their day. With this in mind, Alister Clarke's photo (5) showed drivers how empty the motorway could be if only, somehow, they could persuade themselves to get up early. This was how the consumer could benefit from Blend 43, part of Nescafé's Australian product range. The fourth and final argument is based on another property of coffee, facilitating social interaction. Drinking coffee is associated with being open to others, listening and exchanging information. "Open Up", created by **Publicis**, became the theme of the brand's communications the world over, and was even used as inspiration for internal corporate communications. The challenge to open up, which was thrown down in a new song written specially, was illustrated in 1997 by Paul Arden in a series of scenarios (4) where unexpected meetings take place around a cup of Nescafé. If it weren't for the coffee, these people would never have met.

4

5

The first cut

Saatchi & Saatchi UK created a campaign for Silk Cut cigarettes, which began in 1984 with a visual enigma. This took the form of a photograph by Graham Ford (1). A commercial followed in 1985, inspired by the curtain Christo had installed across a valley in Colorado, USA, in 1972. This was just the beginning of a long series of intertextual references to the art world (2).

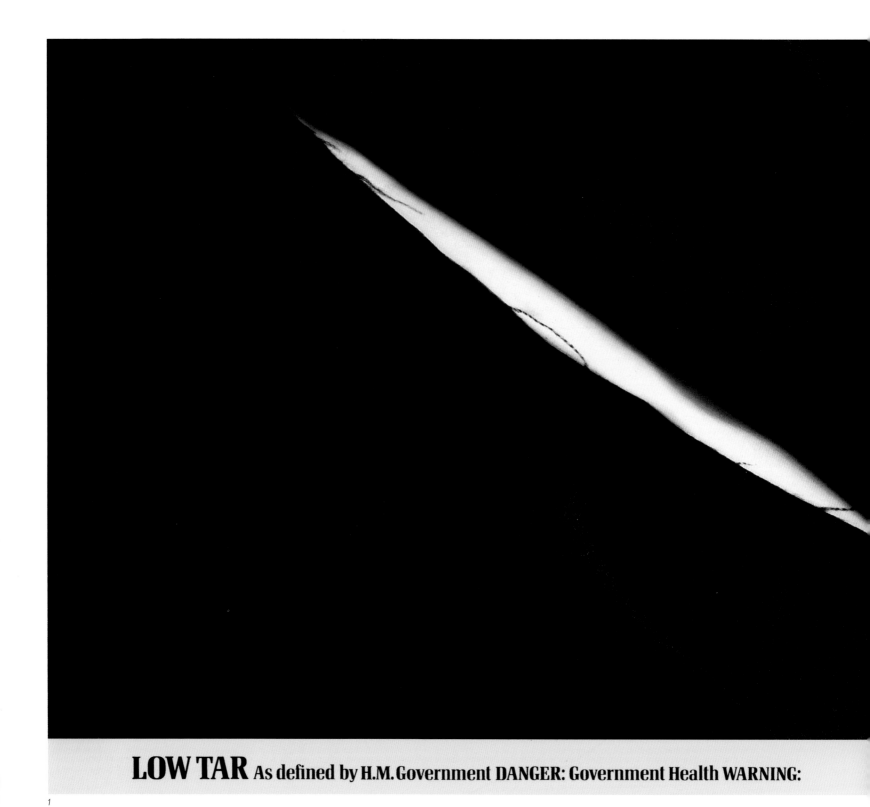

LOW TAR As defined by H.M. Government **DANGER**: Government Health **WARNING**:

1

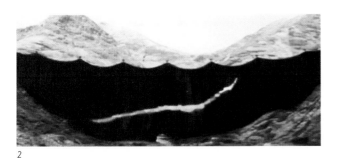

2

CIGARETTES CAN SERIOUSLY DAMAGE YOUR HEALTH

Variations on a theme

Once the concept had been established, the agency rang the changes and played with its audience, throwing in references to the worlds of fine arts, cinema and literature.

2

1

Silk Cut was launched by cigarette manufacturer Gallagher in the United Kingdom in 1964. It was intended as an especially low-tar product, with a name to match. When **Saatchi & Saatchi** UK began to advertise for the brand in 1983, its image was good but sales were down slightly. The agency decided to turn its back on the strategy to date, which prioritised the rational, low-tar argument. It chose instead to turn the brand into a very '80s lifestyle icon —urban, cutting-edge— with appropriately sophisticated, slightly cryptic communications. The campaign was launched in June 1984. Sales of Silk Cut doubled, and in 1992 it was the second-biggest British cigarette brand. This was quite an achievement in an overall declining market. Supreme elegance: the brand name and the pack disappeared from the advertisements. One serious indicator of the Silk Cut advertisements' success was a literary mention, in 1988, courtesy of David Lodge in "Nice Work".

3

A "shrink's" delight! *The Silk Cut campaign opened with the famous rip in a piece of purple silk, cutting like a wound through soft skin. Once the code had been established, it was no longer necessary to reproduce all the symbols to conjure up the brand image. Thus in 1992 a rhinoceros' horn tears the silk, photo by Tyen (2) but, in 1991, the rip is no longer visible, it is merely suggested by the ominous, hovering presence of the iron, inspired by Man Ray, photo by Daniel Jouanneau (3). In 1993, scissors, photographed by François Gillet, created the same effect (1). To the delight of semioticians, sometimes the threat of a tear is itself represented figuratively, by the reference to a thriller such as Hitchcock's "Psycho", photo by Graham Ford (5) or "Dial M for Murder", photo by Barney Edwards (4). It is important to remember that this campaign was dreamt up when cigarette advertising was severely restricted. So Silk Cut also delighted advertising regulators!*

4

LOW TAR As defined by H.M. Government **Warning: SMOKING CAN CAUSE FATAL DISEASES** Health Departments' Chief Medical Officers

5

For love of money

The need to send money to friends or family is growing in line with people's mobility. At the same time, the pressures of economic life have lent immense value to the small pleasures in our private lives.

1

In 1851, a group of businessmen from Rochester, established the New York and Mississippi Valley Printing Telegraph Company which, five years later, would become the Western Union Telegraph Company. Originally created to send messages from one side of the USA to the other, in 1871 the company launched the Western Union Money Transfer, which would become its speciality. After 150 years in business, the company was present in over 140 countries and had 100,000 agents worldwide. In 2003, **Publicis Ambience**, the Indian agency created in 1987 by Ashok Kurien and Elsie Nanji, used figures such as Abraham Lincoln to express the idea of transferring money. Lincoln grasps the banknote for dear life, suggesting to us that it is moving at top speed (1). In 2004, the agency depicted this notion once again by playing on the similarity between two national flags (2).

POLAND

MONACO

2

The roots of Citigroup, of which Citibank is now part, are not only long-established but also very varied. The main financial establishments behind the group were from the United States, but establishments from other countries like Poland or Mexico also contributed. Most of these joined less than a decade ago. Traditionally, many were more focussed on business than private customers. This all meant that when Citibank turned to **Fallon** for its advertising in 2000, the brand's attractiveness had not kept pace with the bank's strength. The advertising had to be created in a difficult context: after years of growth, stemming from the boom in Internet startups, business on the stock exchange was sluggish. The target audience comprised people seeking balance in their lives (4) and a 2001 commercial expresses the same idea, showing a child who is being spun round by his father (3).

3

4

Smart animals

In many commercials, animals talk and behave like human beings. However, there are more interesting and effective ways to explore the potential of animals to its fullest.

The founders of DHL were named Dalsey, Hillblom and Lynn. In 1969, they transported via airplane the bills of lading for ships connecting the two harbours of San Francisco and Honolulu, a service which eased custom procedures and saved time and money. By the end of the '70s, besides mail, DHL also started to carry small parcels. Later, the carrier assigned its advertising in Australia to **Saatchi & Saatchi** Sydney and, in 1991, the agency aired a first commercial. A facetious parakeet, tired of being terrorised by the cat of the house, pressed the keys of a telephone set and ordered DHL to ship the cat to Africa (1). In 1992, came the cat's revenge. He stuck a DHL pick-up label for Siberia on the parakeet's cage (2). Finally, in 1993, the bird opens a big box that DHL has just delivered. An enormous dog jumps out and the cat runs away –a perfect, cartoon-style chase sequence. The parakeet lands on his new friend's head, the dog who triumphed over the cat (3). Derek Hughes directed all three commercials. In 2002, Deutsche Post World Net would acquire the company.

4

5

American Family Life Assurance Company, founded in Columbus, Georgia, in 1955 and a leading insurer, decided to go by the acronym, Aflac, in 1989. Ten years later, their advertising is assigned to **The Kaplan Thaler Group**, created in 1997. The agency finds a straightforward and brilliant solution to make this name, Aflac, known, rapidly increasing its awareness among the public. To the agency's team, the word Aflac sounded like a duck quacking —and thus the idea was born! In the first commercial, aired on 31 December 1999, two businessmen having lunch in a park, discuss how supplemental insurance helped manage finances when one got hurt and missed work. The other asks: "Supplemental insurance? What's that?" A duck in a pond nearby answers "Aflac!" Since the two men do not seem to hear, the duck keeps quacking vociferously. This hilarious character would be the hero of more than twenty commercials, including a spot where the duck offers advice to Father Christmas blocked in a chimney (4), another where the duck pays the bills for somebody who cannot move because of a broken leg (6) and another one where the duck and a seductive young woman swap their personalities (7). The animal becomes the company's genuine icon and is given a place in the brand logo (5). Today, Aflac counts 40 million clients worldwide and is the number one foreign insurance company in Japan.

6

7

Life is but a dream

Today, as yesterday, games of chance evoke the hope of an unexpected win. But we now have electronic means of pursuing our dreams.

1

"If real life was this exciting you wouldn't need a Sony Home Theatre": this commercial aptly illustrates its own slogan. It was shot by Josh Frizzell in Bollywood in 2000 on behalf of **Saatchi & Saatchi** Singapore and used in many countries, notably India (1). A busy executive from Mumbai is going home after a hard day's work. On his way across town, he witnesses a series of strange events, worthy of a spectacular action film. A Sony-Ericsson joint venture, established in 2001, used a similar approach while working with **Publicis Ad-Link** Hong Kong to promote its mobile phones in the People's Republic of China. Publicis turned to the famous film director Derek Chang. He produced a commercial featuring Maggie Cheung and Michael Wong, in which mobile phones, the essential tools of a subterfuge, were used to organise a romantic encounter in the middle of a formal reception and to order a sumptuous firework display. The phones add an element of fantasy to our humdrum everyday lives (2).

2

¡Psst, mira lo que tenemos para ti!

FLORIDA LOTTO

3

4

Hope goes hand in hand with risk. In 1986, the
State of Florida authorized a lottery and 2 years
later, the first Florida Lotto tickets went on sale.
Sanchez & Levitan, which joined **Publicis** in 2001
and merged with Bromley in 2004, was given the
task of devising communications to appeal to the
Hispanic population: "Hey! Look what we've got
for you!" (3). In 1993, the UK Parliament approved
the National Lottery Act. **Saatchi & Saatchi** UK
handled the launch of the first national lottery
and developed a commercial by Kevin Molony,
showing that the finger of fate could pick anyone (4).
Several new lottery games were introduced,
including the "Instants" scratch cards in 1995 (5).

5

Web of intrigue

Brands sometimes target narrow audiences which conventional advertising can't quite reach. This is when new approaches and communication channels need to be invented.

2

penetrate the hype www.hypegallery.com

1

That rare breed, the professional graphic designer was the particular species on which the reputation of Hewlett-Packard, a manufacturer of printing machinery, would be built. These designers are key opinion leaders. **Publicis** London therefore suggested in 2003 that the printer division at Hewlett-Packard organise an exhibition: the Hype Gallery. Young artists could take part by creating digital work containing the letters 'h' and 'p'. The exhibition was held virtually, at www. hypegallery.com (1) and also for real, at the Truman's Black Eagle Brewery in the East End of London (2), welcoming nine hundred artists and nine thousand visitors in a single month. This whole operation was repeated a few months later at the Palais de Tokyo, in Paris (3).

3

The typical BMW customer in the United States is a wealthy, fashionable man who spends more time in front of a computer than he does in front of the television. Using this customer specification as a basis, **Fallon** began to commission 5-10 minute films in 2000 from Joe Carnahan, John Frankenheimer, Alejandro González Iñárritu, Wong Kar Wai, Ang Lee, Guy Ritchie, Tony Scott and John Woo. The films all have two heroes: the mysterious driver, Clive Owen (4), and his BMW. Their release was orchestrated like a feature film launch, yet these commercial films could only be seen at a specially-created website (5). The site also showed images from the preparation (6) and filming stages (7). This approach lead to 100,000,000 film views.

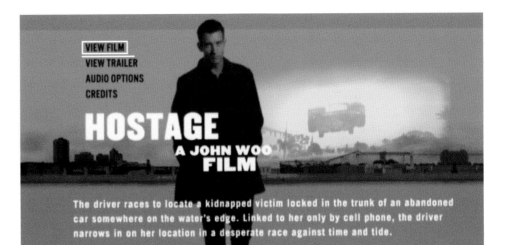

4

5

6

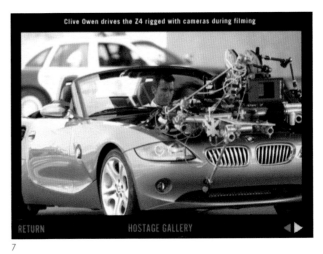

7

Star-struck

Two General Motors brands were stars of innovation. Saturn built a reputation on the new rules of the automotive industry, while Pontiac called on a television star to tap into the stuff of its customers' dreams.

1

At the end of the '70s, manufacturers in the US began to worry about the share of the market held by Japanese models. The Japanese industry had signed an agreement on Voluntary Export Restraints yet had also been getting round these restraints by setting up "transplants" to make Japanese cars in the USA. Then General Motors blasted off its Saturn project. A special team would create a car based on a completely new approach. The aim was not to show off technical expertise but to calm industrial relations –the United Auto Workers union was very concerned about job security. In 1990, the first cars came off the production line at Spring Hill, Tennessee, a factory located a long way from Michigan, the cradle of the US automotive industry. In a commercial by Leslie Dektor, **Hal Riney**, in charge of the launch, told the story of a Detroit worker finding new dignity and motivation at Saturn (2). In his 2001 advertisement, Arthur Grace conveys the same message: "A new kind of company. A new kind of car" (1). The firm sold a million vehicles in just five years.

2

The successful launch of the new Pontiac G6 was the result of a meeting between Oprah Winfrey, the star and host of "The Oprah Winfrey Show," who wanted to do something special for her studio audience, and General Motors, who wanted to introduce its new model to women. The show, organized by Oprah Winfrey, Harpo Productions, **Vigilante, Chemistri** and **Starcom** unfolded as follows. First, eleven audience members won a Pontiac G6. Then, Oprah announced that there was one car left and distributed a small gift box to all of the remaining 265 members of the audience. Everyone opened the boxes and, crazy with joy, discovered inside a key to a brand, new car. They had all won: "Congratulations! Your wildest dreams have come true!" (3). They immediately ran to their new cars, which awaited them wrapped in a magnificent red bow (4). Seen by more than 27 million women, "The Oprah Winfrey Show" is aired on more than 200 stations in the United States, and in the 24 hours that followed the show, there were 25,000 visits to the Pontiac Web site.

3

4

Papa? Nicole!

Seven years was long enough for the British viewing public to learn this French dialogue by heart —especially as it only consisted of two words, 'Papa' and 'Nicole'. They also had plenty of time to admire a neat, new, French-built car.

2

1

The Nicole of the advertising is a vivacious, young, free-spirited French girl. She has several suitors and a consistently charming French father (1). Some other characters appear in supporting roles, such as Nicole's mother, who calls from time to time but never puts in a personal appearance, and Papa's close female friends. Papa's mother arrives and causes a bit of a stir, and there's a very stuffy butler (2). All are French, bien sûr. But the real star of those endless adventures of Nicole and Papa is the lovely Renault Clio. And yes, you've guessed it, the car also has a certain frisson of Frenchness (3). **Publicis** London started the saga in April 1991 and ended it in 1998, employing a series of directors, including Michael Serrasin, Richard Loncraine and Paul Weiland. The first commercials were set in Provence —all cicadas, siestas, apéritifs and rendez-vous. In a country which loves its soap operas as much as the United Kingdom, this series was the longest-running car campaign.

3

Nicole's real name was Estelle Skornik. Papa's was Max Douchin. Nicole's big wedding went down in history –it was screened on ITV in 1998 in a commercial break in the famous TV soap opera "Coronation Street". And who could forget the names of her last two lucky suitors, Bob Mortimer and Vic Reeves (5). Nobody could ignore the phenomenon that was Papa and Nicole, which almost made the characters come to life for real (6). Above all, no one can deny that Renault sold 300,000 Clios in the United Kingdom between 1990 and 1998, increasing its market share from 3.4 % to 8 % of new vehicles. This success was due in large part to the Clio (4). Thus Renault, with an image initially forged by the good old Renault 5, became a fashionable modern manufacturer. The next icon to become spokesman for the Clio brand was Thierry Henry –someone with more than a "certain je ne sais quoi".

Vic or Bob? May the best man win Nicole's hand

A shoot and stars: Bride Nicole, played by Estelle Skornik, with Shooting Stars presenters Vic Reeves and Bob Mortimer and, right, with her Papa

by GERVASE WEBB

THE NATION was left on tenterhooks yet again today as the most popular guessing game of the moment — the identity of the man who will marry Nicole in the Renault Clio ad — was unveiled. However, there was a sting in the tail.

Comedians Vic Reeves and Bob Mortimer feature in two of three alternative endings for the latest instalment of the £7million campaign for the car in which Nicole, played by Estelle Skornik, will be led up the aisle by her Papa. The 60-second commercial will be screened tomorrow night during Coronation Street, but Renault bosses were today refusing to say what the ending would be. A heavy clue was let slip by Papa, played by French classical actor Max Douchin, who hinted that Nicole might be jilted at the altar.

"In a French wedding the words are very simple. All you have to say is oui or non — and it has been known for people to change their minds at the last minute and say 'non'," he said.

Today he presented his screen daughter in her £5,000 silk and lace wedding dress at a wedding breakfast in the Savoy, together with Reeves and Mortimer.

For the comedians, the cliffhanger ending of the seven-year advertising campaign remains a mystery.

Three were shot under conditions of tight secrecy in Provence — one with Reeves, one with Mortimer and one still secret — but neither knows which will be screened. "I know it sounds daft but we have no idea either," said Mortimer. "It was tremendous fun though, and we both thoroughly enjoyed doing it."

Ken Pritchard, Renault's UK advertising manager, said only four or five executives in the company knew what all three endings were and which one would be used.

"We have had to have the most extraordinary secrecy during filming," he explained.

"Normally when shooting in Provence we have British tourists who recognise Nicole and Papa, coming up to us, but this time we had to be much more careful."

Security around the shooting location included the use of former SAS and French foreign legionnaires at the tiny church in the village of Saigon, where the wedding was filmed.

Despite repeated questions, pleas and even offers of money, Mr Pritchard resolutely refused to disclose the denouement of the campaign. He, too, may have given a hint when he said Renault wanted to keep the campaign open-ended.

"Who knows what the future might hold? We wanted to keep all our options open. But whatever ending viewers see I'm sure it will bring a smile to their lips."

M Duchain, slipping confusingly between his real-life persona and that of Papa, grinned and said: "Whatever happens, Nicole is going to be happy."Renault estimates the commercial will be seen by half the British population, 15 times as many as those expected to watch the cliffhanger wedding scene in the American comedy Friends.

Mr Pritchard admitted that a long list of potential suitors had been drawn up, including Hugh Grant and David Ginola. "Vic and Bob are funny, well-known people and we thought they would be ideal for this particular ad," he said. "The whole purpose is to give viewers something to smile at and I don't think they'll be disappointed."

Main picture JEREMY SELWYN

5

Living in space

For Renault, more than performance and social status, cars equal lifestyles. The company took up the challenge and from 2000 onwards positioned itself as: "créateur d'automobiles".

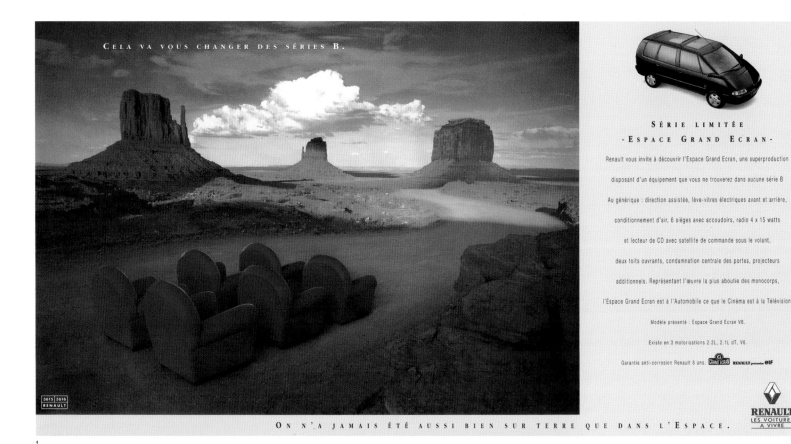

CELA VA VOUS CHANGER DES SÉRIES B.

SÉRIE LIMITÉE
- ESPACE GRAND ECRAN -

Renault vous invite à découvrir l'Espace Grand Ecran, une superproduction

disposant d'un équipement que vous ne trouverez dans aucune série B

Au générique : direction assistée, lève-vitres électriques avant et arrière,

conditionnement d'air, 6 sièges avec accoudoirs, radio 4 x 15 watts

et lecteur de CD avec satellite de commande sous le volant,

deux toits ouvrants, condamnation centrale des portes, projecteurs

additionnels. Représentant l'œuvre la plus aboutie des monocorps,

l'Espace Grand Ecran est à l'Automobile ce que le Cinéma est à la Télévision

Modèle présenté : Espace Grand Ecran V6.

Existe en 3 motorisations 2.2L, 2.1L dT, V6.

Garantie anti-corrosion Renault 6 ans. GRAND ECRAN RENAULT présente elf

ON N'A JAMAIS ÉTÉ AUSSI BIEN SUR TERRE QUE DANS L'ESPACE.

RENAULT
LES VOITURES
A VIVRE

1

The idea of the people carrier was born in 1979 at Matra, a French automobile manufacturer, inspired by American vans. In 1983, Renault and Matra signed a production agreement for this new vehicle, marketed the following year as the Espace. Renault launched a special new slogan for the occasion: "Les voitures à vivre" (cars for your life). The Espace was simultaneously family-focussed and fashionable, utilitarian and luxurious. It was certainly unconventional. But, once they got over their astonishment, the press and public wholeheartedly welcomed the new vehicle. Renault built several versions: the limited edition Espace Grand Écran (big screen) was one of these, as photographed by Paul Wakefield in 1994 for **Publicis** Paris. It boasted two glass sunroofs, allowing its six passengers a better view of the surrounding countryside (1). It was only a short step from the 'Espace' (French for 'space') to the idea of luxury: in this 2003 campaign, Sébastien Chantrel showed a man walking the packed streets of New York, insulated from it all by a bubble in the shape of an Espace (2).

2

The *idea of the people carrier* proved fruitful for the Renault designers, who applied it to the whole product range. The small, city runaround market has the Modus, which Renault introduced at the Geneva Motor Show in March 2004. It is highly compact and utterly laid-back, deftly meeting the expectations of young urbanites. In September 2004, **Publicis'** launch campaign, photographed by Daniel Schweizer and illustrated by Geneviève Gauckler, slotted this attitude into an image(3), (4). But the Modus also had some secrets to reveal: it was built on the same platform as Nissan's small car, the Micra. This was a first: in March 1999, the French and Japanese manufacturers had formed an alliance which became more tightly knit as time went on and led to this production rationalisation. As part of its international development, Renault also became a majority shareholder in Romanian manufacturer Dacia in 1999 and, in 2000, bought the automotive arm of the Korean group Samsung to form Renault Samsung Motors.

3

3

4

Car capers

At the end of the '30s, Japan had practically ceased to import all vehicles, although demand was increasing. Sakichi Toyoda, who made looms to weave textiles, saw a chance to diversify. He took it, and created an automotive subsidiary.

1

Toyota began by specialising in small, commercial, sport utility vehicles (SUVs). In 1999, **Saatchi & Saatchi** New Zealand commissioned a Tony Williams TV advertisement. A farmer, not used to the performance of his new Toyota Hilux, constantly makes silly mistakes, exclaiming "bugger!" after each mistake. As he starts the engine, he calls his dog, which leaps towards the back of the 'ute'. But the SUV has started too speedily and the dog lands in the mud. It is now his turn to sigh "bugger!" (3). In 2003, the agency celebrated when, for the twenty-first year in succession, the Hilux was voted most popular light truck in New Zealand (2). The following year, **Saatchi & Saatchi** Los Angeles asked Baker Smith to make a commercial for the Tacoma Double Cab (1). This time, the vehicle is seen as so wonderful that its owner's girlfriend gets jealous. She pushes it off a cliff to destroy it, but the amazing Tacoma is so sturdy it lands on all four wheels, unharmed.

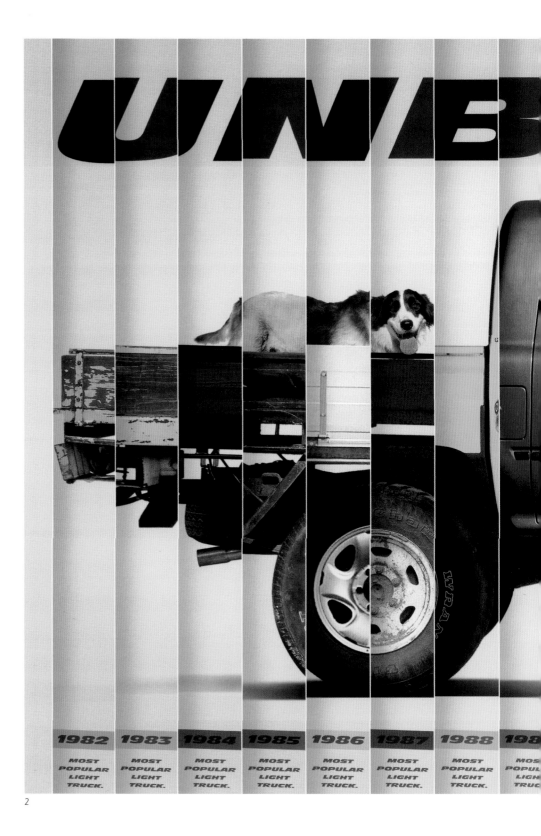

UNB

1982	1983	1984	1985	1986	1987	1988	198
MOST POPULAR LIGHT TRUCK.	MOST POPULAR LIGHT TRUCK.	MOST POPULAR LIGHT TRUCK.	MOST POPULAR LIGHT TRUCK.	MOST POPULAR LIGHT TRUCK.	MOST POPULAR LIGHT TRUCK.	MOST POPULAR LIGHT TRUCK.	MOS POPUL LIGH TRUC

2

BROKEN

3

1990 1991 1992 1993 1994 1995 1996 1997 1998 1999 2000 2001 2002

MOST POPULAR LIGHT TRUCK.

Country cars and city slickers

When Saatchi & Saatchi began working with Toyota in 1975, the manufacturer had a significant share of the Asian market. In a few decades' time, it would occupy one of the prime positions worldwide.

2

THE ALL NEW TOYOTA LANDCRUISER. NOW WITH V8 POWER.

1

Two vehicles in particular represent *Toyota's all-terrain expertise: the Land Cruiser and the Rav 4. In Marc Gouby's poster,* **Saatchi & Saatchi** *France showed with a smile how powerful the new 1994 all-terrain Rav 4 was (3). In contrast, the Land Cruiser has been setting standards in its category for over fifty years. At the end of 1998, a V8 engine was fitted, which granted it even better performance –as this poster explains. The photography is by Simon Harsent (1), and it was produced for* **Saatchi & Saatchi** *Australia. In 2004,* **Saatchi & Saatchi** *Los Angeles was approached to launch the second-generation Toyota Prius, seven years after the first. The Prius is a hybrid car with two engines, one a traditional internal combustion engine and the other powered by electricity. A symbol was developed for this revolutionary technology (2). Its launch in over 25 countries was a success, and during the first month, 10,000 vehicles were sold in the United States and 17,500 in Japan.*

TOYOTA RAV 4 / QUATRE ROUES MOTRICES.

3

A top-of-the-range Japanese car? When the Lexus was launched in the United States, in 1989, this seemed like a contradiction in terms so its manufacturer Toyota urgently sought to create a distinct personality for the car. Toyota organised a network of specific distributors and **Saatchi & Saatchi** formed **Team One**, dedicated to the brand and based in El Segundo, near Los Angeles, California. The team soon opened offices elsewhere in the USA and the rest of the world. A commercial for the Lexus ES 300, directed by Henri Sandbank, showed off its spectacular quality finish. The joints between various body panels were so smooth a ball bearing could follow the line without dislodging (4). Another advertisement appears at first glance to be a traditional comparative advertisement, but appearances can be misleading (5)!

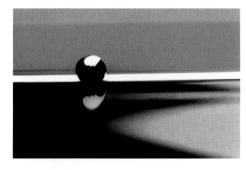

4

THIS IS AN ADVERTISEMENT FOR THE FINEST LUXURY SEDAN IN AMERICA. SO WHICH LOGO BELONGS IN THE BOTTOM RIGHT-HAND CORNER?

DO YOU KNOW? Or is it possible you merely *think* you know? Well, there's only one way to be certain and that's to put aside your perceptions and prejudices and focus purely on the facts: the tangible, measurable, provable evidence. (In other words, you have to completely ignore the emblems and instead scrutinize the automobiles beneath them.)

And that's what the researchers at Automotive Marketing Consultants Incorporated (AMCI) did to identify "The Finest Luxury Sedan in America."*

So what exactly was required to achieve this?

Hallmarks of integrity.

AMCI is the nation's leading independent vehicle testing company. They design objective, third-party studies to substantiate claims that can truthfully be made about an automobile. They drive and evaluate more cars than the federal government, car-enthusiast magazines or any other organization in the United States. Consequently, they have substantiated most claims made in broadcast automobile advertising.

AMCI-substantiated claims are in fact among the most highly respected in the automotive industry. And perhaps that's why they were asked to assist when the federal guidelines were originally established for all forms of comparative automotive advertising.

Trademark thoroughness.

In order to certify this claim, AMCI undertook their most sophisticated study to date, by far.

Their unprejudiced, three-phase evaluation took more than a year and 4,000 man-hours to complete.

Phase one was a comprehensive paper review of the most luxurious sedans available in America. The study imposed a few basic criteria† to identify only the finest automobiles and those most germane to the U.S. buyer. Ten vehicles were then promoted to phase two, initial Comparative Vehicle Assessment (CVA®) Testing. (Of course, many more were eliminated.)

All were carefully examined in an effort to define the most competitive set possible. An example of each vehicle was procured and thoroughly evaluated.

From this a very clear picture emerged of which automobiles could be considered true contenders. In all, just five remarkable luxury sedans proceeded to the final phase of evaluation, Certification Testing.‡

To ensure a nonpartisan evaluation of the facts, AMCI then acquired the most luxurious versions available of each of the finalist vehicles from official

franchised dealers, and began the arduous process of subjecting all of them to a barrage of one hundred and ninety-three dynamic, static and luxury-feature tests and evaluations in seven exhaustive categories.

Success. Not symbols.

Distinguishing a luxury sedan from an ordinary car is rather simple because a luxury sedan has many measurable, defining characteristics—other than the hood ornament. But even more important, these same attributes can also differentiate one luxury sedan from another, and that's what AMCI was looking for.

Here's some of what their evaluation discovered:

For any tests that required driving, AMCI used two of their most experienced test drivers. Each test was repeated until they had both achieved eighteen "perfect" runs in every car for all the tests.

One of the most significant of these trials was the 50–0 mph braking on wet pavement. In this test the BMW 750iL took 95.3 feet to stop. And while this is rather remarkable, it pales when compared to

"The Finest Luxury Sedan in America," which stopped over three feet sooner. And it didn't stop there.

In fact, the 750iL failed to win a single test in the Performance category and only ranked third overall. (So, could the BMW logo be the one? Ultimately, no.)

If a reputation for refinement were all it took to be considered "The Finest Luxury Sedan in America," one brand would certainly have to be acknowledged as the most obvious contender: Rolls-Royce.

But upon closer examination you might begin to question that reputation. For example, if you counted the exposed screw heads and fasteners inside "The Finest Luxury Sedan in America," you wouldn't find a single one. Do the same in a Silver Seraph and you'd find a total of sixty. (From which you can probably surmise that it's not the Rolls-Royce logo either.)

Is it possible that "The Finest Luxury Sedan in America" is also the quietest? AMCI thinks so. With a decibel reading of just 31.1 at idle, measured in the front seat, it's certainly the most tranquil vehicle they have ever evaluated. And when you consider that the background sound in a typical library is a deafening 40 decibels, chances are you will promptly conclude they're more than likely right in their assessment.

All told twelve interior-sound, ride-quality and refinement evaluations were performed. "The Finest Luxury Sedan in America" took the honors in most, and quietly drove off with victory in this category.

Traditionally a concours d'élégance is for cars that have been restored to their former glory. But what if you convened one for brand-new cars? Well, that's exactly what AMCI did. And to judge their concours they enlisted the help of three independent paint experts, three wood experts and three leather experts—all highly respected in their fields.

Yet again "The Finest Luxury Sedan in America" took home the trophies in this category. Sorry, old chaps, it wasn't the Jaguar Vanden Plas Supercharged. In fact, no Jaguar even made it far enough into the study to have the honor of participating in AMCI's concours. (And for those of you who are keeping tabs, that's one less logo for you to contemplate.)

Ergonomics is the science of designing things that people use so that the people and things interact in the most efficient, effective and safe manner.

Sounds rather Germanic, doesn't it? But it seems as though that stereotype is only partly true. You see, while the three independent experts who evaluated this category chose the Mercedes-Benz S600 as one

of the finest German-made sedans, overall it ranked just second to "The Finest Luxury Sedan in America." (Apparently, it's not the three-pointed star either.)

By now you're probably wondering if it could possibly have been a Bentley that was acknowledged as "The Finest Luxury Sedan in America."

However, just like its matriarch, the Rolls-Royce, even the Bentley Arnage Red Label did not make the final round. (Needless to say, that leaves just one logo to take its rightful place in the corner of this page.)

If the badge fits, wear it.

Finally, after meticulous analysis of the results, AMCI certified that only one luxury sedan has earned the distinction of positioning its logo at the bottom of this advertisement for "The Finest Luxury Sedan in America." By now you have probably concluded, as AMCI did, that the Lexus LS 430 is that sedan.

And that's not merely something they happen to believe. It's a fact they can prove conclusively.

FOR MORE DETAILS VISIT FINESTSEDAN.COM.

5

The UK takes off

*British Airways was established in 1974, when several airlines merged.
In the '80s, Lord King formed the new BA: a modern, prestigious, profitable
business. A single agency, Saatchi & Saatchi, forged its image.*

1

*The privatisation of British Airways was yet to be
announced, but a new management team had
already been appointed.* **Saatchi & Saatchi** *UK
began work on its account in 1982, and
immediately developed the slogan: "The World's
Favourite Airline". Although eventually abandoned
in 1999, this slogan became etched on our
collective memory. In 1983, the agency illustrated
just what the slogan meant. A spectacular
commercial produced by Richard Loncraine
showed that BA transported the equivalent of the
entire Manhattan population every year (3). But
competition was increasing, and in 1984 the first
Virgin Atlantic route to New York was launched.
Saatchi & Saatchi reacted by producing this
advertisement, which explains that BA flew to
New York twice a day (2).*

2

BA was privatised in February 1987. Saatchi & Saatchi wanted to show how friendly and how powerful this major airline was. The result was this 1989 Hugh Hudson commercial (4). Schoolchildren –4,500 of them– dressed in red, white and blue, stood in the Utah desert to form a smiling face. In the background, we heard music from Léo Delibes' opera "Lakmé", as arranged by Malcolm McLaren. The commercial was adapted into eleven different languages and used in thirty-eight countries. In 1991, when air traffic was waning after the war in the Persian Gulf, British Airways launched a very popular coupon offer (1). The advertisement went out just once, on the same day, in sixty-nine countries and over three hundred publications. More than a hundred million people saw it, and as many as six million sent off the coupon.

3

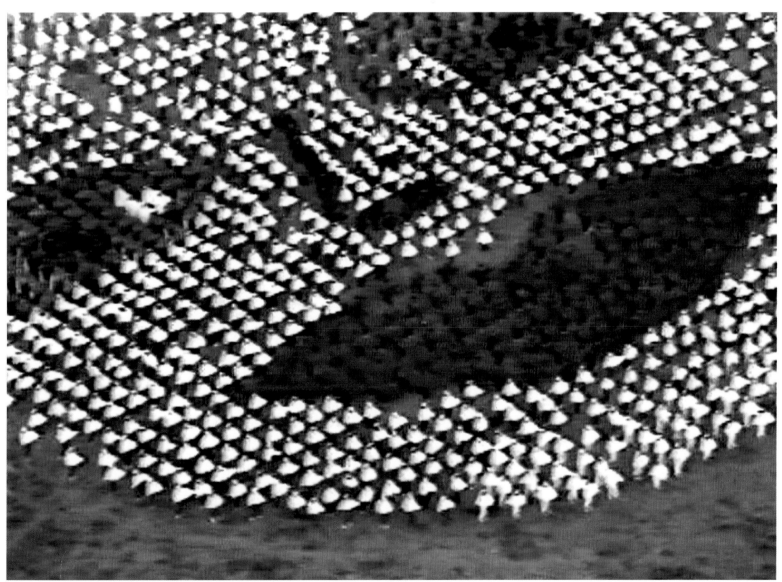

4

France takes off

This international corporate campaign emphasised the airline's strengths —a certain finesse and a top-flight crew— at a time when Air France was still state-owned.

2

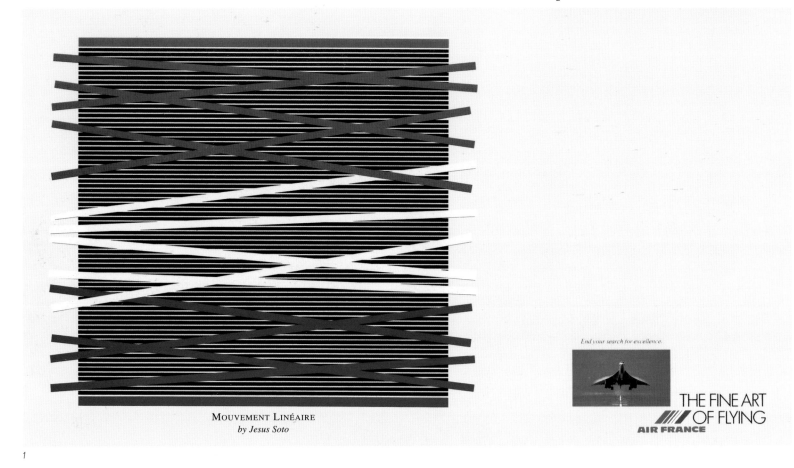

MOUVEMENT LINÉAIRE
by Jesus Soto

1

End your search for excellence.

THE FINE ART
OF FLYING
AIR FRANCE

Air France had long been using a distinctive winged seahorse emblem. This was the insignia of one of its founder companies, which merged in 1933. On 21 January 1976, a new logo was launched in an advertisement for the first commercial flight on Concorde, the supersonic jet with interiors designed by Raymond Loewy (2). This new visual identity was designed by **Eca 2**, which joined **Publicis Events** some time later. From 1988 onwards, Air France worked with **Publicis** on international campaigns aimed at business travellers. "The Fine Art of Flying" emerged from this partnership and was a regular theme in magazines illustrated by major contemporary artists. The Venezuelan Jesús Soto portrayed the criss-cross pattern of Air France's many flight paths in "linear movement" (1). In "F-BVFA", French artist Jacques Monory showed Concorde, which linked Paris and New York in 3 hours 40 minutes (3).

F-BVFA
by Jacques Monory

3

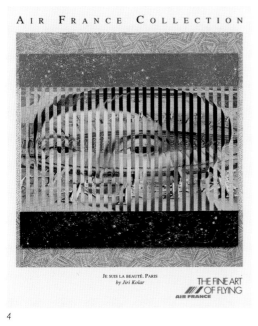

JE SUIS LA BEAUTÉ, PARIS
by Jiri Kolar

THE FINE ART
OF FLYING
AIR FRANCE

4

JOYRIDE
by Martin Bradley

THE FINE ART
OF FLYING
AIR FRANCE

5

These were specially commissioned works,
portraying precise messages. Czech artist Jirí
Kolár pictured Paris' Charles de Gaulle airport
hub by interleaving a view of the airport with a
charming and delicate portrait of "Mademoiselle
Rivière" by the classical painter Jean Auguste
Dominique Ingres: "Je suis la beauté. Paris" (4).
"Joyride", by British artist Martin Bradley, was
inspired by the non-stop flights between Paris and
Tokyo, Rio de Janeiro, Los Angeles and
Bangkok (5). In "Magic table", the Greek sculptor
and graphic artist Pavlos portrayed the quality
of the on-board catering using his paper cutting
technique (6). Many other works illustrated
different issues and amongst notable advertisements
were "Phenomena Points North, South, East,
West" by Paul Jenkins from the United States,
"Mucha gente" by the Argentinean Antonio Segui,
"Rhythmic space" by the Israeli Yaacov Agam,
"The tree of freedom" by Japanese artist
Yasse Tabuchi and "Desire for the sky" by
Konrad Klapheck. The airline acquired all these
works and Air France used this collection in
various ways, by organising exhibitions and
reproducing them on posters, lithographs,
postcards and many other promotional items.
This campaign would give Air France both
standing and status: the standing of a major
global player and the status of a refined airline.

LA TABLE MAGIQUE
by Pavlos

THE FINE ART
OF FLYING
AIR FRANCE

6

Sun, sand and see

In this age of leisure, nothing is more vital than a vacation. Holidays are a time to do what we value most: singles meet people and people meet their true self.

2

Club Med

re-born

生まれ変わる、バカンスへ。

1

The first holiday village opened in 1950: a collection of tents on the island of Djerba, Tunisia. The initial inspiration came from Gérard Blitz, the tents from Gilbert Trigano's family. In 1954, the owners decided to replace the tents with chalets. This was the start of the Club Med success story. Fifty years on, one hundred and twenty Club Med villages are dotted around the world's most beautiful tourist destinations. By now, the "G.O."s (gentils organisateurs, "our kind hosts") have welcomed over one and a half million "G.M."s (gentils membres, "our esteemed guests") into the club. In 1998, Club Med turned to **Publicis** Paris for its international advertising. Here was an agency which understood that holidays were not just about travelling, or even getting away from it all, but about replenishing depleted resources. This "re-freshing" idea was reflected in an advertising campaign. In French, "être re" ("to be re?") sounds the same as "être heureux" ("to be happy"). The posters were by François Deconinck (1), (3) and the TV commercial by Bruno Aveillan (2).

Club Med

re-splash

Etre-re

3

Club 18-30 organised its first holiday in 1965. The holidays began as a means of marketing seats on night flights, for which there was no demand. *Saatchi & Saatchi* UK got to the bottom of the Club's young, relaxed brand image in this 1997 advertisement (4). The brand was sold to Thomas Cook in 1999, and in 2002 the photographer Trevor Ray Hart included a few cheeky details in his posters (5), (6).

4

5

6

"Die drei Streifen"

Legend has it that Adi Dassler, who established Adidas in Germany in 1949, sewed three strips of leather onto the sides of his sports shoes as "stabilisers". However they originated, these "three stripes" ("die drei Streifen" in German) became known worldwide as the brand's logo. They fed fertile advertising imaginations resulting in a stylish advertisement commissioned by D'Arcy Copenhagen in 2002, photographed by Peter Boel.

Street fighting men

Shoe manufacturers no longer dare call them "sports" shoes. They are now the biggest fashion item for a whole generation. These shoes have engendered creativity, borrowing shamelessly from the worlds of sport, cinema and video games.

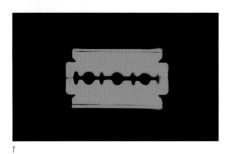

1

Four men were behind Nike. *Number one was Phil Knight, a young middle-distance runner from Portland (Oregon), who decided to import Japanese Onitsuka Tigers sports shoes in 1963. Number two was his business partner, coach Bill Bowerman, who would establish Nike with him in 1972. Third was Jeff Johnson, their first employee, who is credited with the name Nike, which he borrowed from the Greek goddess of victory. Lastly, US track athlete Steve Prefontaine became the first sportsman to wear Nike shoes. Although originally designed for sport, the shoes soon became the street footwear of choice. Shortly after the 2003 Rugby World Cup in Australia, Steve Rodgers made the commercial "Keep the ball alive" for* **Publicis Mojo** *Sydney (2). In it, men of all ages and levels of fitness play a game of rugby on the streets. Nike's communications used symbols to stand for the values associated with the brand and the game: an all-seeing eye for vision, a shark for attack and a razor blade for slicing through the defence (1).*

2

All runners want to reach their maximum possible speed. In the 1890s, when Joseph William Foster from the UK had the idea of fixing spikes to running shoes, they proved an immediate success. A long time later –in 1958– Foster's descendants named the business Reebok, after a type of antelope found in South Africa and **Leo Burnett** was commissioned to advertise the brand in several countries. The agency worked in the Hong Kong market between 1994 and 1998, producing a notable poster illustrated by Even Lee, with photography by Andrew Lau: "Jackie Chan Pump Fury" (5), for the launch of a limited edition trainer bearing the actor's name in 1997. In the face of competition from the Air Force 1, Nike's 1982 shoe which was the first to use its patented Air system, Reebok had launched the Pump ERS in 1989 which was renamed Pump Fury in 1996. **Saatchi & Saatchi** was also working for Reebok and the Amsterdam agency produced this advertisement in 1997 for the Sidewinder Evolution GSC, the first football boot to have such good grip that it didn't need conventional studs (3). The agency in Singapore created this 'Owl' advertisement in 2002 (4) for a fluorescent shoe designed for night-time use. The advertisement formed part of an optical illusion series, including a butterfly and a tiger, all photographed by Ian Butterworth and retouched in the Electric Art studio. Advertising played a pivotal role in fitting the brand to the rhythm and style of street life.

Originality

Jeans are ubiquitous, spanning centuries, sexes, generations, classes and countries with the most famous brand, Levi's, firmly linked to the enviable, enduring idea of freedom.

1

Levi's was born in California at the end of the 19th century when Oskar Levi Strauss cut trousers from blue cloth which had been originally intended to make tents for gold diggers. The fabric is originated in the city of Nîmes in France, and thus 'de Nîmes' (French for 'from Nîmes') gave 'denim'. The dye is from Genoa in Italy, hence the name 'jeans'. After their long and colourful history, the brand turned to **BBH** London in 1982 for its UK advertising and just when everyone had become used to wearing blue jeans, Levi's introduced us to black jeans. This poster by photographer Alan Brooking explains their appeal (1). Although Levi 501's had been created in 1918, it was 1985 before many people first discovered them. In Roger Lyons' commercial, a young man played by Nick Kamen undresses in a launderette to put his jeans in the wash (2). Every time Nick took his trousers down, sales went up: they rose by 820% in the first ten years. BBH went on to become Levi's worldwide advertising partner.

2

In 1990, a BBH campaign showed us the reality of feelings between jeans and their wearers. Instead of using models, it showed real New York dockers. Handwritten testimonials illustrated their favourite qualities, not least the fact that the jeans felt like a second skin. The photograph shown here is by Richard Avedon (3). In 2002, the agency found yet another approach to keeping the legend alive. It sought to make the 'Engineered' jean embody both modernity and traditional brand values, while giving the wearer the freedom to move. A young man runs through walls to music by Handel, and is soon joined by a young woman. Thus they escape everyday restrictions and the daily grind, fleeing into the night sky (4). The commercial was directed by Jonathan Glazer, with special effects supervised by Mark Nelmes from the Framestore CFC studio.

3

4

When a man loves a woman

Selling to men and women can involve very different tactics, even when selling the same brand. Some challenging experiments in underwear advertising by Dim were also indicative of socio-cultural changes.

1

Dim, the hosiery specialists had decided to diversify. Their first attempt involved socks, which was not a success and now the brand was to try bras (1). Once again, the initial results were not promising: the brand's image was a bit too throwaway and trendy for women to take Dim bras seriously. A second attempt finally brought success and Dim went to number one on the French market. This time, **Publicis** Paris created a campaign around the idea of "real women, real bras". There is always a man in the frame, and the atmosphere is one of romance and tenderness. The first commercial dates from 1979 and shows a writer and his muse appreciating Dim's cotton "nicely curved" bra: "Le Bien Galbé (2). A 1980 commercial for the "soft underwired" bra "Le Douce Armature" shows a smouldering young woman waiting for her lover to return (3). Alain Franchet produced these two advertisements as mini-dramas. The final example was designed to promote the brand's latest diversification. The mood is still tender, the women have a gentle humour and the ever-present men are very appreciative. We can see the magic at work in this 1981 commercial produced by Diane Kurys (4).

2

3

4

DIM. ÇA VA FAIRE MÂLE.

5

For a brand like Dim, being firmly rooted in the world of women, the idea of reaching out to men seemed like a very tall order. Even more so, considering the company decided to use exactly the same brand name and personality. As with its women's range, Dim wanted its underwear for men to become synonymous with comfort, quality, affordability and modernity. Naturally, **Publicis'** communications continued to use the music which had brought about the brand's breakthrough, and recreated the relaxed atmosphere of the women's advertisements. Coming as it did after the Dim unisex socks of the late '70s, Dim underwear for men was launched with the idea of "Très mâle, très bien" ("Very male, very good", which sounds like "very bad, very good"). For example, this 1987 advertisement stated "Ça va faire mâle" ("It's going to be male", which sounds like "it's going to hurt"), above a photograph by Chico Bialas (5). In 1988 came "Mâle bâti" ("Male-ishly built", sounding like "Badly built"), the inscription above a photo by A. McPherson (6). After conquering many European markets, Dim had spread into North America and the brand, bought by the US company Sara Lee in 1989, had become a credible presence on both women's and men's underwear markets.

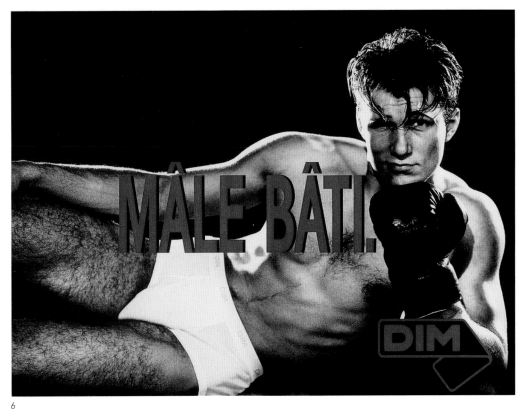

MÂLE BÂTI.

DIM

6

Because it's worth it

Breaking out from fortress Europe, L'Oréal opened up its prestigious brands to the United States and Japan and conquered the Chinese market with new angles on cosmetics.

1

Right from its 1908 beginnings, Eugène Schueller, the creator of L'Oréal, saw the importance of hairdressers in diagnosing and prescribing hair care products. The company supplied salons worldwide with L'Oréal Professionnel brand products and services, which were tailored to their trade. Other products, such as the Garnier range which Publicis introduced across seventy countries, were aimed at the public. This was the brand name behind the launch of Fructis shampoos in 1997, a brand which combined the benefits of nature and technology, benefits later extended to gels launched to help people with the latest trendy hairstyles, photograph by Guy Aroch (1).

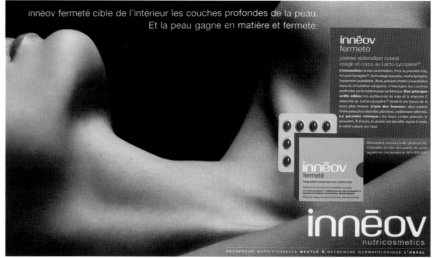

2

3

When he created Lancôme in 1935, Armand Petitjean made some truly spectacular gestures. First, he launched his brand with five fragrances. The following year, he launched Nutrix, a skincare cream with a futuristic formula —so far ahead of its time that it remains the same to this day. Then came its Rose de France lipstick, the first pink lipstick scented with rose. These three products each spawned a Lancôme product line and each had its own symbol: a cherub for makeup products, a lotus flower for beauty products and a rose for perfumes. When L'Oréal acquired Lancôme in 1964, it retained only the rose; this was redesigned the same year and came to represent the brand as a whole. In 1983, Publicis relaunched Lancôme, employing the actress Isabella Rossellini. She gave the brand a glow of international glamour and a universal appeal, elegance and timeless beauty, as illustrated in Paolo Roversi's picture (3). For twelve years, she was Lancôme's muse and the face of the perfume Trésor, as shown here in a photograph by Peter Lindberg (4). The perfume had been launched in 1952, but it was Rossellini who would make it a true success. In a completely different but complementary approach to beauty, Innéov mounted an original initiative in 2002. It was the first time a global nutrition brand —Nestlé— had joined forces with a global beauty specialist —L'Oréal. The research departments of the two companies thus created a new, 'nutricosmetic' name. The new products would be nutritional supplements for beautiful skin, hair and nails. Publicis Paris was asked to advertise the launch. The 2004 advertisement shown here promotes a re-densifying nutritional supplement for face and body, with a photograph by John Akehurst (2).

4

A rose by any other name…

Behind the Lancôme image were women with beautiful faces and exceptional personalities. Behind its success lay the two thousand people who worked in its laboratories.

1

They say women's beauty has many layers and because every woman is different, other famous actresses succeeded Isabella Rossellini in bringing colour to the brand. Fresh inspiration came from Juliette Binoche (who represented the perfume Poême from 1995 to 2000), Cristiana Reali (the face of the brand's makeup products, and in particular of the Idole foundation), Marie Gillain (who represented the skincare products), and Uma Thurman (an ambassador for Miracle perfume). Inès Sastre was the face of Trésor, and was photographed wearing a new lipstick by Nick Knight in 2000 (1). The rose theme grew and developed and, twice restyled since its creation in 1935, it was used from 2000 onwards as an integral part of the brand's communications, with subtle changes according to the campaign and product in question. In 2004, a petal was used to represent the flower and the signature became handwritten in an audacious makeup advertisement. Sølve Sundsbø took this picture for **Publicis** to highlight the colour, texture and power of a lipstick (2). The brand is now distributed in over 140 countries, with a turnover balanced equally between Europe, the United States and Asia.

LANCÔME
PARIS

LE ROUGE ABSOLU
MES LÈVRES SE DÉSALTÈRENT D'UNE COULEUR SUBLIME ET GALBANTE

CRÈME DE ROUGE - GALBE ET HYDRATATION INTENSE - SPF 15
> UNE TEXTURE VOLUPTUEUSE QUI NOURRIT ET RE-HYDRATE INTENSEMENT
> UNE COULEUR GALBANTE AUX CONTOURS IMPECCABLES
> SOUPLES ET PULPEUSES... MES LÈVRES SE GORGENT DE SOIN ET DE COULEUR

24 teintes satinées. Hydratation continue 6 heures   www.lancome.com

2

"Don't make anything ugly, someone might buy it"

This aphorism was uttered by Jean-Louis Dumas, who has been President of the Hermès group for the past twenty-seven years. He appears to take a more realistic view of human nature than top designer Raymond Loewy, who once said "Ugly does not sell".

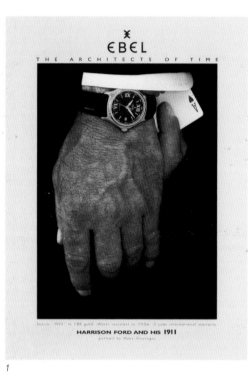

1

Chaux-de-Fonds, *in the French-speaking part of Switzerland, is known for its clock making. This was where Eugène Blum and his wife Alice Lévy began to manufacture watches. They fashioned the company name Ebel from their own initials (Eugène Blum et Lévy). He looked after the technical side, while she took care of the artistic aspects, and the brand built a good reputation in select professional circles. In 1969, Pierre-Alain Blum, the founders' grandson, took the reins and breathed new life into the business. In 1999, the firm was taken over by LVMH, a group which, at the time, wanted to develop its jewellery and watch-making business, and then passed into the hands of Movado, a luxury clock and watch-making group, a few years later. Ebel turned for its advertising to* **Publicis Étoile,** *the Paris agency which became Publicis Dialog in 2004. Publicis conducted a campaign in 1996 to show several celebrities, "The architects of time", wearing Ebel watches. This gallery of portraits were shot by Hans Gissinger. They include the actress Meg Ryan (2) and the actor Harrison Ford (1) —shown here wearing one of the firm's most prestigious timepieces, the impressive 1911 model.*

"Beluga" in steel with diamonds. Water resistant to 30m. 5 year international warranty.

MEG RYAN AND HER BELUGA
portrait by Hans Gissinger

2

LE SOUFFLE ET
L
A
S
I
E

Carré "Grands Fonds"
(détail) en twill de soie.

3

Hermès was established in Paris by a saddler from German origin named Thierry Hermès. Founded in 1837, the shop moved to 24, rue du Faubourg Saint Honoré in 1880. With the growing popularity of the automobile, Hermès moved into the luxury accessories market and in 1920, it launched the beautiful bag that Grace Kelly made famous in Life magazine in 1956. In 1937, Emile Hermès designed the company's first scarves, those legendary 90cm squares of silk. In 1945, Hermès adopted the horse and carriage emblem. In 1949, it launched ties, and in 1951 perfumes. Every year, since 1987, Hermès selects a theme to inspire its creators. In 2001, Hermès has been looking for the world's beauty. This inspired two campaigns which included these two advertisements by Publicis EtNous, an agency established in 1997. John Clang photographed the first "essential encounters" featuring Hermès objects confronted with the main elements of life: water, air, earth (3), and Guido Mocafico the second, "encounters with the Earth's beauty" which promoted the encounter of Hermès products with naturally orange Earth's elements: animal, mineral, and vegetable (4).

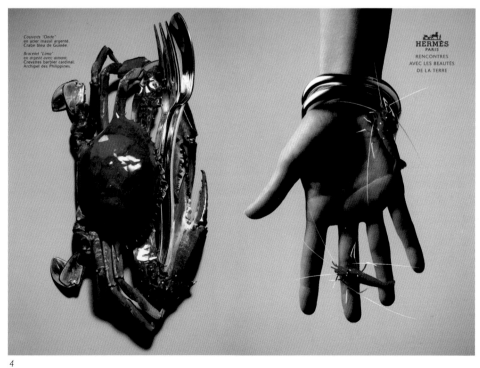

4

How low can you go?

The main mission of modern distribution is to ensure customers benefit from low, low prices. The challenge facing communications is to find original, convincing ways of repeating this message without the consumer ever tiring of it.

2

1

3

A phrase coined by the agency Success in 1988 entered everyday usage: "Avec Carrefour, je positive!" ("With Carrefour, I (feel) positive!") (2). In 1998, to celebrate the supermarket's 35th birthday, the agency (who was to join Publicis) came up with another campaign: "A month like you've never seen". It planned to offer limited quantities of certain products at highly attractive prices every day in October –usually a slack period– and emphasise that only limited stocks were available. Three catalogues were issued featuring a wooden packing crate to represent a consignment of goods (1). Sales increased by 18.6% over the previous year. On the basis of this success, the company went on to repeat the promotion every year. It took the idea to several countries. **Publicis** Shanghai took the concept to China: "The 30 days you've been waiting for" (3). Also visible in the advertisement is Carrefour's name, "Jia Le Fu", made up of three ideograms for family, happiness and good luck.

To stick with low prices or move towards the more sophisticated end of the market, in parallel with the competition? This was the choice facing the British supermarket Asda in the '80s. On the basis of a survey showing what mums wanted, **Publicis** London recommended in 1991 that Asda go back to basics (5). The Asda price promise was carved in stone and displayed prominently in every store. The whole company was galvanised towards becoming the cheapest place to buy groceries. Over forty commercials a year were made to convey this message, and all contain a scene in which a customer pats their back pocket, listening with satisfaction to the jingle of their savings (4).

POCKET THE DIFFERENCE

4

5

White goods are hot stuff

Retailers have traditionally called them "white goods". But these mini domestic helpers for home and kitchen, cookers, cleaners and freezers are now quite colourful.

1

SEB stands for "Société d'emboutissage de Bourgogne" (Burgundy metal stamping company). SEB was established in Burgundy at the end of the 19th century. The first product it made was the famous "Cocotte Minute" pressure cooker. Following this success, SEB moved into domestic appliances in 1967 with the deep-fat fryer and in 1968, the group acquired Tefal, a company that had made its name in non-stick frying pans. SEB's growth continued, as it bought Calor in 1972, a company specialising in irons and hairdryers, Rowenta in 1988, the Brazilian firm Arno in 1997, the Latin American market leader Volmo in 1998, part of Moulinex-Krups in 2001 and All-Clad in 2004. The latter was a US subsidiary of the Irish Waterford Wedgwood group. This 2002 advertisement for the Brunch coffee maker was photographed by Dimitri Tolstoï (2). This advertisement for a Krups coffee maker is by Markus Wendler, a German photographer who specialises in luxury cars (1). Both campaigns were created by **Publicis**.

2

3

It was billed as a long transition. When Whirlpool from the Unites States formed a joint venture with Philips from the Netherlands in 1989, the two companies agreed one thing for sure. The large domestic appliances that the new subsidiary would sell should eventually only bear the US brand name. But in order to give consumers time to get used to the name, Whirlpool agreed with **Publicis** that products would be 'co-branded' for a transitional period. Dates and figures were stipulated: the Whirlpool brand had to achieve sufficient awareness before it was used on its own. The figures were actually achieved in 1993, five years earlier than anticipated. This was when a campaign featuring 'goddesses' began. These female forms represented heat, when they advertised cookers (3), cold, for refrigerators (4) or cleanliness, for washing machines and dishwashers. The theme "Brings quality to life" was created for Western Europe, but went on to be used in Eastern Europe, Asia, Africa and even America, the brand's birthplace!

4

The art of demonstration

Here were three simple demonstrations of a product's effectiveness. They were all the more convincing as the viewer/consumer is addressed in a knowing way with humour helping to sugar the didactic pill.

1

The place: a Spanish convent. The people: two young novices, trying to repair a statue of a cherub from which the penis has become detached (1). They take the broken member to the Mother Superior, who gets out a tube of Talens glue to rectify the situation. While the Mother Superior works on the statue, a voice off camera cites the advantage of using Talens glue: it is very flexible. For a short time it allows you to reposition an item if you have misplaced it. On hearing this, one of the novices places the penis at a jaunty angle. This commercial was produced by **Casadevall Pedreño** in 1992 and directed by E. Maclean; the agency joined Publicis in 1998. The second adhesive commercial is from 1985 and was made for Pattex, the new glue from Henkel, by **BMZ**. BMZ was established by Georg Baums, Thomas Mang and Peter Zimmermann in 1971 and has been part of Publicis since 1992. Director Hans-Joachim Berndt shows an HGV driver sticking a pin-up to the radiator grill of his truck. He balances the tube of glue on the mudguard. As he makes to leave, he forgets the glue, which slips off the mudguard and under the wheel. It splits and sticks. No matter what the driver does, he cannot get his truck to budge —it really is stuck in the mud. This provides the ideal moment to flash up "Only Pattex sticks like Pattex" on the screen (2).

Pattex

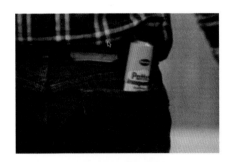

2

The kiwi, or apteryx, is an unusual little bird, with small wings and a shiny plumage. It is also the national bird of New Zealand. William Ramsay's wife was from New Zealand, and that is why he named his 1906 shoe polish Kiwi. The business was bought by Sara Lee in 1984, and now has a presence in over two hundred countries. In late 2002, when **Publicis Casadevall Pedreño** created a campaign for Kiwi in Spain, Sara Lee's brands were already market leaders, with Kiwi at the forefront, but polishing shoes was not a popular pastime. The strategy therefore aimed to put polishing back on the map, since bringing growth to the market was certain to benefit the leading brand. Photography for the posters was by Béla Adler and Salvador Fresneda, who likened unpolished shoes to dirty cars and, like everywhere, some people have etched graffiti in the grime (3), (4) as a 'protest' against dirt!

3

4

Keep it clean

When it was just powder in laboratory water, Tide was known simply as "Product X". Once it hit the shops, the Tide turned to Procter & Gamble's advantage.

2

1

3

The discovery of synthetic detergents, which were more effective than soap at low temperatures —even in hard water— was a real breakthrough. Tide, launched by Procter & Gamble in the United States in 1946, was one of the new synthetic products. A **Benton & Bowles** campaign from 1950 linked the brand's name to the slogan: "Tide's in; dirt's out" (1). The brand then went to Compton in 1962 and stayed with the agency after the latter had been taken over by **Saatchi & Saatchi** New York. The agency launched a campaign centred on the idea "It's got to be Tide" in 1998. With these advertisements, Tide talked to the consumer exactly when and where washing powder was really needed most (just after staining their clothes). The campaign's media of choice were therefore small posters on the streets, aimed at people driving (3), paper cups at drinks dispensers (4) and posters for people enjoying sauce with their food (5). Another Procter & Gamble brand, Cheer, was relaunched in 1987 by **Leo Burnett** USA. With the promise of "White stays white. Colors stay bright", the agency used the comic actor Jobe Cerny, very well known also for lending his voice to Pillsbury Dough Boy, who has become a regular presenter of the brand (2).

4

Immaculate concept

A huge white board and a tiny stain. The board represented the brand's international strategy; the stain expressed a national strategy; both showed impeccable creativity!

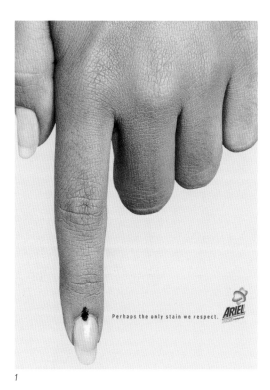

1

Some stains were too stubborn for even synthetic detergents, so Procter & Gamble set out to perfect washing powders containing enzymes. Enzymes are biological catalysts which speed up the breakdown of stains such as egg, fruit and blood. In 1967, Ariel was launched as the first Procter & Gamble washing powder in this new, biological generation. In 2001, **Saatchi & Saatchi** Mumbai took advantage of a typically Indian tradition during a promotional campaign which coincided with the general elections to the House of the People (Lok Sabha). The Ariel advertisement also encouraged citizens to do their civic duty. After voting, each citizen receives a mark on the index finger of their left hand, made in ink which only fades after three months. This is aimed at preventing fraud, hence the slogan to this advertisement with photography by Prasad Naik (1). The same agency gave a consummate demonstration of whiteness, in line with the brand's international strategy, with this giant billboard produced by Prabhakar Bolar in 2003. Its eloquence lies in its simplicity, offset by urban surroundings full of colour and neon lighting (2). Ariel is one of thirteen Procter & Gamble brands, which between them net over a billion US dollars a year.

2

Advertising age

In 1987, the magazine Advertising Age devoted a special issue to Procter & Gamble's 150th anniversary. Among all the agencies that wished their client well were six which are today part of the Publicis Groupe.

Procter & Gamble, they said you'd play it straight as an arrow when it came to maintaining the absolute highest standards in business. That you'd be as rigid with your advertising as you are with your marketing approach. They said you'd be one tough client, unbending in your commitment to excellence. But they never told us that in order to attain the excellence that has become your trademark you would throw away the book sometimes. That as firmly as you stood, you could still bend in the name of innovation. They didn't tell us you have the marketing savvy it takes to allow creative freedom. Procter & Gamble, you sure threw us a curve.

Congratulations, Procter & Gamble, on 150 years of marketing leadership. Sincerely, Burrell Advertising Inc.

2

Here's to a match made in heaven.

1

Leo Burnett, which had first worked with the company in 1950, was proud of his work for brands such as Lava and Camay soaps, Pert Plus shampoo, Secret deodorant, Joy and Era liquid detergents, Cheer washing powder and the revolutionary Dryel Fabric Care System. The agency's logo (designed to reflect Burnett's maxim "When you reach for the stars, you may not quite get one, but you won't come up with a handful of mud either") stretches up towards Procter & Gamble's logo. The P&G logo was created in 1882 and redesigned fifty years later by the sculptor Ernest Haswell; the stars symbolise the original thirteen colonies which together formed the United States (1). **Benton & Bowles** had looked after the soap brands Ivory Snow and Zest, the shampoo Prell, the toothpaste Crest, the detergent Tide, Charmin toilet paper and Pampers nappies since 1941. When D'Arcy, MacManus and Benton & Bowles merged in 1985, they created **DMB&B** and this was another agency showing their loyalty to P&G on this special occasion (3). **Burrell**, which had recently become one of P&G's advertising partners, also sought to congratulate the company on its success (2).

There were 26 stars on the flag.
The U.S. Constitution was only 50 years old.
The light bulb wouldn't be invented for another 42 years.
And William Procter and James Gamble had a vision.

DMB&B salutes 150 years of what was, what is, and what will be.

3

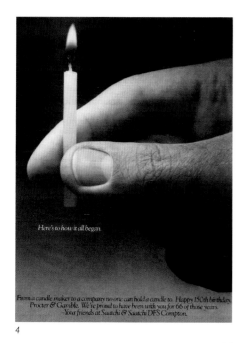

Here's to how it all began.

From a candle maker to a company no one can hold a candle to. Happy 150th birthday, Procter & Gamble. We're proud to have been with you for 66 of those years. —Your friends at Saatchi & Saatchi DFS Compton.

4

Thank you P&G for letting us take you to the doctor.

You let us take you to the pediatrician for Pampers, the dentist for Crest, the gastroenterologist for Pepto-Bismol, the dermatologist for Safeguard, the geriatrician for Attends, and in general to thousands upon thousands of general practitioners.

For that we thank you.

We appreciate that, along the way, you also let us take you to other healthcare professionals such as nurses and pharmacists, to hospitals as well as nursing homes, and to just about everywhere a white coat is hung.

And not just in the U.S.A., but internationally. So, our offices in the United Kingdom, West Germany, Italy, Japan and Canada thank you, too.

We enjoyed the privilege of helping you build successful professional programs worldwide during the last 15 of your 150 years.

Incidentally, thanks for helping us become the world's largest healthcare advertising agency.

Congratulations!

Medicus Intercon

5

One candle to celebrate 150 years? *It might look strange, but* **Saatchi & Saatchi DFS Compton**, *one of P&G's partners for 66 years, was, as ever, in the know. After all, William Procter did make candles all those years ago* (4). *Compton (still named Blackman at the time) was the first P&G partner in 1922, advertising Crisco oil and Ivory soap. Dancer Fitzgerald Sample (DFS) was the second, promoting Oxydol washing powder.* **Medicus** *emerged from Benton & Bowles in 1972 specialising in medical communications and, for fifteen years, the agency had been bringing brands such as Crest and Safeguard* (5), *Pampers and Pepto-Bismol medicine closer to the medical establishment.* **Ayer** *was in charge of advertising P&G's Folgers coffee, Citrus Hill biscuits, Crush and Hawaiian Punch fruit juice, Duncan Hines cake mix and Puffs tissues* (6).

Congratulations Procter & Gamble. America's oldest agency is proud to be your newest agency.

6

Experience tells

For brands, firms and institutions events are an especially effective way of expressing their ideas as participants in these events become equal players in the communications game.

1

To announce the launch of a new business class on Delta Air Lines, **Saatchi & Saatchi** New York and **Zenith** USA (a media company in the Publicis Groupe) installed a "living poster" near Times Square, New York, in 1997. This was a life-size reproduction of the new business class cabin, with real-life passengers and crew (1). The organising committee for the 1998 football world cup, held in France, turned to **Eca2** to organise its opening and closing ceremonies. This global events creation and production company, established by Yves Pépin in 1974, joined **Publicis Events** in 2004. For the opening ceremony, the Stade de France in Paris was transformed into a giant garden —complete with massive flowers, each unfurling to reveal an enormous football (2). In 2001, in Spain, Starcom, another Publicis Groupe media company, wanted to demonstrate that a judicious choice of place can make or break an advertisement. It asked **Vitruvio Leo Burnett** to create a series of advertisements showing posters in inappropriate places. Michel Selley took the photographs. Here, he shows that location can have quite an impact (3).

2

3

4

5

The dawning of the new millennium was an occasion for major festivities the whole world over. In Paris, the Société Nouvelle d'Exploitation de la Tour Eiffel asked **Eca2** to organise a firework display around the famous Paris landmark. They duly obliged, with a display timed to the millisecond. The show started at three minutes to midnight on 31 December 1999, and lasted exactly 6 minutes 54 seconds. It took almost a year to prepare and was watched by a million people on the ground plus two billion people watching on 250 television channels worldwide (4). On 25 March, the 2005 World Exposition, at Aichi, Japan, opened. The theme was "Nature's wisdom", at the crossroads of ecology, sustainable development and new technology. The communications for the major Toyota pavilion were entrusted to the agency **Dentsu** and Eca2 was asked to produce a show. The spectacle "Life is Movement" was the culmination of two years' work, involving a troupe of artists, a large technical crew and much equipment. Every day for 6 months, they put on 14 shows a day. The show was a 21st century opera featuring thirty futuristic prototypes of individual transport (autopiloted "i-units" equipped with 'Intelligent Transport System' technology) and three robot transporters (6). Meanwhile, after Sanofi-Synthelabo's bid to take over Aventis, 10,000 of the new company's employees met in Las Vegas for three days in 2005. The convention was organised by **Publicis Events**, and besides the normal speeches boasted acts such as singer Sheryl Crow (5).

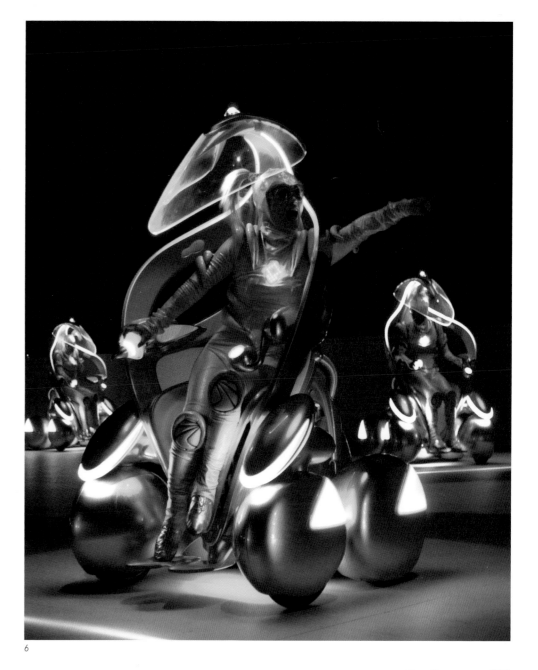

6

Cultural aspirations

Man cannot live by bread alone. You also need hopes and dreams for nourishment. This is the realm in which advertising operates, addressing music fans and art lovers. Advertisements resonate with people seeking to make their dreams a reality.

1

2

In 1989, the Soviet Space Agency Glavcosmos was looking for British candidates to fly to the Mir space station –the lucky Brit chosen would take part in 'Mission Juno'. **Saatchi & Saatchi** UK produced this advertisement for the occasion. It only appeared once, but generated some 1,500 applications, including one from Helen Sharman who eventually became the first British cosmonaut in 1991 (1). In 1999, the Times of India group opened the first Planet M shop in Mumbai. Planet M shops specialise in music, books and videos. **Ambience D'Arcy** created this advertisement for the chain in 2001 (4). In the early noughties, Argentina was facing a major economic crisis. **Del Campo Nazca Saatchi & Saatchi** created a campaign in 2001 to help the Buenos Aires Zoo raise funds. The campaign featured Julieta Garcia Vazquez's photographs in this example: "Get much more for much less" (3). In 2002, the Vltava river flooded, threatening the Charles Bridge in Prague. **Leo Burnett** was approached by the authorities to help them raise the funds needed for restoration. The bridge's statues of saints provided the inspiration for Jakub Kohak's commercial (2).

3

4

Atten-shun!

Geopolitical change was sweeping the world, and a wind of change also blew through the post World War II armed forces. However, 'joining up' remained a big decision for any young man or woman.

2

1

The human cost of the Vietnam War weighed heavily on the US Army's image in the early '70s. Yet with the end of conscription in 1973 it would once again become an entirely professional force, with a need to recruit. Against this backdrop, **N.W. Ayer & Son** dreamed up a campaign, beginning in 1971, which promoted new values, including openness to all, which were given greater weight than the traditional warfare expertise. In 1974, the campaign slogan changed (1) and in 1980, another major change took place: Congress voted in favour of a systematic census of all people aged 18, so the country would be ready to reintroduce conscription, should the need arise. In the meantime, the army was an increasingly technical place to work. In 1983, Ronald Reagan launched the Strategic Defence Initiative, aimed at creating a space-based system to intercept nuclear attack. That same year, Ayer started a new recruitment campaign around the idea of "Army: Be all you can be" (2) but by the end of the '90s there was a demographic hurdle to overcome. On top of the poor image of soldiering itself; there were now considerably fewer people aged between 17 and 24 who constituted the traditional target of army recruitment. **Leo Burnett** had now been entrusted with the US Army's communications and adopted the theme "An Army of One". The agency wanted to emphasise human values (6) and respect for the personality of each soldier, within a strong collective framework (4). The campaign was also innovative in its presentation of a nine-week series following young soldiers through their basic training on the internet.

3

4

5

The British Army faced similar recruitment problems in the '90s. The pool of potential soldiers was drying up, both for demographic reasons and due to the fall in unemployment. The cold war had ended, raising questions about the army's role, and troop reductions impacted on army morale. So **Saatchi & Saatchi** UK launched a campaign in 1994 encouraging potential recruits to "Be the best". This 1997 advertisement, aiming to increase the quality of recruits, updated the famous First World War poster (3). The quantity of recruits was another issue and to encourage diversity the army ran the line: "Britain is a multi-racial country. It needs a multi-racial Army". Another change came when the army began to use electronic media, such as this interactive internet-based game from the year 2000 (5).

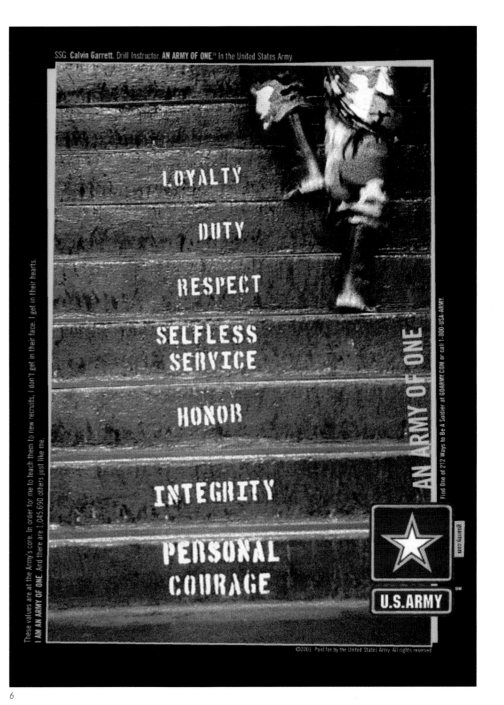

6

Europe

European citizens were sometimes confused by the complexity of the new European institutions and they wanted clear communications. When these were supplied, the response was usually enthusiastic.

EUROPE.
WE ARE BUILDING A DEMOCRACY

Responsible for its environment.

17 JUIN 1984

Your Voice In Europe
The European Parliament

1

The first crucial aspect of European democracy took 27 years to emerge. In 1952, a consultative assembly, with members nominated by national parliaments, was agreed. By 1962, it had decided, of its own accord, that it would take the symbolic title of 'parliament' and, in 1979, for the first time, all European citizens were permitted to elect Members of the European Parliament. In 1984, the ten Member States each conducted an identical six-week information campaign. **Publicis** created a campaign around the idea of "Europe: democracy unites us" (3). Four TV advertisements looked at the new rights of Europe's citizens, solidarity in a crisis, environmental protection and cooperation with emerging countries. Each theme was presented by a variety of Members of European Parliament from all political persuasions and nationalities. Here, Kent Kirk from Denmark, Joyce Quin from the UK and Konstantinos Gontikas from Greece present: "Your voice in Europe. The European Parliament" (2). In Germany, Denmark and the Netherlands, the television advertisements could not be shown, so advertisements appeared in the press instead (1).

UNE DEMOCRATIE NOUS REUNIT. L'EUROPE.

3

4

6

5

A 1999 press release stated: "The Governing Council of the European Central Bank (ECB) has selected **Publicis** as the agency which will assist in conducting an information campaign in preparation for the introduction of the euro banknotes and coins on 1 January 2002." Twelve countries would be adopting the currency: Austria, Belgium, Finland, France, Germany, Greece, Ireland, Italy, Luxembourg, the Netherlands, Portugal and Spain. The currency changeover meant getting used to new coins, notes and words. Information was important, but so too was Europeans' trust in their new point of reference: the euro (4), (5), (7). Publicis was also in charge of the ceremony at which the new euro notes and coins were unveiled at the ECB in Frankfurt-am-Main on 31 August 2001 (6).

7

Red border, blue pencil

Everyone is entitled to their own point of view, be they a journalist or an advertiser. Free speech is sacrosanct.

1

People who are willing to die

for freedom shouldn't be buried

in the middle of the newspaper.

Understanding comes with TIME.

2

Time, which was the first US weekly news magazine, is an institution. From its launch in 1923 by Briton Hadden and Henry Luce, the magazine's freedom of expression (and its inverted sentence structures) set it apart from the competition. It also began the tradition of voting for a 'Person of the Year' and applied a red border to its front page as a distinctive visual trademark. In 1989, the magazine became part of the Time Warner group, which owns AOL, CNN and Warner Bros. In 1991, the agency **Fallon** –which would join Publicis in February 2000– began a partnership with Time which would last 15 years. The first campaign to be born of this cooperation arrived in 1994. It used the famous red border, as shown in this 1998 advertisement (1). Later, the border remained, but the slogan changed (2). The Neue Zürcher Zeitung, a Swiss daily newspaper established in 1780, has steadily acquired various other local titles and diversified into electronic, online and off-line editions. **Publicis Farner** Zurich created the blue pencil symbol for the paper, which is used to embody the paper's qualities. This 1995 advertisement illustrates 'Persistence' (3).

3

The problem faced by Rolling Stone, the magazine Jann Wenner launched in San Francisco in 1967, was the gap between its real and imagined readerships. Advertisers saw the magazine's readers as broke, ageing hippies. Unsurprisingly, the publication did not feature in their media campaign plans. Equally obviously, this had an impact on the magazine's finances. The **Fallon** campaign began in 1985, to coincide with the magazine's move to New York, where it was closer to the world of communications (4). The campaign proved highly effective –the number of pages given over to advertising grew by 82% in five years. Meanwhile in Europe, after Tito died in May 1980, tension increased between the peoples who had inhabited Yugoslavia together since 1919. Slovenia was the first new, independent country to break away in June 1991. It was followed by several others. The breakaway was not without violence, a fact to which an independent journalists' association alerted public opinion. This poster contains photos by Alexander Kujucer and was created for **Saatchi & Saatchi** Yugoslavia (5). On yet another continent, Campaign Brief Asia, a professional journal created in 1996, believed in supporting creativity in the region's advertising. In 2002, **Saatchi & Saatchi** Hong Kong illustrated the unexpected consequences a good idea can have in this humorous photograph by Stanley Wong (6).

4

5

6

What if?

Information, now so readily available, has made our world smaller. Sometimes, it feels like the troubles of the whole world rest on our shoulders. And we have only to switch on the television or read an e-mail to be approached for help.

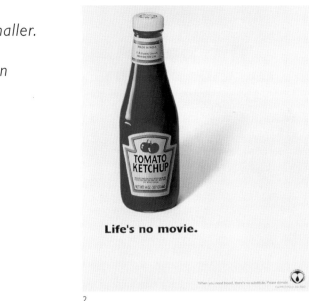

Life's no movie.

2

IS THERE ANYBODY OUT THERE?

YES. THE SAMARITANS, 24 HOURS A DAY.
YOU'LL FIND US IN THE PHONE BOOK.

1

These days, several organisations offer a listening ear to people who are lonely, depressed or suicidal. One of the very first organisations to do so was the brainchild of Edward Chad Varah, a young London-based clergyman, in 1953. The Daily Mirror christened his new helpline "The Telephone Good Samaritans", and the name stuck. From 1991 onwards, **Saatchi & Saatchi** UK conducted several campaigns for the Samaritans. One featured the image shown here, taken by Barney Edwards (1). In the movies, ketchup can be used to represent blood. But in real life, blood is irreplaceable. That was the rationale behind this poster encouraging people to give blood, which **Leo Burnett** Mumbai created in 1999. The photography was by Vipul Patel (2). Anti-personnel mines were banned by the 1997 Ottawa Convention, but they continue to be used by warring parties in many conflict zones. In Colombia in 2001, the President was coming to the end of his term of office when he attempted to highlight this tragic problem. He commissioned **Leo Burnett** Bogota for a campaign showing how easily a child could be killed. Reini Farias took the pictures (3).

no more landmines
Kids can't be part of armed conflict.

PRESIDENT'S OFFICE

3

The Red Cross was established by Henry Dunant, a Swiss who had witnessed the deadly battle of Solferino, Italy, in 1859. He wanted to take care of those wounded and taken prisoner in wars, without discriminating between them. Later, the Red Cross would also help civilian populations. In 1986, the organisation became the International Red Cross and Red Crescent Movement. In 1999, **Casadevall Pedreño & PRG**, which had been in charge of advertising for the Red Cross in Catalonia since the '80s, began a campaign to refer potential volunteers in Spain to its website (4). There, visitors could find the answers to four basic questions: where help was most urgently needed; when the Red Cross needed help, photograph by Q. Sakamaki, what to do and why it was imperative to act immediately, photograph by José Manuel Navia. **Saatchi & Saatchi** Wellington conducted a fund-raising campaign for the Red Cross in 1995, in which it trod the ground between fresco and graffiti. Shown here is one of the three themes Evan Purdie illustrated on the city's streets (5).

4

5

What next?

Our societies are increasingly sensitive to moral issues. We are also increasingly able to discuss people's private lives, which were previously taboo.

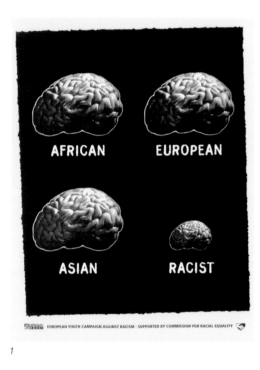

AFRICAN   EUROPEAN

ASIAN   RACIST

EUROPEAN YOUTH CAMPAIGN AGAINST RACISM · SUPPORTED BY COMMISSION FOR RACIAL EQUALITY

1

2

In 1679, the English Parliament passed the Habeas Corpus Act to protect individuals against unlawful detention. This was an inspiration to the Enlightenment philosophers and lead to the idea of human rights and, ultimately, to the United Kingdom's 1965 Race Relations Act, which was amended in 1968, and again in 1976. This was when positive action (to prevent discrimination or to overcome past discrimination) was first enshrined in law. In 1997, the Commission for Racial Equality replaced two existing bodies. It was awarded the requisite legal powers to combat all forms of racism. In 1993, **Saatchi & Saatchi** UK was asked to draw up a programme to raise public awareness of racism (1). In 1995, the same agency was approached to conduct a campaign for Anti-slavery International. It wanted to let people know that a hundred million people worldwide were still in slavery. The agency expressed an extremely violent, humiliating tone (3). In doing so, it mirrored the tone a master would take when addressing a slave.

If you're offended by this advertisement, you should be.

Nobody should be treated like this.

Yet unfortunately, there are millions of people around the world who are.

For many, a verbal lashing is the very least they have to worry about.

In Brazil, for example, Amazonian estate workers face a punishment called 'the trunk'.

A man who hasn't felled his quota of trees, is stripped, tied up and left in a hollowed out tree-trunk for three days.

As if that isn't punishment enough, the trunk is first smeared with honey to attract ants and other insects.

In India, children face similar horrors. Kids as young as six are sold to work in carpet factories.

When the loom-masters can't find enough children to buy, they kidnap them.

The kids are made to work all day. If they slow down at all, they are not allowed to sleep at night. If they make a mistake, they are beaten.

One child was doused with paraffin and set ablaze because he asked for time off. Six others were so viciously beaten for just playing, one of them died.

In Nepal, slavery is just as widespread. Ten year old girls are abducted and sold into prostitution in India.

First, they have to go through a 'grooming' period. Stripped naked, they are locked in a tiny room for days at a time without food.

They are burnt with cigarettes, beaten and raped until eventually they become totally submissive. Only then will they fetch the highest prices from Bombay's brothel keepers.

Just as prostitution can be a form of slavery, so can marriage.

In many parts of the world parents still control who their daughters wed. Who they choose very much depends on what the groom's family offers in exchange. The bride's welfare matters little.

Consequently, there are many women forced to marry against their will. Some even as young as nine. One twelve year old Nigerian girl hated her husband so much, she kept trying to run away from him.

To stop her, he hacked off both her legs. As you can see, slavery isn't a thing of the past.

Nor is it just a problem of the Third World.

In Britain alone, there have been 1700 cases of abused domestic servants reported since 1987. Most of them are young girls from poor backgrounds overseas. They see working in Britain as an answer to their problems.

But when they get here, they are often treated no better than animals. Many are made to sleep on the floor and just fed scraps. They have to work an 18 hour day. If they complain, they're beaten or caned. Some aren't even allowed out. Some are raped.

The list of atrocities goes on and on.

There are still over 100 million slaves in the world. Each one probably has a story as pain-filled as these.

Anti Slavery International campaigns for the abolition of slavery. We know that it's only by making the facts of these people's lives known and by bringing slavery out into the open that we'll ever destroy it.

Indeed, by lobbying and by raising world awareness of these issues, we've persuaded governments and the UN to tackle the problem.

In some countries like Thailand, India and Pakistan we've even pushed them into changing the law.

None of this would have been possible without the help of our supporters. They have sent letters and asked questions of individuals, companies and governments all around the world.

To keep the pressure on them, we need your help in our forthcoming campaigns.

If you'd like to be involved, fill out the coupon below and become a member. In time, we'll make sure no one knows what it feels like to be treated as a slave.

ANTI-SLAVERY
INTERNATIONAL

Anti-Slavery International, Stableyard, Broomgrove Rd, London SW9 9TL.
Tel: 0171-924 9555. Fax: 0171-738 4110.

READ THIS YOU PIECE OF SHIT.

I would like to join ASI: £15 Individual membership ☐   £5 Student, Unwaged ☐   I would/would not like more information. Name _____
Address _____ Postcode _____ I would like to donate £ _____ Payment can be made by cheque or postal order (payable to Anti-Slavery International) or by credit card. Mastercard ☐ Visa ☐ Amex ☐ Diners ☐ Number ☐☐☐☐☐☐☐☐☐☐ Expires ☐☐☐

3

![Billboard poster with handwritten text: "One in every eight people who walk past this poster was abused as a child." NSPCC A cry for children.]

4

Unicef, the United Nations International
Children's Emergency Fund, was established in
1946. It had been present in China for 25 years
when, in 2001, **Saatchi & Saatchi** Beijing
produced a commercial to support its work,
directed by Li Wei Ran. The advertisement
reminds the viewer: "One day someone else's
child will help or protect you. Give that child a
chance to grow up, just as you would your own
child" (2). The National Society for the Prevention
of Cruelty to Children (NSPCC) was founded in
Britain in 1884 by the Reverend Benjamin
Waugh. In 1994, **Saatchi & Saatchi** UK developed
this billboard poster for the Society (4), and in
2002 produced this commercial, directed by
Frank Budgen. It shows an angry father
mistreating his son with mounting rage. The
commercial was shot with real actors, but the boy
is represented by a cartoon character. To begin
with, the boy recovers from the abuse and can
still move around. But in the end, a heavy blow
leaves the real boy in a heap (5).

5

What are you on?

Living as part of a society can sometimes mean protecting individuals against themselves. People's individual behaviour is sometimes judged to be too costly for society as a whole.

2

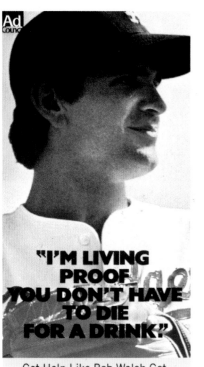

"I'M LIVING PROOF YOU DON'T HAVE TO DIE FOR A DRINK."

Get Help Like Bob Welch Got.
Call The National Council on
Alcoholism In Your Area.
Or write NCA, 733 Third Avenue,
N.Y., N.Y. 10017

1

In the United States in 1985, N.W. Ayer created a campaign for the National Council on Alcoholism (now the National Council on Alcoholism and Drug Dependence – NCADD) at the Advertising Council's instigation. Famous faces who have faced this addiction testify in the advertisements. This ad features baseball player Bob Welch (1). In Spain in 2000, **Publicis Casadevall Pedreño & PRG** ran a campaign for San Miguel, a beer with 0.0% alcohol, using photography by Sisco Soler. These suggested what you could still get up to –drive, for example, if all you had been drinking was San Miguel (2). In 1985, Louis Hagopian was Chairman of **N.W. Ayer** and also in charge of the American Association of Advertising Agencies (AAAA). In 1986, he convinced his colleagues to join forces with the government in a Partnership for a Drug-Free America (3).

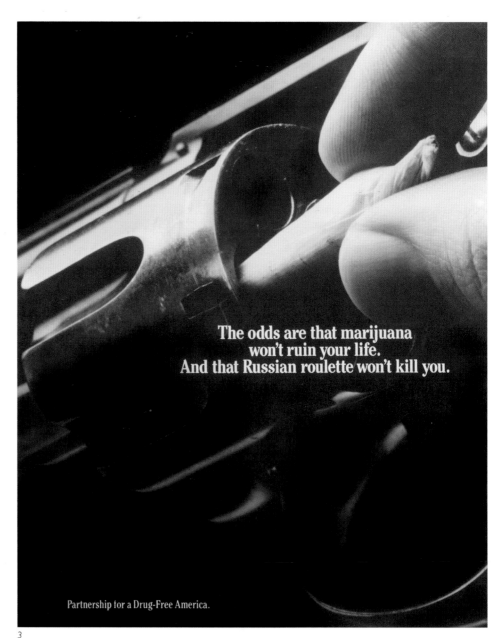

The odds are that marijuana
won't ruin your life.
And that Russian roulette won't kill you.

Partnership for a Drug-Free America.

3

5

The Advertising Council turned to Leo Burnett USA in 1985 for the campaign it planned to conduct on behalf of the National Highway Traffic Safety Administration. The agency came up with Vince and Larry, two crash test dummies (6). In five years, seat belt usage rose from 21% to 70%, and our heroes became highly popular —so much so that they continued to appear on the screen until 1999. In 1993, **Saatchi & Saatchi** Singapore created a commercial for the Traffic Police about the dangers of drinking and driving —it was directed by Larry Shiu. We are sitting in the driver's seat of a car in traffic on an urban highway. "Just one" glass appears before our eyes, then another, then another. Each time, our view of the other cars gets a bit more blurred. Suddenly, we hear the screech of brakes and a crash (4). In 1994, **Saatchi & Saatchi** New Zealand produced this highly effective poster campaign on the subject of road safety, with photographs by Peter Bannan (5).

6

What can be done?

Communications on the issue of AIDS were not just aimed at raising awareness and funds, although these were important objectives. The advertisements sought, above all, to change people's behaviour.

2

COVER YOUR LOVER.

Condom. Giggle and blush all you like, it's better to die of embarrassment than AIDS.

Because the fact is, of the estimated eight million HIV positive people, over a third are women. By the year 2000 the figures are going to be even more frightening. Half of all people with AIDS will be women.

Until there is a cure for AIDS, condoms are the best protection you've got (next to abstaining from intercourse altogether). So if he says he loves you, get him to prove it. Make him wear a condom.

"But I'm safe, I'm married," you say. Unfortunately if your husband doesn't respect your wedding vows neither will AIDS.

And if you've never bought a pack of condoms, now's the perfect time because today is World AIDS Day.

In Singapore, it will be commemorated with a forum at the Carlton Hotel and the distribution of 10,000 free cassettes of the song "Save the Day". To get your copy, read "8 Days".

For more information on AIDS, write to Action For AIDS Singapore c/o Singapore Council of Social Service, 11 Penang Lane, #01-01, Singapore 0923.

Tell him. Wear it or forget it.

1

The first cases of AIDS were documented in the United States in 1981. The first description of the virus, which was known as Lymphadenopathy Associated Virus (LAV) at the time, was produced by a group from the Institut Pasteur in Paris, and published in the journal Science in May 1983. In 1985, sequencing of the LAV virus was completed, and the first detection tests finalised. This virus would come to be known as HIV. In 1996, **Leo Burnett** Hong Kong issued this advertisement on behalf of Aids Concern, which aimed to prevent the pandemic ravaging the most at-risk communities. Ah Chung, an artist of Cantonese origin, painted a very blunt, bleak picture: "You can be proud. All you caught was the 'Vietnam rose' [a venereal disease]. But you'd better wear a condom, because next time you might not be so lucky" (2). In 1997, **Leo Burnett** Mumbai ran an education campaign for the Indian public (5). The advertisement was the work of D. Radhakrishnan, and ran only once –in Debonair, an adult publication. But a leading figure in the gay community so liked the advertisement he reproduced it in the form of small posters for distribution among the homosexual community.

HELP PREVENT, TREAT AND CURE AIDS. SEPTEMBER 21, 2003 aidswalktoronto.org

AIDSWALK
TORONTO

3

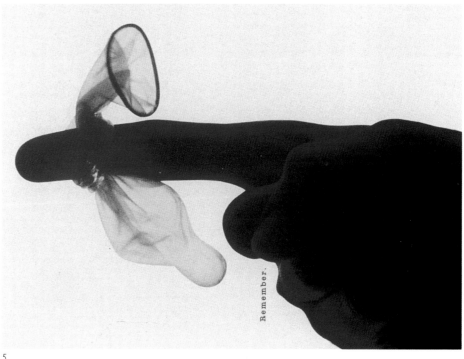

PENIS WITHOUT A CONDOM.
Get free ones by calling 250-8629.

4

Remember.

5

In 1998, *Saatchi & Saatchi* Singapore designed this advertisement for a day of action on AIDS. The text is written by and addressed to women. "Because the fact is, of the estimated eight million HIV positive people, over a third are women. By the year 2000 the figures are going to be even more frightening. Half of all people with AIDS will be women (...) So if he says he loves you, get him to prove it. Make him wear a condom. 'But I'm safe, I'm married,' you say. Unfortunately, if your husband doesn't respect your wedding vows neither will AIDS (...) Tell him. Wear it or forget it" (1). The following year, this advertisement produced by **Badillo Nazca Saatchi & Saatchi** Puerto Rico for Iniciativa Comunitaria de Investigación AIDS, struck an even more direct note (4). Later still, **Publicis** Toronto assisted with communications for the Aids Committee of Toronto (ACT), a community-based, charitable organisation that provides support, HIV prevention and education services for people living with and at risk from HIV/AIDS, established in 1983. In 2003, the agency produced this poster to publicise the annual AIDS walk, with photography by Shin Sugino (3).

Which planet?

Most citizens of the world are united in their belief that protecting the flora and fauna, restricting their use of the Earth's resources and respecting the balance in nature are vital to all our futures.

1

The Seub Nakhasathien Foundation *takes its name from a forestry officer who worked in the vast Huai Kha Khaeng nature reserve in western Thailand, close to the border with Myanmar. The reserve was designated to protect this unique area, full of plants and animals, from all human acts of aggression. In 2001,* **Leo Burnett** *Bangkok dreamed up this image for a photograph by Boonsunh Chalard to raise awareness of this issue: "Every kilometre of road built in the forest kills 290 wild animals, not to mention all the trees" (1). The S.O.S. Mata Atlântica Foundation, created in 1986, seeks to protect the rainforest on the Brazilian Atlantic coastline. In 1999,* **F Nazca Saatchi & Saatchi** *São Paulo signed off this advertisement (photograph by Rodrigo Ribeiro) (2).*

2

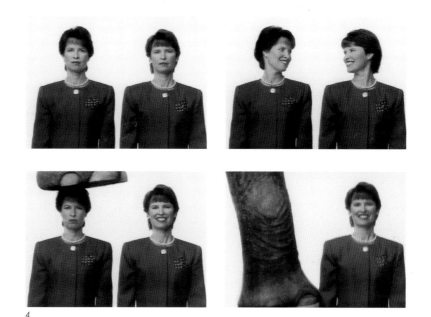

During Canada's infamous cod crisis, the fisheries minister and many sealers justified calls for a larger seal hunt by wrongly blaming harp seals for eating all the fish. This advertisement created by **BBH** in 1992 for International Fund for Animal Welfare successfully influenced public opinion (3). In its search for an efficient way of collecting donations, the Environmental Federation of California (EFC) got the idea of giving straight from your salary. Employees who signed up would have money deducted all year round, and could choose where it should go. In 1992, **Team One** LA produced two commercials to publicise the scheme. One is shown here: "One of these women showed her respect for nature by donating part of her pay cheque to the Environmental Federation of California. The other did not. Now, you may not know which one gave to the environment but an elephant never forgets. Support nature at the office by donating to the payroll deduction plan for environment" (4).

4

Getting a life

Who could imagine a more modest medium than a T-shirt worn by volunteers?
Who could imagine a more wonderful legacy than to pass on a part of
your being after you have passed away?

1

For many sick people, *an organ transplant
represents their last chance at life. Of course, this
absolute generosity can be difficult for the donor's
family to accept. But to encourage the general
public to consider this difficult issue, the Brazilian
Health Ministry regularly runs campaigns on
organ and tissue donations. The country's health
system has long been especially good at
transplants, but the number of potential
recipients continues to grow, and they still wait a
long time. The campaign was intended to raise
awareness of the need for donations, explain
the procedure and reassure people of the
organisation's ethical credentials. This 2005
campaign was launched in São Paulo and ended
in a nation-wide week of events on the issue.
The* **Publicis** *agencies in Brasília and São Paulo
both worked for the Ministry on this campaign.
Among the media they used were volunteers who
walked the streets of the cities of São Paulo,
Rio de Janeiro, Belo Horizonte, Pôrto Alegre and
Recife, getting in touch with their populations.
Giving the volunteers a uniform would make
them easily visible in the throng, hence the idea
of producing five thousand T-shirts, some of
which were distributed to the public* (1), (2).

2

DONATE ORGANS • www.saude.gov.br

2006-

David Droga

Pat Fallon

Miguel Angel Furones

John Hegarty

Bob Isherwood

Linda Kaplan Thaler

No is harder than yes

by David Droga   Worldwide Chief Creative Officer, Publicis

From the alarm clock that wakes them to the movie that puts them to sleep at night —like never before, we now have the opportunity to communicate with consumers everywhere and in every way. Everything is a potential canvas and everything an improvised pulpit. We have both the technology and know-how to cocoon them with our messages 24/7. Literally.

But in our industry's race to innovate and clients' to rush to convert, we need to safeguard our one true asset. Consumer understanding. Otherwise, we risk bombarding them into rejection. Certainly the 30-second television commercial and full-page press ad are no longer a must-have option for all clients. However, that doesn't mean the migration to online advertising or hypertag messaging is any more effective. And just because you can advertise in a toilet or on the side of a popcorn bucket, doesn't mean it is the right solution.

We need to ensure that as an industry we are not seduced by our own cleverness. In fact, at what point do we cross that line, that blurred line between ingenious communication and intrusive marketing? While every consumer is different, surely they are united by one human truth. If it is not relevant to them, they don't want to know about it. From the most overt hard-sell to the cleverest stealth campaign.

"Just because you can, doesn't mean you should." When my father said this to me many years ago, he was obviously trying to cobble together some make-shift wisdom to steer me through the perils of my teenage years. But in reality these words probably mean more today in my professional life, than they did in my pimply youth.

Understanding the consumer is much more than knowing how and when to talk to them. It's also about knowing when not to. Solutions need options. But options are not solutions.

Six famous names from the communication business give their point of view on the challenges the industry will be facing.

Who really owns the brand?

by Pat Fallon *Chairman, Fallon Worldwide*

Time Magazine's Red Border/Know Why campaign uses the entire environment as media. An ideal example from the long-running campaign is this billboard, featuring a motorized pendulum in the shape of the Time Magazine red border, which swung back and forth across images of candidates George W. Bush and John Kerry during the 2004 U.S. Presidential election.

In September 2003, a young iPod owner discovered that a replacement battery would cost as much as a new machine. He created a short film about the corporate brush-off he got from Apple and 'aired it' online. Apple promptly announced new battery replacement. Dan Rather, a veteran news anchor, was ousted after bloggers reacted violently to a '60 Minutes' segment during the 2004 election.

So what's the point? In a world where every individual person can be a media content provider, it is naïve for marketers to assume they own and control their brands. As these examples show, the general public can bring iconic brands to their knees if they have the will.

That same public can also be the most powerful marketing machine of all. By letting people participate in a brand's public persona, a marketer can trigger infectious word-of-mouth goodwill. If someone wants to create their own commercial with their video camera and PC, let them. Better still, spread it all over the world and provide fun commentary on the ad. Monitor and occasionally participate in blog conversations about your brand, but do it openly.

Occasionally, someone will take liberties with your brand that make you nervous. One of our client's brands ended up in the title of a racy rap song. We didn't sue and let it go. The brand made it into popular culture in a non-sanctioned but authentic way.

It's time to embrace the public as co-marketers of brands. They have the tools —easy multi-media editing of content, distribution by e-mail, blogs, pod-casts, etc.— and are ready and willing to join in. The brand, as David Ogilvy once pointed out, exists inside the minds of consumers, but now they have the means to show and tell the world their version of it. This will be one of the central issues for marketers to grapple with over the next few years. It will require ingenuity, subtlety and good judgment to get it right. And that, frankly, is kind of exciting.

Romeo@Juliet.com

by Miguel Angel Furones *Worldwide Chief Creative Officer, Leo Burnett*

The emotion has been converted into a virus which navigates throughout the network.

Qian Fuzhang is a writer who is very famous in China for his love stories. But what has made him especially famous is the medium he uses to spread such stories: the mobile telephone. Twice a day, his readers receive a mini-series of seventy ideograms. They pay the charges by SMS and anxiously await the following 'chapters'.

They say there is nothing more intimate than love. However, in Qian's work, this interior clutter that love rouses reaches the reader via satellite. A return trip to the stratosphere in which passions land on the screens of mobile telephones as if they had fallen from the heavens.

Perhaps this is the third generation of globalization. The first one was technology, the second one economy, and now we find ourselves before the globalization of feelings. This phase has been possible thanks to the fact that new readers descend directly from digital literature. Chats and text messages have provided them with a new language in which they can express their emotions in the same way as previous generations have expressed theirs with the language of Shakespeare.

And if that's the way it goes, if a text message can disturb the epicentre of the human soul with the same strength of a haiku poem, the power of shared emotions can reach proportions that until today were unimaginable.

Gutenberg drove the leap from an iconic communication to a textual one. Thanks to him, democratized text allowed him to share ideologies and feelings that changed the world.

But now the leap is infinitely greater: The text can be received, read, rewritten, and instantly forwarded within horizontal communities of planetary dimensions. The emotion has been converted into a virus which navigates throughout the network.

All this makes our work in advertising today a thousand times more complex. More holistic. More intellectual. But that is precisely the reason why it is also, fortunately, more exciting.

Youthful thinking

by John Hegarty   *Chairman & Worldwide Creative Director, BBH*

A modern interpretation of "A Midsummer Night's Dream" by William Shakespeare. Once again, proving Levi's Anti Fit Jeans are the original.

In advanced consumer societies we are witnessing an ageing population. How national structures deal with this phenomenon will determine future economic growth. However, the problem for marketers isn't how to talk to an ageing population. It's how to talk to a 'youthening' population.

There's a general misconception that as people grow old they want old things. As any old person will tell you, the last thing they want is to be old. We constantly have to remind ourselves this is the generation that came of age listening to rock'n'roll, that grew their hair long and created the protest movement. The women burnt their bras and the men their draft cards. It was the age of liberation. Today's 55-plus's are younger than the 55-plus's of ten years ago. And this trend is set to continue. As we live longer, we want to live younger. It's all about psychographics rather than demographics.

The real task for marketers is: how do you talk to a group of people who are sharper, smarter and 'younger' than they've ever experienced before? This generation will still be open to persuasion. What they won't be open to is vacuous nonsense. They're people who, for obvious reasons, put a high value on time and its worth. And the need for brands to deliver even better value also extends to their communication programmes. The usual bland, inane, cliched advertising, founded on half-truths and general misconceptions, will be given very short shrift. Integrity, ingenuity and originality will be values that are sought and rewarded.

Something that advertisers have traditionally found hard to deliver.

It's time for us all to get smarter.

Cynical Consumers, Shrinking Budgets, TiVo, Fragmented Media, Fear of Litigation, Censorship – The Future Looks Great for Creatives

by Bob Isherwood   Worldwide Creative Director, Saatchi & Saatchi

Dog runs from driveway into the back of a parked car. Caption reads: "The New Celica. Looks Fast".

For the record, it's 16th November 2004.

Creativity is a constant. What changes are the means of delivery for creative ideas, and the challenges that technology and society throw at it. Here's an example. By the mid-1990s in most major markets, we couldn't advertise cars on the basis of speed.

Saatchi & Saatchi tackled the problem with humour. Picture a Toyota Celica parked in a suburban street. A dog rushes out from the driveway of a nearby house, yapping its head off. It runs full speed into the back of the parked car. The dog whimpers away, tail between its legs, back to where it came from. A simple, laconic title appears above the stationary car. "Looks Fast."

Creativity has answers to TiVo, too. One is to develop strong ideas for programme content that spring from clients' brands.

And in a TiVo world, boring advertising won't do. We have to stop treating people as slavish consumers, but as human beings with hearts as well as minds.

The best advertising has always made emotional connections. Until now, of course, we've had only our audience's senses of sight and sound to help us do this.

But imagine a future where the air in cinemas is changed instantly and frequently to re-create the scents that go with each scene.

Imagine outdoor sites that give off the aroma of the advertised product. The sumptuous leathery smell of a luxury car, for example, or the mouth-watering smell of fresh baked bread.

What about "mouthphones" to experience the taste of food and drinks? Or "fingerphones" to experience the feel and texture of a lion's mane, or the touch of Jennifer Aniston's lips.

Science fiction can become science fact all of a sudden. And when this happens, creative opportunities get a big boost.

The future of creativity threatened by social change, legislation, technology, cynicism or censorship? Crystal balls.

"Getting heard & Getting it right"

by Linda Kaplan   *CEO & Chief Creative Officer, The Kaplan Thaler Group*

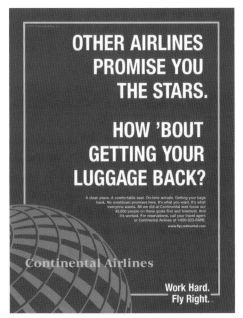

The Continental Airlines campaign makes a big bang by using a simple and straightforward approach. This ad underscores that Continental understands what's important to the customer and is focused on addressing their most fundamental needs —not celebrating the 'joys' of air travel.

The job we have in this industry is to be advocates of our clients and their brands. That said, there are certain products which our agency refuses to advertise or promote.

However, most all other consumed products are not health risks in themselves, if they are consumed within reason. This applies to areas like the fast food industry, in particular, which is the usual target of advocacy groups. A cheeseburger and fries taken in moderation, does not directly lead to a life-threatening illness. Alcohol, in moderate consumption, actually has beneficial side effects, although, if abused, can be life-threatening. However, it is the amount of consumption that can lead to health risks, and this is solely the responsibility of the consumer, not the company nor the advertiser.

What we can do in our industry is to make sure that when promoting these products, we are clearly showing them consumed in moderation, and be cautious not to create advertising for alcoholic beverages that will entice teenagers to buy their product.

We can also work with our clients to be cautious about the messages they are sending, tactfully pointing out media venues which could possibly engage the wrong target, or send an inappropriate or potentially damaging message.

Young and old, women and men of all backgrounds
and colours unite and haul huge ropes. This is
the theme of the film –directed by Ian Wilson
in 2004 for the South African Breweries,
the largest brewery in the country– to show
how people working or "pulling together" for a
common goal on achieve the extraordinary. The
commercial, created by **Publicis** Johannesburg,
ends with an incredible scene: under the effect
of this joined effort, the continents move closer
together! In reality, the movie, which featured the
brewery's staff, didn't move mountains. It did much
more: it helped the people of this country regain
confidence –in themselves and in the future.

1842-2006

List of Important Names

Francis Wayland Ayer

John Bartle, Nigel Bogle, John Hegarty

William B. Benton

Chester W. Bowles

Some of the personalities, agencies and institutions which have been important to the history of advertising and to that of the Publicis Groupe.

Advertising Age. Launched in Chicago in 1930 by G.D. Crain Jr., this professional magazine has become an international reference. Equivalents include Campaign in the UK (1968) and Stratégies in France (1971).

Advertising Council. Created in 1942 by American advertising executives to curb the loss of credibility their profession was facing. John Webb Young, university professor and advertising professional, played an important role in its creation. During the Second World War the 'Ad Council' sensitised public opinion to the war effort and when peace came switched to promoting issues of public interest. The United States also helped create similar organisations in Mexico and Japan.

Alliance Graphique Internationale (AGI). Started in Basel in 1950 as a club of five artists of international repute who had already worked in advertising. Five years later the AGI counted 48 members and was organising its first exhibition at the 'Musee des Arts Décoratifs' in Paris on the theme "Art and Advertising in the world". 11 countries were represented: Switzerland with Hans Erni, Herbert Leupin and Donald Brun; the United States with Herbert Bayer, Joseph Binder, Leo Lionni et Paul Rand; the United Kingdom with George Him and Jan Le Witt; and France with Jean Carlu, A.M. Cassandre, Paul Colin, André François, Marcel Jacno, Jacques Nathan, Raymond Savignac and Bernard Villemot. Publicis was the only agency present. In 2006 the room in which this exhibition was held was named after Bleustein-Blanchet.

Ambience. Founded in Mumbai in 1987 by Ashok Kurien, the agency joined D'Arcy in 1999 and on integrating with Publicis in 2002 was renamed Ambience Publicis.

American Advertising Museum. Founded in 1986 in Portland, Oregon. Some of the advertising documents housed in this museum date back to 18th century.

American Association of Advertising Agencies (AAAA). Founded in 1904 by a group of the professionals in the advertising business and known as the Associated Advertising Clubs of America a campaign was launched in 1911 on the subject of 'Truth in Advertising'. Three years later in Toronto, the annual congress proposed the creation of a worldwide federation. In 1917 the American arm counted 111 members and became the American Association of Advertising Agencies. The same year, in London the Association of British Advertising Agencies was formed which went on to become, in 1927, the Institute of Incorporated Practitioners in Advertising (IPA).

Other countries created similar organisations as in France in 1972 with the Association of Consultancy and Communication Agencies in 1980.

Arc Worldwide. Founded in 2004, this network united certain marketing services agencies of Publicis and BCom3. It was created from Frankel (founded by Bud Frankel in Chicago in 1962) IMP (International Marketing and Promotions founded in London in 1968) Semaphore Partners (interactive communication agency created from the fusion in 2002 of Giant Step and Novo) iLeo (the result of merging Leo Burnett Customer Group, Chemistri and Leo Burnett Database Marketing Services). The name ARC was inspired by the original D'Arcy agency name with the removal of the first and last letters.

Arge. Advertising agency founded in 1959 in Madrid by Emilio Pardo Soleparte, joined Publicis in 1990 and was renamed Publicis España in 1999.

Ariely. Advertising agency founded in 1965 in Tel Aviv by Amnon Ariely. Joined Publicis in 1997.

Art Directors Club. Founded in New York in 1920. Similar associations were later set up around the world: Design & Art Direction (London, 1962), Club des Directeurs Artistiques (Paris, 1968). These clubs issue an annual selection of the best advertising campaigns in their respective countries.

Association of National Advertisers (ANA). Founded in 1899 as the Association of American Advertisers, adopting its current name in the '20s. Similar associations: Incorporated Society of British Advertisers (United Kingdom, 1900), Union des Annonceurs (France, 1916).

Ayer, Francis Wayland (1848-1923). Born in Lee (Massachusetts), he was the son of a schoolmaster called Nathan Wheeler Ayer. During the American civil war, at the age of 14, he became a schoolteacher for five years. After the war, a friend of his fathers, the editor of "The National Baptist" (one of the principal religious weekly newspapers in Philadelphia), offered him a commission of 25% on all the advertising space he could sell. In 1869 he decided to start his own agency but because of his tender years he used the name of his father – NW Ayer. He invented the 'Open Contract' whereby the agent worked for the client and not the media and which established the foundation for the advertising industry.

Badinter, Élisabeth. Holder of the highest philosophy degree in France, professor at the Ecole Polytechnique. Her passion for the philosophy of the Enlightenment makes her an avid follower of the intellectuals of the 18th century and her writings on the relationship between the sexes are in the tradition illustrated by Simone de Beauvoir. She has published several works: "Mother Love: Myth and Reality, Motherhood in Modern History" (MacMillan, 1981), "Man/Woman; The One is the Other" (London, Collins Harvill, 1989), "XY, On Masculine Identity" (New York, Columbia University Press, 1995), "Les passions intellectuelles" (Fayard, 1999 & 2002), "Fausse route" (Odile Jacob, 2003). Élisabeth Badinter is Marcel Bleustein-Blanchet's daughter and President of the Supervisory Board of the Publicis Groupe.

Barthes, Roland (1915-1980). Influential French figure of structuralism and semiotics. Applies these 'studies of signs' to ordinary objects and communication issues.

Basic. Agency founded in Manila in 1978 by Tony Mercado and Herminio Ordonez. In 1996 it became Publicis's network first partner in the Asia Pacific region.

BBH (Bartle Bogle Hegarty). Agency founded in London in 1982 by John Bartle, Nigel Bogle and John Hegarty. In 1997 Leo Burnett Group bought 49% of the agency and opened offices in New York, Singapore, Tokyo and São Paulo. The network joined the Publicis Groupe in 2002. The symbol of a Black Sheep epitomising 'independent spirit' which was used in a poster for Levi's in 1982 has since become the agency logo.

Bcom3 Group. Holding company resulting from the merger of the MacManus Group and the Leo Group in 2000 with Dentsu acquiring a 20% stake.

BCP (Bouchard, Champagne, Pelletier). The first French speaking advertising agency in Québec created by Jacques Bouchard, Paul Champagne and Pierre Pelletier in 1963. Joined Publicis in 1996.

Beacon Communications. Agency created in Tokyo in 2001 by Bcom3 through the merger of Leo Burnett's and D'Arcy's Japanese operations. Dentsu also made a significant investment in the venture.

Benton & Bowles. Agency founded in New York in 1929 by William B. Benton (1900-1973) and Chester W. Bowles (1901-1986), joined by Atherton W. Hobler (1890-1974) in 1932. In 1936 Benton retired followed in 1941 by Bowles but the agency kept the names. In 1940 Ted Bates had left to form his own agency and took with him Rosser Reeves and the Colgate Palmolive client which the agency replaced by winning Proctor and Gambles. Merged in 1985 with D'Arcy-Masius-McManus to form DMB&B.

Bernbach, William (1911-1982). American advertising figure, one of the most prominent personalities in the profession. Founded DDB in New York in 1949 along with Ned Doyle and Maxwell Dane. Is considered to be the originator of the new creative spirit that emerged in the 60's with memorable campaigns such as "You don't have to be Jewish to love Levy's", "Think small" for Volkswagen and "We try harder" for Avis.

Bleustein-Blanchet, Marcel (1906-1996). Founding President of Publicis and one of the pioneers of modern French advertising. Born on 21st August 1906 he lived with his family in Monmartre, a busy quarter of Paris. When, at a very young age, he decided to work in advertising his father said to him "You are going to sell a load of wind!?" to which he retorted "But isn't that what makes windmills work?" At 20 he founded Publicis making the name a combination of Publicity and Six (pronounced 'cis' in French) – six being his lucky number. At that time Havas dominated French advertising in the press so he decided to try to create new opportunities in the growing radio medium. He created his own radio station "Radio-Cité" and persuaded clients to sponsor the programmes. In parallel, he became interested in another emerging media – Cinema – and he created a network of cinemas willing to show advertising. In 1938 he started a network of newspapers and magazines with the creation of "Régie-Presse". World War 2 interrupted all professional advertising in France and he left for London to join General de Gaulle, becoming press officer to General Koenig, commanding officer of the Free French Forces. Returning to Paris after liberation he added his nom de guerre "Blanchet" to his real name and became "Bleustein-Blanchet". In 1946 he refounded Publicis and in 1948 the agency gained its two first international clients Colgate-Palmolive and Nestlé. In 1957 the agency moved to 133 avenue des Champs-Elysées in the old Astoria Hotel building which served until 1950 as the headquarters of SHAPE (Supreme Headquarters of the Allied Powers in Europe). In 1958 Marcel Bleustein-Blanchet opened, in Paris, the first "Drugstore Publicis" and in 1960 he created the Foundation de la vocation" (Foundation for vocations). With Gallup and Dichter he became acquainted with the techniques of opinion polling and motivational research and the agency took the name Publicis Conseil (Publicis Consulting). On 27th September 1972 the Publicis building was partially destroyed in a fire but the following day Marcel Bleustein-Blanchet addressed the workforce from a balcony amonst the ruins of the fire announcing "Publicis goes on". The company started to develop first regionally and then internationally by buying the two European networks, Intermarco and Farner. In 1987 Bleustein-Blanchet promoted Maurice Levy to executive director and the following year Levy announced the signing of an alliance with the American network Foote Cone & Belding. This alliance was rescinded a little later because Publicis wished for greater urgency in acquiring visibility and credibility on the international stage. On 21st April 1996 Marcel Bleustein-Blanchet died and the whole industry paid homage. His daughter Elizabeth Badinter, long prepared to continue his mission, became President of the Supervisory Board of Publicis.

Marcel Bleustein-Blanchet

2

3

1

4

5

6

Marcel Bleustein-Blanchet speaking at the N.B.C
during a trip to New York in 1938 (1). On board
an Allied Forces bomber in 1944 (2). Publicis sets
up in the Hotel Astoria, Headquarters of SHAPE
in 1950 where Marcel Bleustein-Blanchet
creates the Eisenhower museum (3). In front
of the burning building in the night of
27th September 1972, surrounded by his daughter
Élisabeth Badinter and Jean Pierre-Bloch, an
old friend (4). With pianist Arthur Rubinstein in
1977 during presentation of the Bourse de la
Vocation (5). Speaking with Maurice Lévy in his
office in 1978 (6). In 1990 on the Champs-Élysées
celebrating the "Harvest Festival" (7).

7

Leo Burnett

Thomas J. Burrell

Richard Compton

John P. Cunningham

Glen Sample

Bloom. *Agency founded by Sam Bloom in 1952 in Dallas, joined the FCA! network in 1991 and Publicis in 1993. Absorbed D'Arcy USA in 2003 to create Publicis USA.*

BMZ. *Agency founded in Düsseldorf by George Baums, Thomas Mang and Peter Zimmermann in 1971. Joined Publicis in 1990. In 1992 it made up a network of six countries and, by 1993 had merged with the FCA! network to create FCA!BMZ.*

Bromley. *US based Hispanic communications agency founded by Lionel Sosa in 1981 in San Antonio, Texas, as Sosa & Associates. Joined DMB&B in 1989, becoming Bromley in 2000, with the arrival of Ernest Bromley. It absorbed Miami-based Publicis Sanchez & Levitan in 2002.*

Brose. *Founded in Frankfurt in 1947 by Hanns W. Brose who had worked as a consultant between the Wars for Odol, Henkel, etc. The agency was taken over by Benton & Bowles in 1978.*

Burnett, Leo Noble *(1892-1971). Born in St John's, Michigan, where his family had settled nine years earlier, the man who would choose his father's pencil (an Alpha 245) as a company symbol, was one of the most prominent figures in the global advertising world. He embodied all of the virtues of the profession, which were set out in his 20 point speech given in 1967 in front of his 900 fellow workers: "When to take my name off the door". He was hired by Cadillac in Detroit in 1915 as writer of a sales magazine where he would meet MacManus, his first mentor in the industry. He subsequently became head of advertising at Cadillac, then of La Fayette Motors in Indianapolis. He became 'creative chief' of the Homer McKee agency where he was taught the advantage of the "warm sell" over the "soft" and "hard" sell. In 1930 he joined the Chicago office of Erwin, Wasey and on 5th August 1935 he opened his own agency on the request of three of his clients. He set up at the Palmer House Hotel with five other colleagues and, from 1955 onwards, his agency would be consistently ranked among the top ten American agencies.*

Burrell. *Agency specialised in communications targeted at the African-American community, founded by Thomas J. Burrell and Emmett McBain in 1971 in Chicago. In 1999 Publicis took a 49% stake.*

Calkins, Earnest Elmo *(1868-1964). A pioneer of modern American advertising, as both theorist and practitioner, he was successful in imposing his ideas regarding the creation of advertising concepts and the rigour involved in their application at the beginning of the 20th century.*

Casadevall Pedreño. *Agency founded in Barcelona by Luis Casadevall and Salvador Pedreño in 1991. Joined Publicis in 1998.*

Cassandre, A.M. *(1901-1968). Pseudonym of Adolphe Mouron, French artist born in Russia. He was a lithographer, painter, and creator of typefaces. Especially well known for his posters reconciling avant-garde pictorial movements (cubism, surrealism and Neue Sachlichkeit) with the demands of commercial communication.*

Chaitra. *Agency founded in Mumbai in 1972 by fourteen advertising professionals. Leo Burnett got involved in this project in 1995 and acquired it in 1999 to create Leo Burnett India.*

Coiner, Charles T. *(1898-1989). American art director recognised as one of the most influential of the 20th century for his pioneering efforts in the use of fine art in advertising. During his forty year career at N.W. Ayer & Son (1924-1964) he made the general public and companies aware of art.*

Compton. *In 1908, Oscar H. Blackman founded his agency in New York. In 1909, the agency was renamed Blackman-Ross after partnering with Frederick Ross, with the agency reverting to its original name when Ross left in 1920. In 1921 the agency began working with the client Procter & Gamble, a relationship that is ongoing today. In 1934, the agency moved to the Rockefeller Center and the partners of the time sold it to three employees, Richard Compton, Alfred Stanford and Leonard T. Bush. In 1935, the agency took the new chairman's name: Compton. It acquired J. Stirling Getchell in 1943 and in 1960 began to expand internationally, taking a significant stake in S.T. Garland in London to create Garland Compton. In 1962, expansion ensued in Australia, in 1963 in the Philippines, in 1964 in France (with R.L. Dupuy) and in Italy, in 1968 Hong Kong, etc.*

Conill. *Rafael Conill founded Mestre, Conill and Co. in Cuba in 1953. In 1968, the agency moved to New York under the Conill name, as an agency specialising in marketing to the Hispanic community. It was purchased by Saatchi & Saatchi in 1987 and in 2002 became part of its Caribbean and Latin American network, Nazca Saatchi & Saatchi.*

Cunningham & Walsh. *Agency founded in New York in 1919 under the Newell-Emmett name, creator of the first radio 'jingle' for Pepsi-Cola: "Pepsi-Cola hits the spot". In 1950, the nine managing partners disbanded; two of those, Fred Walsh (1875-1964), and John P. Cunningham (1898-1985), creative director, took over the agency. Purchased in 1982 by Mickelberry, the agency was taken over by Ayer in 1986.*

Dancer Fitzgerald Sample. *Agency founded in Chicago by Hill Blackett and Glen Sample in*

Frank Hummert

William C. D'Arcy

Abraham De la Mar

Pat Fallon

Francis Elvinger and Dr. Rudolf Farner

1923 as Blackett Sample. The arrival of Frank Hummert in 1927 saw the agency renamed: Blackett Sample Hummert. In 1944 Blackett withdrew and Glen Sample, with two executives from BSH, H. Mix Dancer and Cliff Fitzgerald, founded Dancer Fitzgerald Sample. In 1948, this agency moved to New York to get closer to the budding television industry. In 1969, DFS partnered with Dorland agencies in Germany and in the UK and, in 1971, the Australian Fortune joined the venture. In 1979, DFS could offer a network of 46 agencies spread across 19 countries. In 1986, Saatchi & Saatchi purchased DFS and merged it with Dorland which it had previously acquired in 1981, to form DFS Dorland Worldwide. In 1987, the DFS part of the network was then merged with Saatchi & Saatchi Compton.

D'Arcy. Advertising agency founded by William Cheever D'Arcy and six collaborators in Saint Louis in 1906. Subsequently opened offices in Atlanta, Cleveland, New York, Toronto, Los Angeles, Mexico and Chicago. Merged with MacManus John & Adams in 1971 and in 1972, with Masius Wynne-Williams and its European network. Was renamed D-MM and in 1985, merged with Benton & Bowles to become DMB&B. In 1999, the agency returned to its original name, D'Arcy, before being absorbed by Bcom3 in 2000 and then the Publicis Groupe in 2002.

D'Arcy, William Cheever (1873-1948). Began his career at an agency in Saint Louis, Missouri, where in 1906 he was to create his own agency with Coca-Cola as his first client. Played a crucial role in the launch of the 1911 movement "Truth in Advertising" at the Associated Advertising Clubs of the World convention. Co-signed the "Declaration of Advertising Principles" in 1913. In 1915, Anheuser-Busch, Saint Louis' big brewery, awarded him its advertising account and the agency would handle one of their brands, Budweiser, until 1995. His name is also associated with the Riverfront Memorial set up in 1936, "Gateway to the West", a monumental arch along the banks of the Mississippi, designed by Eero Saarinen.

De la Mar, A. Agency founded in Amsterdam in 1880 by Abraham De la Mar. The founding agency of the European network Intermarco, created in 1960 by a partnership with French agency Elvinger, which would be acquired by Publicis in 1972.

Dentsu. The origins of the agency go back to 1901, when Hoshiro Mitsunaga was heading both a telegraphic service, Telegraph Service Co., and an agency, Japan Advertising. Mitsunaga obtained advertising space from the newspapers in barter for telegraphic dispatches. In 1936, the company refocused on its advertising activities and in 1943, acquired sixteen companies and opened offices in

Osaka, Nagoya and Kyushu. It was renamed Dentsu Advertising in 1955 and in 1974 was ranked the number one advertising agency in the world in terms of billings. In 2000, Dentsu made an investment in the Bcom3 Group, which Publicis acquired in 2002; Dentsu acquired a 15% stake in the new entity, Publicis Groupe.

Dichter, Ernest (1907-1991). Born in Vienna, the founder of motivational studies, opening an institute in New York in 1946. Especially known for his pioneering research on Chrysler's Plymouth and Procter & Gamble's Ivory soap.

Duke University. Founded in 1924 in Durham, North Carolina, notably houses the D'Arcy Collection, a series of records of D'Arcy, Benton & Bowles, D-MM, and DMB&B.

Elvinger. Agency founded in 1923 by Francis Elvinger. Joined the Intermarco-Farner network in 1972 and later merged with Publicis Conseil.

Fallon. Agency created in Minneapolis in 1981 by Pat Fallon (1945-) and Thomas McElligott (1943-). Set up a network of agencies in New York, London, São Paulo, Singapore, Hong Kong and Tokyo. Joined Publicis in 2000.

Farner. Agency created in Zürich in 1951 by Doctor Rudolf Farner (1917-1984) acquiring Nestlé's agency BEP (Lausanne) in 1955. Set up a network with agencies notably in Italy, Austria and Germany. On purchase by Publicis in 1973, Farner is merged with Intermarco, acquired in 1972, creating Publicis' first European network.

FCA! (Feldman, Calleux, Associés). Agency founded in Paris in 1966 by Jean Feldman, Philippe Calleux and Alain Ossard. After opening several offices, most of them in Europe, joined Publicis in 1993. The French agency merged with Success and the FCA! network merged with the BMZ network to give birth to the FCA!BMZ network.

Festival International de la Publicité. Created in 1954 by Jean Mineur as Festival International du Film Publicitaire (International Festival of Advertising Films). At its beginnings, took place alternatively in Venice and Cannes where it definitely settled as of 1984. Other similar industry gathering: Clio Awards (1959), Effie (1968) organised by New York American Marketing Association, Euro Effie (1996).

Freud. Public relations agency founded in London in 1985 by Matthew Freud. Joined Publicis Groupe in 2005 as part of the "Public Relations & Corporate Communications" division.

Gallup, George W. (1901-1984). American pioneer of opinion polls, he worked at D'Arcy and at Northwestern University before joining Young & Rubicam in 1932 where he set up a research department. In 1935 he founded the American Institute of Public Opinion and, in 1947, he launched his famous "Gallup polls".

Gebrauchsgraphik. *Magazine launched in Berlin in 1924 by the Professor K.H. Frenzel. Bilingual (English-German), aimed at graphic designers, it settled in Munich in 1950, taking on the name Novum Gebrauchsgraphik in 1971 and later being renamed Novum World of Graphic Design in 1996.*

Getchell, J. Stirling *(1899-1940). Born in New York, he participated in the war against Pancho Villa in Mexico in the ranks of General Pershing. After various positions, returned to New York in 1925 to work at George Batton (later to become BBDO) where he shared an office with W.B. Benton and C.B. Bowles, and then at J. Walter Thompson. In 1931 he created his own agency, J. Stirling Getchell. Hired Ernest Dichter and propelled his agency to one of the top ten in the country. Compton absorbed the agency in 1943.*

J. Stirling Getchell

Graphics. *Agency created by Mustapha Assad in 1973 in Beirut. Built a seven country network to serve the Middle East. Joined Publicis in 1999.*

Graphis. *Magazine launched in Zürich in 1944 by Walter Herdeg, subtitled "The International Journal of Visual Communication". Transferred to New York in 1986 when it was acquired by B. Martin Pedersen, the graphic designer and publisher born in Norway who started his career at Benton & Bowles mail service.*

Hal Riney

Hal Riney & Partners. *Advertising agency founded by Hal Riney (1932-) in San Francisco. Opened agencies in New York, Chicago and Atlanta and joined Publicis in 1998, being renamed Publicis & Hal Riney.*

Havas, Charles *(1783-1858). Created in 1832 in Paris the very first press agency in the world where Julius Reuter and Bernhard Wolf worked (future founders of respectively the press agency Reuters in the UK and the financial news agency Wolfs Bureau in Germany). His interest for advertising began in the late 1830's yet, in the early 1850's, his operation is taken over by Société Générale d'Annonces, founded by Charles Duveyrier in 1845. In 1920, the SGA, which took the name of Havas, included a press agency, a booking agency branch (selling media advertising space) and a branch of media buying agencies. After the Second World War, the press agency was spun off as Agence France Presse. In 1968 the agency Havas Conseil was set up and in 1991 the agency RSC&G (Roux, Séguéla, Cayzac & Goudard) acquired. The group recovered the name Havas in 2002 and is today the 6th ranking group worldwide.*

Linda Kaplan Thaler

Hemisphere. *Agency founded by Virgilio A. Yuzon and Gregorio D. Garcia III in 1971 in Makati (Philippines). Joined Leo Burnett in 1983.*

History of Advertising Trust. *Archive centre established in Norwich, Great Britain, in 1974,* aiming to conserve British advertising and encourage its study.

Hopkins, Claude C. *(1866-1932). Hired at the age of 41 as copywriter at Lord & Thomas by Albert Lasker. In 1923, the agency published his book "Scientific Advertising" which argued that the only objective of advertising was selling. Published his memoirs "My Life in Advertising" in 1927.*

Intermarco. *Advertising network of Dutch origin including over twenty agencies in a dozen European markets, such as Elvinger in France. Acquired by Publicis in 1972 and merged with the Farner network, it was renamed Publicis in 1986.*

Intermarco-Farner. *Network created by Publicis in 1973 by bringing together the Intermarco network (acquired in 1972) and Farner (1973), adding the British agency McCormick Richards in 1979.*

Interpublic. *Holding company founded in 1961 by Marion Harper Jr, successor in 1948 to H.K. McCann at the head of McCann-Erickson. Today the group is ranked third worldwide and counts six divisions (McCann, FCB, Lowe, Draft, Constituent Management and Interpublic Aligned Companies) with a presence in 130 countries.*

Jackson Wain. *Agency founded in 1946 in Sydney by Hadley Cousins. The first Australian agency to set up an international network. Joined Leo Burnett in 1970.*

Kaplan Thaler Group. *Agency founded in 1997 by Linda Kaplan Thaler. Joined the MacManus Group in 1999 but kept its own identity.*

Lápiz. *Originally set up in Chicago in 1987 as the Hispanic communications division of Leo Burnett USA. Became an agency in its own right in 1999 and as a Bcom3 entity, became part of Publicis Groupe in 2002.*

Lasker, Albert Davis *(1880-1952). In 1898 joined Lord & Thomas, an agency founded in Chicago in 1881, taking over with Charles Erwin (who would later found his own agency: Erwin Wasey). Hired talents such as John E. Kennedy and Claude C. Hopkins. Stepped down in 1942, leaving the agency in the hands of three directors: Emerson Foote (New York), Fairfax Cone (Chicago) and Tom Belding (Los Angeles) who subsequently renamed it FCB which remains one of the most important American agencies.*

Leo Burnett. *Agency founded in 1935 in Chicago by Leo Burnett. Opened an office in New York in 1941, Los Angeles in 1946, Toronto in 1952 and Montreal in 1959. The acquisition of D.P. Brothers & Co. in Detroit allowed it to join the General Motors roster. Acquired the British London Press Exchange in 1969 which brought its European and African network and in 1970 the Australian agency Jackson Wain, providing it with* a foot in the Asian market. Completed its international expansion by acquiring agencies in the Nordic region and acquiring German agency Lürzer Conrad in 1980. Partnered with Homsy & Chehab in the Middle East in 1981 and branching out into Central Europe in 1991. In 1992, it set up in China. In 1997, took a stake in BBH and launched Starcom (formerly Leo Burnett Media).

Leo Group. Holding company formed in 1999 encompassing Leo Burnett, Starcom and the 49% stake in BBH, along with other marketing services companies. Became Bcom3 in 2000 with MacManus Group and an interest from Dentsu.

Leupin, Herbert (1916-1999). Swiss poster artist. The Basel School which he led with Stoecklin, Brun and Birkhauser was to dominate Swiss advertising for over twenty years.

Lévy, Maurice (1942-). Joined the Publicis Groupe in 1971 to set up its data management system. Became Secretary-General of Publicis Conseil in 1973, General Manager in 1976 and President in 1984. In 1986 he was named Vice-President of Publicis S.A. and took over operational control. In 1988 Marcel Bleustein-Blanchet, wishing to organise his succession, modified the statutes of the company and created a Supervisory Board of which he took the Presidency, and a Management Board of which he nominated Maurice Lévy as President. Under his initiative a vast international development programme was put into place which would lead Publicis to become the biggest advertising network in Europe and later one of the most important players in the communications industry in the world. As someone tuned into the expectations of influential economic leaders, he rapidly identified a need for providing a diversified services offering. This led him to set out to protect the variety of cultures and personalities of the important players that make up Publicis Groupe. In Spring 2001, he first introduced the idea of holistic communications at a speech given at a 4A's event, the American Association of Advertising Agencies. During this period, Publicis Groupe saw strong growth, continuous improval of its creative offering, and innovation in terms of client services, building the foundations of a company set for growth. Outside of Publicis Groupe, Maurice Lévy is co-founder of the ICM (Research Institute for the Brain and Spinal Cord) and President of the Palais de Tokyo, an important site housing contemporary art situated in Paris. He is member of the Consulting Committee of the Banque de France and, since 2002, co-president of the French-American Business Council. In 2004 he received the "Benjamin Franklin Award" from the Franco-American Foundation and the "Scopus Award" from the Hebrew University of Jerusalem. Maurice Lévy is a Commander of the Legion of Honour and Commander of the Nation Order of Merit.

Loewy, Raymond (1893-1986). Considered as the father of industrial design, this American designed products, packaging and logos for over 200 companies. The Lucky Strike cigarette packet is one of his most well known creations.

London Press Exchange. Agency founded in London in 1892. Developed an international network of 24 agencies in 19 countries. Its acquisition by Leo Burnett in 1969 marked the beginning of the American agency's international expansion.

Lürzer, Conrad. Agency founded in Frankfurt in 1975 by Walter Lürzer and Michael Conrad. Joined Leo Burnett in 1980. Lürzer left the agency in 1982 to start the trade magazine Lürzer's Archiv. Conrad became creative director of the Leo Burnett network in the '90s.

MacManus. Agency founded by Theodore F. MacManus (1872-1940) in Detroit in 1911. Merged with the W.A.P. John and Jim A. Adams agency created the previous year in Detroit to form MacManus, John & Adams. Joined D'Arcy in 1971.

MacManus Group. Holding company created in 1996 with the acquisition of the Ayer agency and Medicus, Televest and MS&L (Manning, Selvage & Lee) by DMB&B (D'Arcy Masius Benton & Bowles). Merged with Kaplan Thaler Group in 1999 and with the Leo Group in 2000 to form Bcom3.

Manning, Selvage & Lee. Public relations agency founded in 1938 in New York under the name Selvage and Lee by Morris M. Lee Jr. and James Selvage. Merged in 1972 with Farley Manning Associates, taking on its current name. Acquired by Benton & Bowles in 1980 and absorbed into Leo Burnett's public relations department. Became part of the "Public Relations & Corporate Communications" division of Publicis Groupe in 2005.

Markkinointi Topitörmä. Agency founded in 1962 in Helsinki by Topi Törmä, merged with Erkki Yrjölä's agency Oy in 1993, becoming Publicis International Oy in 1996.

Masius. Began as the London branch of American agency Lord & Thomas. American Leonard Michael Masius began managing the agency in 1929, leaving the parent company in 1943 to start his own agency with Ferguy Ferguson: Masius & Ferguson. It became Masius, Wynn-Williams in 1964 when Ferguson left the company to be replaced by Jack Wynn-Williams. It became one of the top agencies in Europe at the end of the '60s and merged with D'Arcy MacManus in 1976 to form D'Arcy-MacManus Masius.

McCann, Harrison King (1880-1962). Founded his agency in New York in 1911. Pioneer of the advertising networks, he quickly expanded his activity to a presence in London, Paris and Berlin.

Leo Burnett

Theodore F. MacManus

Leonard "Mike" Masius

During the Depression of 1930, he partnered with Alfred W. Erickson's agency, founded in 1902, to create McCann Erickson. In 1954, McCann acquired the agency Marschalk & Pratt and to enable it to handle competing clients to McCann Erickson by retaining its own identity, invented the concept of holding company in the advertising industry. This holding was called McCann Erickson Inc. in 1960 and became Interpublic in 1961.

McCormick Richards. Agency founded in 1969 in London by John McCormick and Tom Richards. Joined the Intermarco-Farner network in 1979, taking on the name McCormick Intermarco Farner. Renamed Publicis in 1989 and proceeded with a number of important acquisitions including Geers Gross in 1992.

MC&D. Born in 1989 from the advertising department of Siemens, with a presence in both Munich and Erlangen. Joined Publicis in 1991.

McLuhan, Marshall (1911-1980). Canadian sociologist and media specialist, publishing "Understanding Media" in 1964. Insisted upon the preeminance of media on the message and upon the social effects of electronic communications.

Médias & Régies Europe. Branch of the Publicis Groupe bringing together operations in the booking agency sector (commercialisation of media advertising space). Traces its origins back to the foundation of Régie-Presse in Paris in 1938. Added activities in cinema (Jean Mineur, Cinéma & Publicité, Mediavision), radio (Régie 1) and urban transport advertising (Omni Media Cleveland.)

Medicus. Medical communications agency founded in 1972 in New York by Edward Dent, William G. Castagnoli and Lawrence Lesser as a joint venture with Benton & Bowles. Joined Publicis Healthcare Group in 2003.

Mojo. Advertising agency founded in 1979 in Sydney by Alan Morris (Mo) and Alan Johnston (Jo). Opened offices in Melbourne, Brisbane (Australia) and in Auckland (New Zealand). Joined Publicis in 1997.

Mundocom. Agency specialised in publishing, created in 1995 with the merger of Mundoprint, publishing department of Publicis Conseil (Paris), and Mundocom, publishing subsidiary of Intermarco (Amsterdam).

Musée de la Publicité. First imagined by Roger Marx in 1899 and founded by Geneviève Gaëtan-Picon in 1978 in Paris. It started life as the Poster Museum, taking its current name in 1982.

Museum of Broadcast Communications. Founded in 1987 in Chicago by Bruce DuMont.

Museum of Television and Radio. Founded in 1975 in New York by William S. Paley as the Museum of Broadcasting, taking its current name in 1990. Opened in Los Angeles in 1996.

National Museum of American History. One of the Smithsonian Institution museums, founded in Washington in 1964 under the name of the Museum of History and Technology, taking it current name in 1980. Notably conserves the Ayer Collection.

Nazca. Saatchi & Saatchi's Latin American and Carribean network, launched in 1994 by a group of executives of Saatchi & Saatchi agencies in the region, under the direction of Angel Collado-Schwarz.

Nelson. Medical communications agency founded in New York in 1987 by Wayne K. Nelson. Joined Publicis in 2000 and became part of Publicis Healthcare Communications Group in 2003.

Norton. Agency founded in 1946 in São Paulo by Geraldo Alonso and acquired by Publicis in 1996. Became Publicis Norton and after merging with Salles D'Arcy in 2003, took the name Publicis in 2005.

N.W. Ayer & Son. Agency founded by Francis W. Ayer in 1869 in Philadelphia. In 1877, it took control of Coe, Wetherill & Co., successors of Volney B. Palmer's agency. Became N.W. Ayer in 1974 when it set up in New York and absorbed Cunningham & Walsh in 1986. Became part of the MacManus Group in 1999 and the Kaplan Thaler Group in 2001.

Ogilvy, David (1911-1999). Born in England, he interrupted his studies in 1931 to first work in Paris, in the kitchens of the Hotel Majestic, before returning to England, as a door-to-door salesman of cookers. He wrote a salespersons' instruction manual which his older brother, working at the time at Mather & Crowther showed to the heads of the agency who subsequently hired him. In 1938, he arranged to be sent to the United States where he would undertake several different jobs and notably work for 3 years with George Gallup. In 1948, he opened his own company in New York with help from English agencies Mather & Crowther and Benson. An emblematic figure in the industry, in 1963 he published the highly successful "Confessions of an Advertising Man" (New York, Ballantine). He presented his own vision of advertising and illustrated it with examples of some of his most successful campaigns such as Hathaway shirts, Schweppes or Rolls-Royce.

Ogilvy & Mather. Agency founded in 1948 in New York under the name Hewitt, Ogilvy, Benson & Mather (HOB&M) with Anderson Hewitt from J. Walter Thompson as President and David Ogilvy as Vice-President in charge of studies and research. The agency merged with Mather & Crowther in 1965 and, on Hewitt's departure, took the name Ogilvy & Mather International then Ogilvy Group in 1985. The WPP Group acquired control in 1989.

Volney B. Palmer

 PUBLICIS

Omnicom. Holding company founded in 1986, notably houses three important advertising networks (BBDO, DDB and TBWA) and two media buying networks (OMD and PHD). Ranked number one communications group in the world in 2004.

Palmer, Volney B. (1799-1864). The first modern advertising professional, founded the first advertising agency in Philadelphia in 1842, opening offices in New York, Boston and Baltimore four years later. Like many professionals of the time, he was a booking agent, that is to say he sold media advertising space, but was unique in that he was the only representative of 1,200 publications out of the 2,000 listed in the country. More importantly, he applied his 'system of advertising' which consisted of creating and writing the advertisements on advertisers' behalf – forming the basis of today's advertising agency.

Partnership in Advertising. Agency founded in 1974 in Johannesburg by Vasco Zoio and Greg Muller. Joined Publicis in 1993.

Prakit. Advertising agency founded in 1978 in Bangkok by Prakit Apisarnthanarax. A part of the company joined Publicis in 1997, firstly under the Prakit Publicis name, and from 2004, as Publicis Thailand.

Publicis. Agency founded in Paris in 1926 by Marcel Bleustein-Blanchet. Starting out in Montmartre, the village-like area of Paris, the agency would set up at the top of the Champs-Élysées in 1957 and be renamed Publicis Conseil at the end of the '60s. It is the founding agency from which the Publicis network and Publicis Groupe have grown.

Publicis Consultants. Strategic communications agency founded in Paris in 1993. Today encompasses activities in the domains of corporate and financial communication, industrial marketing, press relations, design (Carré Noir), publishing, and with the integration of MédiaSystem in 2005, in human resources communications. The Publicis Consultants network has an international presence, including Johnston & Associates and Winner & Associates in the United States, and has been part of the Publicis Groupe "Public Relations & Corporate Communications" division since 2005.

Publicis Dialog. Customer relationship marketing agency, resulting from the 1996 merger of Publicis Direct and ID Marco Polo (group FCA!) in Paris. Became Publicis Dialog in 1998 and under this banner, a network of agencies have been created across the world.

Publicis Groupe. Holding company resulting from the 2002 acquisition of Bcom3 by Publicis. Comprises three advertising networks present throughout the world (Publicis, Leo Burnett and Saatchi & Saatchi), two multi-hub creative

networks (BBH and Fallon) and two regional agencies (Kaplan Thaler Group and Beacon Communications). The Groupe also has a media agency division which counts two networks (ZenithOptimedia and Starcom MediaVest) and a division of "Specialised Agencies and Marketing Services" (SAMS). Publicis Groupe is present in almost 200 cities across more than 100 countries. It is ranked 4th communications group in the world.

Roberts, Kevin (1949-). Began his career at the end of the '60s as brand director of famous British couture house Mary Quant. Subsequently became marketing director at Gillette and Procter & Gamble in Europe and in the Middle East, then President of Pepsi in the Middle East and later Canada. Moved to Auckland in 1989 as managing director of the Lion Nathan brewery, joining Saatchi & Saatchi in 1997. Today he is global CEO of Saatchi & Saatchi, based in New York, and a member of the Publicis Groupe Management Board.

Rockwell, Norman (1894-1978). The most famous of American illustrators. A chronicler and realist, moved by everyday life, he notably produced 322 front covers for the weekly newspaper the Saturday Evening Post between 1916 and 1963.

Romero. Advertising agency founded in 1951 in Mexico by Paulino Romero under the name Paulino Romero y Asociados. First agency acquired by Publicis in Latin America in 1996. Merged with Arredondo de Haro, bought in 2002, to form Publicis Arredondo de Haro.

Rowland. Public relations agency founded in New York in 1957 by Herb Rowland. Acquired by Saatchi & Saatchi in 2000, and became part of the "Public Relations & Corporate Communications" entity of Publicis Groupe in 2005.

Rubicam, Raymond (1892-1978). Began his career in Philadelphia at N.W. Ayer & Son as a copywriter. Founded Young & Rubicam with colleague John Orr Young in 1923. Moved to New York in 1926 then opened an office in Chicago in 1931, recruited George Gallup to manage what was one of the first consumer studies and research departments in an advertising agency. Young left the company in 1935 and Rubicam in 1944. Listed on the stock exchange in 1998, the network was taken over by WPP in 2000.

Saatchi & Saatchi. Agency founded in London in 1970 by the brothers Charles and Maurice Saatchi. In 1974, the acquisition of Notley led to it doubling in size and it took another substantial leap when it acquired control of Garland Compton in 1975. The public would first hear the name Saatchi & Saatchi when it signed a campaign for the Conservative Party in 1979 and in 1986, after the purchase of Ted Bates, Dancer Fitzgerald Sample and Backer & Spielvogel, it became the number one network in the world. After the departure of its founders in 1995, the network joined Publicis in 2000.

Saatchi & Saatchi Healthcare. Started in 1944 in New York when Paul Klemtner founded Klemtner Advertising, agency specialised in medical communications. Acquired by Compton in 1979 and converted into Saatchi & Saatchi Healthcare which then comprised three agencies: Saatchi & Saatchi Healthcare Advertising, Saatchi & Saatchi Consumer Healthcare and Saatchi & Saatchi Healthcare Innovations. In 2003, Saatchi & Saatchi Healthcare joined Publicis Healthcare Communications Group.

Salles. Advertising agency founded by Mauro Salles in 1966 in São Paulo as Mauro Salles Publicidade. Became Salles Inter-Americana in 1977 and began a partnership with DMB&B in 1982. In 2000, the agency was rebranded Salles D'Arcy and in 2002, joined the Publicis network. Merged with Publicis Norton in 2003 to give birth to Publicis Salles Norton which became Publicis in 2005.

Sanchez & Levitan. Agency specialised in Hispanic communications, founded in Miami in 1986 by Fausto Sanchez and Aida Levitan. Publicis acquired 49% in 2001 and at the same time took control of Siboney agencies in Dallas and Los Angeles. The three entities were merged under the name Publicis Sanchez & Levitan, and absorbed by Bromley in 2002.

Savignac, Raymond (1907-2002). One of the most prominent French poster artists of the second half of the 20th century. Brought to prominence in 1949 by Eugène Schueller, founder of L'Oréal and by his poster of a cow for Monsavon.

SMW. Advertising agency founded in 1975 in Toronto by Lewis Smith, Tony Matthew and Frank Waldock. Acquired by Publicis in 1998.

Starcom MediaVest Group. Media agency network created in 2000 by Bcom3 through the bringing together of The Media Centre (media department of DMB&B founded in 1991 and baptised MediaVest in 1997) and Starcom (media department of Leo Burnett created in 1999). Joined Publicis Groupe in 2002 and, with 110 offices across 76 countries, is today the largest media agency network in the world.

Steichen, Edward J. (1879-1973). American photographer originating from Luxembourg who pushed advertising photography to reach the highest levels of artistic rigour. Set the precedent for several generations of important artists such as Richard Avedon, Irving Penn and William Klein.

Thompson, James Walter (1847-1928). Began his career in 1868 as accountant at advertising agency Carlton & Smith which, founded in 1864 in New York, was the booking agent for several religious magazines. He bought the agency in

1877 and renamed it J. Walter Thompson. He had the idea that he would sell more advertising space if he also wrote the advertisements and so hired copywriters and illustrators to work in a specially created department, which was a major innovation at that time.

Vigilante. Advertising agency founded in New York in 1997 by Marc Stephenson Strachan and Danny Robinson, in partnership with Leo Burnett, to bring to its clients the inspiration of urban trends.

Vitruvio. Advertising agency founded in Madrid in 1980 by Miguel Angel Furones. Joined Leo Burnett in 1990 to become Vitruvio Leo Burnett.

Warhol, Andy (1928-1987). Starting out as an advertising illustrator, becoming a world famous painter producing thousands of canvases in his New York "factory". He was also a film maker, producer, publisher, and above all an icon of artistic life in the '70s. His work is a reference of American art in the second half of the 20th century.

Welcomm. Advertising agency founded in 1987 in Seoul (Korea) by Tae-Hyoung Kim, Woo-Duk Park and Ae-Ran Moon. Joined Publicis in 1999.

Wet Desert. Advertising agency founded in 1945 in Kuala Lumpur (Malaysia) by Lee Yuen Hong under the name Union. Became Union Forty Five in 1970 and after his daughter founded Adsell Advertising in 1973, the holding company Wet Desert was created in 1997. Joined Publicis in 1998.

WPP. Holding company founded in 1985 by Martin Sorrell, previously the financial director of Saatchi & Saatchi, by taking a stake in shopping cart manufacturer: Wire & Plastic Products. He used this as a base for building a communications group which was to become the 2nd ranking in the world, thanks to numerous acquisitions such as J. Walter Thompson in 1987, Ogilvy & Mather in 1989, Young & Rubicam in 2000 and Cordiant in 2003.

ZenithOptimedia. Media agency network created in 2001 through the merging of Zenith (created by Saatchi & Saatchi in London in 1988) and Optimedia (created by Publicis in Paris in 1989). Publicis Groupe took full control of the newly formed entity in 2003.

Charles and Maurice Saatchi

SAATCHI & SAATCHI

Bibliography

Cover of "The Ayer Idea in Advertising"
by Francis W. Ayer, 1912.

General History

Bargiel, Réjane
150 ans de publicité
2004   Paris: Union Centrale des Arts décoratifs

Bertherat, Marie
100 ans de Pub
Préface de Marcel Bleustein-Blanchet
1994   Paris: Éditions Atlas

Cohen Selinger, Iris
The Advertising Century. Special Issue
1999   New York: The Advertising Age

Datz, Philippe
Histoire de la publicité depuis les temps
les plus reculés jusqu'à nos jours
1918   Paris: J. Rothschild

French, George
20th Century Advertising
1926   New York: Van Nostrand

Holme, Bryan
Advertising: Reflexions of a Century
1982   New York: The Viking Press

McDonough, John; Egorf, Karen and
Reid, Jacqueline
Encyclopedia of Advertising.
The Advertising Age
2002   New York: Fitzroy Dearborn

Meyerson, Jeremy and Vickers, Graham
Rewind. Forty Years of Design & Advertising
2002   Londres: Phaidon Press

Pollay, Richard W.
Information Sources in Advertising History
1979   Westport, Conn.: Greenwood Press

Saunders, Dave
20th Century Advertising
Foreword by Rupert Howell
1999   London: Carlton

Schuwer, Philippe
Histoire de la publicité
1965   Lausanne: Rencontre

Spiess, Dominique
100 ans d'histoire à travers la publicité
Préface d'Anne-Claude Lelieur
1987   Lausanne: Edita

Turner, Ernest Sackville
The Shocking History of Advertising!
1953   New York: E.P. Dutton & Company

Wood, James Playsted
The Story of Advertising
1958   New York: Ronald Press

Zur Westen, Walter von
Reklamekunst
1914   Bielefeld: Velhagen & Klasing

History by country

Anikst, Mikhail
Soviet Commercial Design of the Twenties
1986   London: Thames and Hudson

Benevolo, Marco
L'arte della pubblicità.
Le grandi campagne del ventesimo secolo
1995   Milano: Lupetti

Bouchard, Jacques
La publicité: toute la publicité, rien que
la publicité
1967   Ottawa: Les Éditions de la Table Ronde

Bruneau, Pierre
Magiciens de la publicité
1956   Paris: Gallimard

Bryden-Brown, John
Ads That Made Australia
1981   Lane Cove: Sydney, Doubleday

Chessel, Marie-Emmanuelle
La publicité: Naissance d'une profession
1900-1940
1998   Paris: CNRS

Elliott, Blanche Beatrice
A History of English Advertising
1962   London: B.T. Basford

Falabrino, Gian Luigi
Effimera & bella: Storia della pubblicità italiana
1990   Torino: Gutenberg 2000

Fox, Stephen
The Mirror Makers: A History of American
Advertising and Its Creators
1984   New York: William Morrow

Goodrum, Charles, Dalrymple, Helen
Advertising in America. The First 200 Years
1990   New York: Harry N. Abrams

Gracioso, Francisco e Penteado Whitaker J.
50 Años de Vida e Propaganda Brasileiras
2001   São Paulo: Mauro Ivan Marketing

Kellner, Joachim
50 Jahre Werbung in Deutschland.
1945 bis 1995
1995   Düsseldorf: Kunstpalast

Kenehisa, Tching
La publicité au Japon. Image de la société
1984   Paris: Maisonneuve et Larose

Marchand, Roland
Advertising: The American Dream
Making Way for Modernity, 1920-1940
1985   Berkeley: University of California Press

Martin, Marc
Trois siècles de publicité en France
1992   Paris: Éditions Odile Jacob

Mayer, Martin
  Madison Avenue, U.S.A.
  1958 New York: Harper & Brothers
Mayer, Martin
  Whatever Happened to Madison Avenue:
  Advertising in the '90s
  1991 Boston: Little, Brown & Company
Nevett, Terry R.
  Advertising in Britain: A History
  Published on behalf of The History of
  Advertising Trust
  1982 London: William Heinemann
Presbrey, Frank
  The History and Development of Advertising
  1929 New York: Doubleday, Dorand & Co
Printer's Ink
  Fifty Years: 1888-1938
  1938 New York: Printer's Ink Publishing
Raventós Rabinat, José M.
  Cien años de publicidad española 1899-1999
  2000 Barcelona: Mediterránea Books
Shudson, Michael
  Advertising, the Uneasy Persuasion: Its Dubious
  Impact on American Society
  1984 New York: Basic Books
Strasser, Susan
  Satisfaction Guaranteed: The Making of the
  American Mass Market
  1998 New York: Pantheon
Weisser, Michael
  Deutsche Reklame. 100 Jahre Werbung
  1870-1970
  Ein Beitrag zur Kunst-und Kulturgeschichte
  1985 Munich: Deutsche Reklame

History by media

Bleustein-Blanchet, Marcel
  Les ondes de la liberté, 1934-1984
  1984 Paris: Jean-Claude Lattès
Fraser, James
  The American Billboard: 100 Years
  1991 New York: Harry N. Abrams
Hettinger, Herman S.
  A Decade of Radio Advertising
  1933 Chicago: The University of Chicago Press
Lelieur, Anne-Claude
  De Bébé Cadum à Mamie Nova
  1999 Paris: Bibliothèque Forney
Maltin, Leonard
  The Great American Broadcast
  A Celebration of Radio's Golden Age
  1997 New York: Dutton
Mineur, Jean
  Balzac 00.01.
  Préface de Jean Anouilh
  1981 Paris: Plon
Mollerup, Per
  Marks of Excellence.
  The history and taxonomy of trademarks
  1997 London: Phaidon Press

Poppe, Fred C.
  The 100 Greatest Corporate and Industrial Ads
  1983 New York: Van Rostand Reinhold Comp.
Sterling, Christopher H. and Kittross, John. M.
  Stay Tuned: A Concise History of American
  Broadcasting
  1978 Belmont, Cal.: Wadsworth Publishing Co.
Timmers, Margaret
  The Power of the Poster
  1998 London: V&A Publications
Weill, Alain
  L'Affiche dans le monde
  1984 Paris: Somogy

Agency Profiles

Davis, Howard; Dunning, Deanne; Lynch,
Brad and Tedesco, Kevin
  125 Years of Building Brands
  1994 New York: Ayer
Fallon, Ivan
  The Brothers: The Rise & Rise of
  Saatchi & Saatchi
  1988 London: Hutchinson
Hower, Ralph M.
  The History of an Advertising Agency:
  N.W. Ayer & Son at Work, 1869-1939
  1939 Cambridge, Mass.: Harvard
  University Press
Kaplan, Linda and Koval, Robin
  Bang! Getting your Message Heard in
  a Noisy World
  2003 New York: Doubleday
Kleiman, Philip
  The Saatchi & Saatchi Story
  1987 London: Weidenfeld & Nicolson
Lefebure, Antoine
  Havas, Les arcanes du pouvoir
  1992 Paris: Grasset
Levenson, Bob
  Bill Bernbach's Book: A History of the Advertising
  that Changed the History of Advertising
  1987 New York: Villard Books
Rowsome, Jr., Frank
  They Laughed When I Sat Down.
  An Informal History of Advertising in Words
  and Pictures
  1959 New York: McGraw-Hill Book Company
Sartory, Karel
  De vierde vrijheid
  1955 Amsterdam: A. De la Mar
Thompson, Mark
  Social Work. Saatchi & Saatchi's Cause-Related
  Ideas Saatchi
  2000 London: -273 Publishers
Webber, Gordon
  Our Kind of People.
  The Story of the First 50 Years at
  Benton & Bowles
  1979 New York: Benton & Bowles

Anthologies

Bernstein, David
  Advertising Outdoors. Watch this Space!
  1997 London: Phaidon Press
Heimann, Jim
  All-American Ads 20s-80s
  Introduction by Willy Wilkerson
  2001 Köln: Taschen
Hunt, Robert
  The Advertising Parade: An Anthology of Good
  Advertisements Published in 1928
  1930 New York: Harper
Margolin, Victor; Brichta, Ira and Brichta, Vivian
  The Promise and the Product
  1979 New York: Macmillan Publishing
Watin-Augouard, Jean
  Marques de toujours
  Préface de Maurice Lévy
  2003 Paris: Larousse
Watkins, Julian Lewis
  The 100 Greatest Advertisements
  Who Wrote Them and What They Did.
  Foreword by Raymond Rubicam
  1959 New York: Dover Publications

Memoirs and Biographies

Applegate, Edd
  The Ad Men and Women: A Biographical
  Dictionary of Advertising
  1994 Westport, Conn.: Preager Publishers
Barnum, Phineas Taylor
  Struggles and Triumphs
  1869 New York: J.S. Redfield
Barthélémy
  À travers le monde de la publicité
  1972 Paris: Stock
Burnett, Leo
  Communications of an Advertising Man
  1961 Chicago: Leo Burnett Company, Inc.
Burnett, Leo
  100 Leo's. Wit & Wisdom from Leo Burnett
  1995 Chicago: NTC Business Book
Bleustein-Blanchet, Marcel
  Sur mon antenne.
  Souvenirs d'une radio libre
  1947 Paris: Marcel Dodeman
Bleustein-Blanchet, Marcel
  La rage de convaincre
  1970 Paris: Robert Laffont
  The Rage to Persuade. Memoirs of a French
  Advertising Man.
  Foreword by David Ogilvy
  1982 New York: Chelsea House
  Ikna hirsi, Bir fransiz reklamcinin
  auilari
  Önsöz David Ogilvy
  1995 Istanbul: Yorum Ajans
  Shori eno Jonetsu
  2003 Tokyo: Dentsu

Bleustein-Blanchet, Marcel
La nostalgie du futur
1976 Paris: Robert Laffont

Bleustein-Blanchet, Marcel
Mémoires d'un lion
1988 Paris: Olivier Perrin

Bleustein-Blanchet, Marcel
Les mots de ma vie
1990 Paris: Robert Laffont

Bleustein-Blanchet, Marcel
La traversée du siècle
Avec la collaboration de Jean Mauduit
1994 Paris: Robert Laffont

Bleustein-Blanchet, Marcel
Les enfants de la radio
Entretiens avec Jean Mauduit
1998 Baume-les-Dames, France: IME

Brose, Hanns W.
Die Entdeckung des Verbrauchers.
Ein Leben für die Werburg
1958 Düsseldorf: Econ-Verlag

Cone, Fairfax M.
With All its Faults.
A Candid Account of Forty Years in Advertising
1969 Boston: Little, Brown & Company

Dupont, Wladir
Geraldo Alonso. O homen, o mito
1991 São Paulo: Editora Globo

Farner, Rudolf Dr.
Erfolg in der Werbung
1983 Zürich: C.J. Bucher

Germon, Marcel
Marcel Bleustein-Blanchet, Monsieur Publicité
Présenté par Jean Boissonat
1990 Paris: Jacques Grancher

Hopkins, Claude C.
My Life in Advertising
1927 New York: Harper

Kufrin, Joan
Leo Burnett, Star Reacher
1995 Chicago: Leo Burnett Company, Inc.

Lasker, Albert D.
The Lasker Story As He Told It
1963 Chicago: Advertising Publications

Loewy, Raymond
Never Leave Well Enough Alone
1951 New York: Simon & Schuster

Lorin, Philippe
5 Giants of Advertising
2001 Paris: Assouline

MacManus, Theodore F.
The Sword - Arm of Business
1927 New York: The Devin-Adair Company Rivers

Ogilvy, David
Ogilvy on Advertising
1983 New York: Crown

Rowell, George P.
Forty Years an Advertising Agent
1906 New York: Franklin Publishing Company

Sarnoff, David
Speech Can Change your Life
1970 New York: Doubleday

Séguéla, Jacques
Ne dites pas à ma mère que je suis dans
la publicité... Elle me croit pianiste
dans un bordel
1979 Paris: Flammarion

Young, James Webb
The Diary of an Ad Man
1944 Chicago: Advertising Publications Inc.

Visual Arts

Baldassari, Anne
Art & Pub 1890-1990
1991 Paris: Centre Georges Pompidou

Bogart, Michelle H.
Artists, Advertising and the Borders of Art
1995 Chicago: The University of Chicago Press

Branshaw, Percy V.
Art in Advertising: A Study of British and
American Pictorial Publicity
1925 London: Press Art School

Cogniat, Raymond
Art et publicité dans le monde
1955 Paris: Musée des Arts décoratifs

Guyon, Lionel
Architecture & Publicité
Préface de Marcel Bleustein-Blanchet
1990 Paris: Pierre Mardaga

Henderson, Sally and Landau, Robert Billboard Art.
Introduction by David Hockney
1981 London: Angus & Robertson

Hoffman, Barry
The Fine Art of Advertising
2002 New York: Harry N. Abrams

Hornung, Clarence P.
Handbook of Early Advertising Art
1947 New York: Dover Publications

Lelieur, Anne-Claude
Savignac, affichiste
2001 Paris: Bibliothèque Forney

Massey, John
Great Ideas 1950-1976
1976 Chicago: Container Corporation of America

Rogue, Georges
Ceci n'est pas un Magritte: Essai sur Magritte
et la publicité
1983 Paris: Flammarion

Schneider, Danielle
La pub détourne l'art
1999 Genève: Éditions du Tricorne

Sobieszek, Robert A.
The Art of Persuasion: A History of Advertising
Photography
1988 New York: Harry N. Abrams

Stoltz, Donald Robert
The Advertising World of Norman Rockwell
1985 New York: Harrison House

Varnadoe, Kirk and Gopnik Adam
High & Low: Modern Art and Popular Culture
1990 New York: The Museum of Modern Art

Warhol, Andy
The Philosophy of Andy Warhol
From A to B and Back Again
1975 New York: Harcourt Brace Jovanovich

Theory and Pratice

Aaker, David
Building Strong Brands
1995 New York: Free Press

Abruzzesse, Alberto
Metafore della pubblicità
1988 Genova: Costa & Nolan

Arren, Julien
Sa Majesté la publicité
1914 Tours, France: Alfred Mame & Fils

Ayer, Francis Wayland
The Ayer Idea in Advertising
1912 Philadelphia: N.W. Ayer & Son

Baker, Stephen
Visual Persuasion
1961 New York: McGraw-Hill

Bates, Charles Austin
Good Advertising
1896 New York: Holmes

Berger, Warren
Advertising Today
2001 Londres: Phaidon Press

Bleustein-Blanchet, Marcel
La publicité et ses métiers
1985 Paris: Chotard et associés

Brochand, Bernard et Landrevie, Jacques
Publicitor
1983 Paris: Dalloz

Calkins, Earnest Elmo
The Business of Advertising
1905 New York: D. Appleton & Company

Calkins, Earnest Elmo and Holden, Ralph
Modern Advertising
1915 New York: D. Appleton & Company

Chandor, P.
Advertising and Publicity
1967 London: The English Universities Press

Coombs, Anne
Adland. A True Story of Corporate Drama
1990 Port Melbourne: William Heinemann

Cummings, Bart
Advertising's Benevolent Dictators
1984 Chicago: Crain Books

De Bono, Edward
Serious Creativity: Using the Power of Lateral
Thinking to Create New Ideas
1992 New York: Harper Collins

Dru, Jean-Marie
Le saut créatif
1984 Paris: Jean-Claude Lattès

Dru, Jean-Marie
  Disruption: Overturning Conventions and
  Shaking up the Marketplace
  1996   New York: John Wiley & Sons
Dzamic, Lazar
  No-Copy Advertising
  2001   Crans-près-Céligny: RotoVision
Elvinger, Francis
  La lutte entre l'industrie et le commerce
  La marque, son lancement, sa vente,
  sa publicité
  1922   Paris: Librairie d'Économie commerciale
Fonteix, J.B. et Guérin, Alexandre
  La publicité méthodique
  1922, Paris: Société Française de Publications
  périodiques et de Publicité
Gérin, Octave-Jacques et Espinadel, Charles
  La publicité suggestive. Théorie et pratique
  Préface de Walter Dill Scott
  1911   Paris: Dunod et Pinat
Gilson, Clive; Pratt, Mike; Roberts, Kevin and
Weymes, Ed
  Peak Performance
  2000   New York: Texere
Hopkins, Claude C.
  Scientific Advertising
  Introduction by David Ogilvy
  1966   New York: Bell Publishing Company
Hyman, Sidney
  The Lives of William Benton
  1969   Chicago: The University of Chicago Press
Kanner, Bernice
  The 100 Best TV Commercials... and
  Why They Worked
  Foreword by Michael Conrad
  1999   New York: Random House
Kapferer, Jean-Noël
  Reinventing the Brand
  2001   London: Kogan Page
Key, Wilson Bryan
  Subliminal Seduction
  1973   New York: Penguin Books
Lagneau, Gérard
  Le faire-valoir. Une introduction à la sociologie
  des phénomènes publicitaires
  Préface de Marcel Bleustein-Blanchet
  1969   Paris: Sabri
Lagneau, Gérard
  La sociologie de la publicité
  1976   Paris: Presses Universitaires de France
Leduc, Robert
  Le pouvoir publicitaire
  1974   Paris: Bordas
Lévy, Maurice and O'Donoghue, Dan
  New Trends in the Promotion of Companies and
  Brands to Stakeholders: A Holistic Approach in
  Marketing Communication in "New Approaches,
  Technologies and Styles", Dan Kimmel,
  Allan J., Editor
  2005   London: Oxford University Press

Ogilvy, David
  Confessions of an Advertising Man
  1963   New York: Atheneum
Opdycke, John B.
  The Language of Advertising
  Introduction by Percy S. Straus
  1925   New York: Isaac Pitman & Sons
Pavitt, Jane
  Brand.New
  2000   London: V&A Publications
Péninou, Georges
  Intelligence de la publicité: étude sémiotique
  1972   Paris: Robert Laffont
Plas, Bernard de et Verdier, Henri
  La Publicité
  1947   Paris: Presses Universitaires de France
Pope, Daniel
  The Making of Modern Advertising
  1983   New York: Basic Books
Pringle, Hamish and Thompson, Marjorie
  Brand Spirit. How cause related marketing
  builds brands
  1999   Chichester: John Wiley & Sons
Reeves, Rosser
  Reality in Advertising
  1961   New York: Alfred A. Knopf
Roberts, Kevin
  Lovemarks
  The Future beyond brands
  2004 New York: Power House Books
Scott, Walter Dill
  The Psychology of Advertising
  1902   Boston: Small, Maynard & Co.
Sell, Henry
  The Philosophy of Advertising
  1882   London: Sell's Advertising Offices
Victoroff, David
  Psychosociologie de la publicité
  1970   Paris: Presses Universitaires de France
Victoroff, David
  La publicité et l'image
  1978   Paris: Denoël/Gonthier
Weil, Pascale
  New Mindscapes in Consumption and
  Communication
  1996   Schidan: Scriptum Books

Key References

Barthes, Roland
  Mythologies
  1972   New York: Hill & Wang
Baudrillard, Jean
  The Consumer Society: Myths and Structures
  1998   London: Sage Publications
Bourdieu, Pierre
  Distinction: A Social Critique of
  the Judgement of Taste
  1984   Cambridge, Mass.: Harvard
  University Press

Dichter, Ernest
  Psychology of Everyday Living
  1947   New York: Barnes & Noble
Dichter, Ernest
  Strategy of Desire
  1960   Garden City, N.Y.: Doubleday
Galbraith, John Kenneth
  The Affluent Society
  1958   Boston: Houghton Mifflin
Kash, Rick
  The New Law of Demand and Supply:
  The Revolutionary New Demand Strategy for
  Faster Growth and Higher Profits
  2002   New York: Doubleday
Keynes, John Maynard
  The General Theory of Employment, Interest
  and Money
  1936   Cambridge, Mass.: Cambridge University
  Press Macmillan
Klein, Naomi
  No Logo
  2000   Toronto: Alfred A. Knopf
Lévy-Strauss, Claude
  Structural Anthropology
  1963   New York: Basic Books
Lipovetsky, Gilles
  L'ère du vide
  1983   Paris: Gallimard
Marcuse, Herbert
  One-Dimensional Man: Studies in the Ideology
  of Advanced Industrial Society
  1964   Boston: Beacon Press
Marcus Steiff, Joachim
  Les études de motivation
  Préface de Marcel Bleustein-Blanchet
  1961   Paris: Hermann
McLuhan, Marshall
  The Gutenberg Galaxy: The Making
  of Typographic Man
  1962   Toronto: Toronto University Press
McLuhan, Marshall
  Understanding Media
  1964   New York: McGraw-Hil
Meadows, Donella H.; Meadows, Denis L.;
Randers, Jorgen; Behrens III, William W.
  The Limits to Growth: a Report for the Club of
  Rome's Project on the Predicament of Mankind
  1972   New York: Universe Book
Packard, Vance
  The Hidden Persuaders
  1957   New York: David McKay
Propp, Vladimir
  Morphology of the Folktale
  1958   The Hague: Mouton

Index

Credits

11: Jean-Luce Huré; 15: Stephanie Owen; 16: Charles E. Martin, 1966, from cartoonbank.com © VG Bild-Kunst, Bonn 2008; 23: Savignac, "Garap", 1953 © VG Bild-Kunst, Bonn 2008; 28: Leonetto Cappiello, "Kub", 1911 © VG Bild-Kunst, Bonn 2008; 29: Pablo Picasso, "Paysage aux affiches", 1912 © Succession Picasso/VG Bild-Kunst, Bonn 2008; 30: Achille Lucien Mauzan, "Prestito Credito Italiano", 1917 © VG Bild-Kunst, Bonn 2008; 34-35: courtesy of The Coca-Cola Company; 36-39: Uneeda® and Nabisco® are registered trademarks of KF Holdings and used with permission; 37: courtesy of Morton's Salt, a division of Rohm and Hass Company; "Cracker Jack" advertisement provided courtesy of Frito-Lay Inc; 40-41: © R.J. Reynolds Tobacco Company; 48: Philips Company Archives; 52: Lucian Bernhard/Rosen, "Reklame Schau", 1931 © VG Bild-Kunst, Bonn 2008; 54: Sonia Delaunay, "Le rêve", 1922 © L & M Services B.V. The Hague 20080103; Stuart Davis, "Odol", 1924 © VG Bild-Kunst, Bonn 2008; 55: René Magritte, "Ceci n'est pas une pipe", 1928 © VG Bild-Kunst, Bonn 2008; Kurt Schwitters, "Pelikan", 1924, © VG Bild-Kunst, Bonn 2008; 58-59: courtesy of The Coca-Cola Company; 60: Cassandre, "Dole", 1938 © MOURON. CASSANDRE. Lic 2008-24-01-02 www.cassandre.fr; Georgia O'Keeffe, "Dole", 1940 © VG Bild-Kunst, Bonn 2008; 63: Norman Rockwell, "The First Corn on the Cob", 1938-1940, Green Giant advertisement; Works by Norman Rockwell. Printed by permission of the Norman Rockwell Family Agency. © 2008 Norman Rockwell Family Entities; 66: © R.J. Reynolds Tobacco Company; 70-71: Cassandre, "Ford V8", 1938 © MOURON. CASSANDRE, Lic 2008-24-01-02 www.cassandre.fr; 75: Photographs by Edward Steichen. Reprinted with permission of Joanna T. Steichen; 80: Philips Company Archives; 83: Albert Champeaux, "Le petit mineur"; 86: Jean Carlu, "Production", 1942 © VG Bild-Kunst, Bonn 2008; 87: Paul Colin, "La Libération", 1944 © VG Bild-Kunst, Bonn 2008; 88: "Save Time", ads provided by Kellogg's Company, all rights reserved, used with permission; "Texaco" images are copyrighted by Chevron Corporation U.S.A. Inc and used with permission; Jean Carlu, "CCA", 1943 © VG Bild-Kunst, Bonn 2008; 92-93: Herbert Leupin, "Pause", 1953, 1957, copyright by C&T Leupin, 5415 Nussbaumen, Switzerland, courtesy of The Coca-Cola Company; 94-95: courtesy of The Coca-Cola Company; 97: Norman Rockwell, "Pigtails" 1954, "Freckles" 1954, "Boy with string", "Girl with string" 1954, © 2008 The Norman Rockwell Family Entities, Stevan Dohanos, "Kellogg's", 1955 © VG Bild-Kunst, Bonn 2008, Kellogg's Company advertisements, ads provided by Kellogg's Company, all rights reserved, used with permission; 102-103: Savignac, "Maggi", 1959, 1964, posters and stills © VG Bild-Kunst, Bonn 2008; 106: Maxwell House® is a registered trademark of KF Holdings and used with permission; 107: "Nescafé", by courtesy of Société des produits Nestlé S.A., registered trademark owners of NESCAFÉ, NESTLÉ and the Red Mug; 108-109, 110-111: Philip Morris, Marlboro and Virginia Slims ads courtesy of Altria Group; 116: Cassandre, "Concentration", 1937 MOURON.CASSANDRE, Lic 2008-24-01-02 www.cassandre.fr; 117: Ben Shahn, "CCA", 1956 © VG Bild-Kunst, Bonn 2008; René Magritte, "CCA", 1963 © VG Bild-Kunst, Bonn 2008; 118: "Berliet", courtesy of Fondation de l'Automobile Marius Berliet, Lyon; 119: Jacques Nathan, "Shell", v. 1950 © VG Bild-Kunst, Bonn 2008; 120-121: Bell Telephone System – Courtesy of AT&T Archives and History Center; 121: Norman Rockwell, "The Lineman", AT&T advertisement © 2008 The Norman Rockwell Family Entities, Courtesy of AT&T Archives and History Center; 122-123: Philips Company Archives; 125: Norman Rockwell, "Portrait of Patricia Patterson" 1958, "Portrait of Mike Hayward" 1958, "Portrait of Janie Carroll" 1957 © 2008 The Norman Rockwell Family Entities, Crest advertisements; 126: Savignac, "André", 1952 © VG Bild-Kunst, Bonn 2008; 127: René Gruau, "Gaine et soutien-gorge Jacques Fath", 1955 © René Gruau, www.renegruau.com; 129: Savignac, "Le Figaro", 1952 © VG Bild-Kunst, Bonn 2008; 132-133: James Rosenquist, "President Elect", 1960 © VG Bild-Kunst, Bonn 2008; 134-135: Andy Warhol, "The American Man", 1964, "Coca-Cola Bottles" 1962 © 2008 Andy Warhol Foundation for the Visual Arts/ARS, New York; 136: Poster and photograph by Richard Avedon. © 2008 The Richard Avedon Foundation; 140: Paul Colin, "Prénatal", 1950 © VG Bild-Kunst, Bonn 2008; Jeanloup Sieff, "Prénatal", 1962 © The Estate of Jeanloup Sieff; 141: Jean Effel, "Ptipo", 1974, © VG Bild-Kunst, Bonn 2008; courtesy of Société des produits Nestlé S.A., registered trademark owners of NESCAFÉ, NESTLÉ and the Red Mug; 143: Andy Warhol, "Campbell's Soup", 1964 © 2008 Andy Warhol Foundation/ARS, NY/TM Licensed by Campbell's Soup Co. All rights reserved; 150-151: Philip Morris, Marlboro and Virginia Slims ads courtesy of Altria Group; 156: "Texaco" images are copyrighted by Chevron Corporation U.S.A. Inc and used with permission; 158: Farman & March; 165: Caroline Schultz; 166-167: Bell System, Yellow Pages – Courtesy of AT&T Archives and History Center; 178: Jeanloup Sieff, "Rosy", 1962 © The Estate of Jeanloup Sieff; 182-183: Jeanloup Sieff, "Dim", 1975 © The Estate of Jeanloup Sieff; 187: Jacques Henri Lartigue, "Woolmark" © Ministère de la Culture – France/AAJHL; 188: Savignac, "Bic", 1960, 1965, 1966 © VG Bild-Kunst, Bonn 2008, with permission from the BIC company; 190: Pablo Picasso, "Mère et enfant" coll. De Beers © Succession Picasso/VG Bild-Kunst, Bonn 2008; 197: René Maltête; 200: Mike Martin; 202: Andy Warhol, "The Last Supper", 1986 © 2008 Andy Warhol Foundation for the Visual Arts/ARS, New York, "Tomato Soup", 1962 © 2008 Andy Warhol Foundation/ARS, NY/TM Licensed by Campbell's Soup Co. All rights reserved; 203: Arman, "Long Term Parking", 1982 © VG Bild-Kunst, Bonn 2008; 206-207: "Perrier" by courtesy of Société des produits Nestlé S.A., registered trademark owners of NESCAFÉ, NESTLÉ and the Red Mug; 208-209: courtesy of The Coca-Cola Company; 223: "Wendy's", reprinted with permission of Wendy's International, Inc.; 224-225: advertisement and associated copyrights and trademarks are owned by H.J. Heinz Company, L.P. and is used with permission; 232-233: by courtesy of Société des produits Nestlé S.A., registered trademark owners of NESCAFÉ, NESTLÉ and the Red Mug; 239: Ted Knutson; 244: Cedric Chambaz; 246-247: General Motors Corp. used with permission, GM Media Archives; 279: Patricia Murphy; 300: © Commission for Racial Equality 2005; 305: Malcolm Walker; 306: Rodrigo Ribeiro; 314: Noam Murro; 315: Chris Smith; 320: Kathleen Blumenfeld; 321: Patrick Le Mervedec "La Fête des Moissons".

The publisher would like to thank the agencies of Publicis Groupe, the campaign creators and the various public and private archives for allowing their works to be published, with full authorisation from the companies and institutions to which they belong. Any error or omission in identifying sources is unintentional. The publisher apologises in advance to the holders of the copyrights and reserves the rights to which they are entitled.